Jeremy Paxman

A Life in Questions

WILLIAM
COLLINS

William Collins
An imprint of HarperCollins*Publishers*
1 London Bridge Street
London SE1 9GF
www.WilliamCollinsBooks.com

First published in Great Britain by William Collins in 2016
This William Collins paperback edition published in 2017

2

A catalogue record for this book is
available from the British Library

ISBN 978-0-00-812833-3

Printed and bound in Great Britain by
Clays Ltd, St Ives plc

MIX
Paper from
responsible sources
FSC C007454

Here richly, with ridiculous display,
The Politician's corpse was laid away.
While all of his acquaintance sneered and slanged
I wept. For I had longed to see him hanged.

Hilaire Belloc

Contents

Foreword

What do we know of our lives? I am certain my blood group is A Negative, because the nurse vaccinating me before some trip to a war zone sent a blood sample off for testing. I noticed that, in private, we all scrawled our blood group onto the back of our helmets, in case something awful happened. I know I passed my Eleven-Plus, took two attempts to get good enough marks at my Common Entrance exam, failed Maths and Latin O Levels at the first attempt, got pretty average A Levels, won an exhibition to Cambridge and got a 2:1 in my final exams. The mere facts which categorise you aren't interesting. If only one could tell children that once you've finished your exams, no one cares much about how you did, or even asks to see your certificates. Instead we expect them to play the game we played.

When the time came for me to start work I applied for the obvious jobs, but without much enthusiasm. I was then astonishingly lucky. One of the irritating characteristics of life is that it can only be understood looking backwards, yet you must live it looking forwards. Though it didn't really seem like that at the time, I now see that there was only one occupation suitable for someone who, like me, was driven by curiosity and loved words. For over forty years I have followed the same trade, whether in radio, television, newspapers or books.

As my own shelves show, the world has a surplus of books. Why perpetrate another? I have no great prescription to dispense. But it's been fun, and along the way I met some interesting people and heard some terrific stories, which I might as well share before I forget them. I have no scores to settle, no unfinished business. I just did things that seemed interesting at the time. A collection of memoirs offers the chance to try to set the record straighter than it might be otherwise, and to laugh at the silliness of so much of life.

The other day I was rootling through some boxes in the bottom of a cupboard. Whatever the reasons for keeping the stuff I found inside – the hours devoted to an essay, the brief moment of insight which seemed so vital at the time, the transitoriness of television – earlier in life I wanted to preserve my past. I have now lost that urge. There, among the Panamanian hotel bills, Swiss speeding tickets, defunct fishing permits, libel-reader reports and now unplayable videocassettes, was the evidence that I was once vain enough to subscribe to a cuttings agency, which dutifully clipped pieces from newspapers and magazines across the land. I suppose I kept the subscription for a year or two, and it is embarrassing to confess. For a while, my head was turned. Even after deciding that the agency was a waste of money, I still occasionally clipped stories from the newspapers in which I had appeared. From them I learn, among other things, that my weather forecasting colleague on *Breakfast Time* was 'a sex machine', and that a Scottish sports reporter on the same show with 'a squashed face' was tipped as the future of broadcasting. I seem once to have told a celebrity magazine called *Best* that 'I find clothes really boring,' and soon afterwards a designer called Jeff Banks nominated me as one of the worst-dressed men in Britain, saying, 'That man should loosen up and get into some soft linen.' In 1994 Ruby Wax told *Options* magazine that she had noticed I had 'huge genitals', and in March 2008 Marks & Spencer took a full-page ad in the *Guardian* to proclaim that I was wrong about the drop in quality of their pants. David Cameron let it be known to some obliging reporter that he detested me. Tony Blair's Health Secretary, John Reid, accused me of disrespecting him after I described him on air as the government's 'all-purpose attack dog' (the ten minutes of foul-mouthed abuse which his assistant afterwards heaped on Kate McAndrew, the producer of the day, was not disclosed), and the next day the *Daily Mirror* quoted a 'friend' of John Reid calling me 'a West London wanker'. In the following weekend's papers the novelist Howard Jacobson accused me of 'coarsening public life'.

The accusation is familiar, along with the suggestion that people like me are responsible for the fact that so many of the public despise mainstream politicians. I reject the charge, of course – all we try to do is to get straight answers to pretty straightforward questions, and often a cloud of obfuscation is as revealing as an unexpected outbreak of frankness. But I accept that if you present yourself uninvited in people's homes, they will take a view on you. That's how it goes. In my case the progression of newspaper-columnist opinion went from 'a breath of fresh air', through 'Who does this cheeky bastard think he is?', to 'peevish old sod'. It is intrinsic to the trade I follow that we constantly seek novelty, and once the novel becomes familiar, it is ripe for aerial bombardment. The only hope then is that in the years when you're wondering where you left your teeth before your afternoon nap, someone reaches for another cliché and deems you to have become a 'veteran' – as if you are a car on the London–Brighton run, and unlikely to get much beyond Croydon. Then you die.

There were dozens of letters in the cupboard, too – a tiny fraction, I suppose, of the total I received, and which I had kept for no rhyme or reason I could discern. I rather enjoyed hearing from viewers, since broadcasting is such a one-way business, and letters often described a first-hand experience of issues which would otherwise be hidden behind clouds of political verbiage. Since anyone who presents news or current affairs programmes on the BBC is effectively an employee of the viewers who are forced to pay the licence fee, they are perfectly entitled to say what they think of them. (Anyone who performs the same role on a commercial channel is also paid for by the viewer, of course, but rather more indirectly.) I relished the exchanges which often followed, and only a handful of times had to use the tabloid editor Kelvin MacKenzie's tactic, which was to tell my correspondent that I would reluctantly have to ban them from watching. This generally led to even angrier letters, protesting, 'You can't do that – I pay the licence fee!'

I discovered that generally, if you've made a mistake it is best to answer a letter of complaint with 'You're quite right. I'm so sorry. I'll try to do better.' This often has the complainant writing back to say, 'Oh, please don't take it too seriously.' The nuclear option is to employ the tactic refined by the former Prime Minister of New Zealand, Rob 'Piggy' Muldoon: 'Dear Mrs Smith, I think you should know that some lunatic is using your name and address to send offensive letters in the post.'* I perhaps sent something similar to the man who wrote from Sutton in Surrey during a journalists' strike I supported in 1985. He described how he had arrived home, 'blessing my luck at not having to look at you on television. Then I picked up the *Standard*, and damn me, there you were, leering in the front rank of the picket line, puffing out your chest like a stuffed ulotrichan and posing with drooping pants.' I must have kept the letter as a vocabulary lesson – apparently 'ulotrichan' means having crisp hair.

Other letters included numerous requests to donate items for sale in charity auctions, or for recipes to be included in fundraising cookbooks – further evidence of the conviction I reached a few years ago, and which is quite the reverse of the impression given

---

* Muldoon lost power in 1984 after calling a snap election when three sheets to the wind. The event became known as 'the schnapps election'.

by most of the mass media, that most people are decent human beings. There are an awful lot of generally unacknowledged individuals doing terrific things in the world.

In one letter, someone said they had managed to read my palms off the television screen: 'You are quite healthy and energetic. Minor ailments are inevitable and may sometimes do you much harm if you neglect them,' followed by similarly vacuous diagnoses. Amateur cartoonists sent awful caricatures they had drawn; singers, songs they had written; and poets their poems. For a while, a kind viewer would post me hand-painted ties every couple of months. A lady still brings pots of jam she has made to recordings of *University Challenge*, and over the years plenty of fishing folk have sent me flies they have tied up with feather and fur, which they claim are 'certain' to catch salmon or trout. When I was blackballed by the Garrick Club (for the crime, apparently, of being beastly to politicians on television) I was bombarded with supportive letters from outraged club members I had never met. They coincided with numerous invitations to join other clubs, including the Crediton Men's Group, where there was 'no danger from bores – if someone's being dull we tell him to shut up and buy us another pint'.

A public life is as inadequate an expression of the whole person as a patient's medical notes – they only record what he or she told the doctor, and often disclose nothing much about the texture of their life. I suppose that when I eventually expire, the likely headline will be 'Man Who Asked Same Question Fourteen Times Dies'. This is no more of a claim on anyone's attention than 'Man Who Collected 5,000 Tin Cans Dies'. It wasn't fourteen times, but the repetition of that number proves that what matters is who produces the first account, and that was the figure used on the radio the morning after the notorious Michael Howard interview. The rest of the caricature – 'Mr Rude', the truculence, the so-called sneering, I just have to live with. Is it just the media which can only deal with a monochrome stereotype, or are we all a bit like that?

You don't learn much more from personal tastes. I am a strong swimmer, love fly-fishing, drink more than the Department of Health says is good for us, and have a dodgy knee. I like dogs, but am allergic to cats. I am easily bored, read a lot, don't watch much television, would love to be able to play a musical instrument but can only sing – badly – in the bath, dislike shopping and enjoy watching birds. For years I had to stay up late, and my real idea of a good time is to be in bed by 10.30. I don't sleep particularly well, and I don't much like kale. Or the parson's nose on a roast bird. I would rather ride a bike than drive a car. I spent several years seeing a therapist, and several more on antidepressants. Though I think I'm an atheist, I have a passion for old churches. Occasionally I sit on the loo and shoot squirrels out of the bathroom window.

Journalists like to brag that their account of events is 'the first draft of history'. Sometimes this is true, although it is really a boast that can only be made by a small minority of our trade. I have been lucky enough to have had an interesting job and to have worked with clever, funny people. We had a lot of laughs, and sometimes we found things out. That's all. What follows does not pretend to be history or rounded portraiture, just some recollections of how it seemed at the time. There is often a disclaimer at the front of novels to the effect that 'Any resemblance to individuals alive or dead is unintended.' In a memoir, the reverse ought to be true – any similarity is entirely intentional. But, just as every witness to an accident tells a slightly different story, others will have discrepant memories from my own. As Bertrand Russell said, 'When a man tells you he knows the exact truth about anything, you are safe in inferring he is an inexact man.'

'The world is a tragedy to those who feel and a comedy to those who think,' that pipsqueak eighteenth-century writer Horace Walpole is supposed to have said. He ignored the fact we can all both feel and think, and I find that what made me weep at the age of twenty made me laugh at fifty. Both responses are right, but as time passes the fierce clarity of youth gives way to a more textured palette, primary colours fading to pastel pigments. I don't like the fact that I have mellowed, but I cannot deny it. For all the sound and fury, there are very few people indeed that I actively dislike: in fact, looking back over the decades I could count them on the fingers of one hand. Assuming I could remember who they all were.

There is, then, nothing all-encompassing about what follows. It's just some stuff that happened, what it felt like at the time, and, maybe, what might be learned from it. I have taken the decision not to write about my family, because what they choose to disclose of their lives is up to them.

As for sources, I have kept many diaries over the years, though some of them were clearly begun as New Year resolutions and petered out by March. Some of the incidents recounted here come from those diaries, some from memory, and others from responses to the sort of letter Auberon Waugh sent when he was invited to produce his memoirs: 'I have been asked to write my autobiography. Does anyone know what I've been doing?' The following were generous with their recollections: Steve Anderson, Peter Barron, David Belton, Keith Bowers, James Bray, Neil Breakwell, Jasmin Buttar, Julia Cleverdon, Frank Considine, Lucy Crystal, Richard Danbury, Peter Davies, George Entwistle, Tim Gardam, Jim Gray, Peter Gwyn, Robert Harris, John Hay, Meirion Jones, Rhodri Jones, Laura Kuenssberg, Anita Land, Adam Livingstone, Barton Macfarlane, Hannah MacInnes, Sally Magnusson, Linda Mitchell, Eddie Morgan, Shaminder Nahal, Andrew Nickolds, Jeff Overs, Charlie Potter, Celia Reed, Peter Snow, Jillian Taylor, Kirsty Wark, Peter Weil and Michael Whale. Carly Wallis, the one person without whom *Newsnight* would fall apart, kindly sent me screeds of paper detailing what happened during my twenty-five years there. To those I have stupidly left off this list, many apologies. I hope it goes without saying that any mistakes are all my own work.

I am grateful to my literary agent, David Godwin, for the occasional lunch, and to Arabella Pike for her encouragement, skill and charm in steering the thing from manuscript to bound copy. Neither is to blame for anything I have got wrong or misremembered.

1

Why Do You Talk Like That?

Some people claim to remember their own birth. I don't believe them, and I certainly can't do so. The night my second younger brother was born, and the day I arrived back from school to find I had a younger sister, I recall vividly. Where I left the book I borrowed from the London Library last week I have no idea.

When I was growing up we lived in an absurdly pretty pink-washed, mullion-windowed cottage at the edge of a village green in Hampshire. Rose Cottage really did have roses around the door, and at weekends we could watch the local team play cricket on the green without leaving the front garden. There was a big old fig tree in the garden which splattered ripe fruit onto the ground each September, and a pump in the middle of the lawn with a white-painted seat around which I learned to ride a bike.

In the cottage next door lived Mr and Mrs Ball. Mrs Ball was very old, and baked a lot. The only thing I can recall about Mr Ball was that he drowned kittens in a sack. Mother wore her long black hair tied back in a bun, and rode a black sit-up-and-beg bicycle with a child's seat over the back mudguard which I occupied as she pedalled the four miles into Fareham for groceries. What little I remember of Dad – he was away at sea a lot – is of a curly-haired figure in loose trousers and lightly checked cotton shirt. There was a black-and-brown family dachshund named Dinah.

My first education was at the redbrick Victorian primary school at the end of the village green. Mum would walk me down to the playground, and was there at the gate when classes finished. The teacher sat at a raised desk, and the classroom was high-windowed and cavernous. I cannot help that it all sounds such a clichéd picture of a vanished England, but that's just how it was.

My father, Keith, was stationed at the Royal Navy base in Portsmouth, and was away at sea when I was born. In the final days of her pregnancy my mother, Joan, took the train north to be with her family, and I was delivered in a nursing home near Leeds. At the time, Yorkshire County Cricket Club operated a selection policy under which only those who had been born in the county were eligible for selection. My Yorkshire father occasionally offered this as an explanation for my mother's long pilgrimage from the Solent to Leeds, though he never seemed to take that close an interest in the game. While I failed to acquire any great skill with bat or ball, I never lost an unreasonable pride (insufferable smugness?) about having come from God's Own County, even though I never really lived there.

We were not a close family – as Mother told it when she was older, there was one occasion when Dad returned from sea service and I ran away screaming, because I had no idea who he was. This must have distressed him, but relations between us never really improved much. I suppose the family would have been classified as middle class, but there was always a slight sense that we were hanging in there by our fingernails. The constant refrain of my childhood was 'We can't afford it,' which I now recognise wasn't really a declaration of poverty so much as mere Yorkshireness, although it didn't seem so at the time. We shared the generally improving standard of living in the fifties, but did not live extravagantly: there was only one foreign holiday, in 1959, when we took a boat from Southampton to Vigo, in Spain – on the return journey the ship carried great numbers of Caribbean immigrants, whom my brothers and I, never having seen a black person, found fascinating.

As a family we did not number doctors, dentists, bank managers or similar worthies in our circle. No one in the immediate family had been to university, though one of my mother's sisters had spent some time at RADA, hoping to become an actress. It was a very brief career which distressed her parents almost as much as her incomprehensible decision to become a Roman Catholic. But my father was a naval officer, and while Mum's father had started out as a travelling salesman, he ended up with his own canning factory and a small country estate in North Yorkshire. It was he who paid the fees when I, my younger brothers Giles and James, and my sister Jenny later went to private schools.

All children like to imagine their parents have heroic histories. In my childhood I believed Dad to have spent the war on convoy duty, protecting the supplies which came from North America to Britain, or those sent from a remote Scottish sea loch to Russian allies in Archangel and Murmansk. Of the many miserable fates which stalked the war generation, unannounced death from a U-boat torpedo in the icy waters of the North Atlantic has always seemed one of the worst. I imagined Dad as the sort of figure played by Jack Hawkins in *The Cruel Sea*, binoculars hanging around his neck, standing on the bridge of a destroyer in a naval duffel-coat, with mountainous seas breaking across the foredeck, calmly ordering 'Full ahead both' into a voice tube as a torpedo wake glows white under the briny. But when I unearthed his records a few months ago his military career turned out to have been rather more prosaic. He seems to have volunteered for the navy straight out of school, giving his civilian occupation as 'bank clerk'. The records show early training at a requisitioned holiday camp at Skegness, from which he emerged as a rating, followed by another training period at an airfield in Luton, as he hoped to become a navy pilot with the Fleet Air Arm.

This did not come off, possibly because, as he later told his sisters, he was grounded for 'hedge-hopping' and flying his aircraft beneath the arches of bridges. Perhaps it was actually for more humdrum reasons – only a very small proportion of those who wanted to become wartime pilots were successful. At any rate, in March 1941 he began a less glamorous naval life as a 'Writer' on board HMS *Fernie*, a largely administrative role aboard a destroyer assigned to escort shipping in the Channel. As it did for many people, my father's war doubtless passed in bouts of intense fear and excitement, separated by very much longer periods of great tedium. By the following year he had been promoted to 'Leading Writer', in which capacity he was shuffled from one ship or shore base to another, either at home or abroad. In 1944 he is recorded as serving in the Persian Gulf on board a series of vessels, including converted Norwegian whaling ships and at the Royal Navy base in Basra, Iraq.

He emerged from the war with five medals, recognising service in home waters and the Indian Ocean. Children generally imagine all medals to have been won in much the way you gain a VC. In fact, most of them testify to more mundane activities. When I was about eight I remember approaching him as he sat slumped in an armchair reading the paper and asking whether he had ever been shipwrecked. 'Six times!' he replied, and reburied himself in the newsprint. He was really saying 'Leave me alone!' But I so wanted to believe him.

At the end of the war, huge numbers of men were demobilised and returned to civilian life. But Dad decided to swim in the other direction, and applied to be commissioned as a Royal Navy officer. In October 1945 he was appointed Temporary Acting Sub Lieutenant. A group photograph of sixty or so young officers gathered at the naval base at Gosport shows him in the third row, one of the few lieutenants with war service medals – an indication that his time in the ranks had resulted in his being older than many of his peers. Within a few years he had been promoted to Lieutenant and given the posting sought by every naval officer, command of his own vessel, a motor torpedo boat.

Quite apart from the awful loss of life, the war deprived a generation of young men and women of the opportunity to enjoy their youth. I imagine the period after the end of hostilities to have been the happiest time of my father's life – the navy then included great numbers of men who would never have joined in peacetime, there were endless practical tasks, the company of shipmates, and – by contrast with his wartime service – freedom from the prospect of imminent death. But what was he like as a Royal Navy officer? In the time I knew and tried to understand him, the blunt, salty humour of the wardroom always seemed his natural environment, and the reports from his commanding officers talk of him as a cheery mess companion, with a well-developed sense of the absurd. Another report, though, worried that he was sometimes too hard on his men. Whether this was because not so long ago he had been one of them is only speculation, of course.

None of the reports answers the great enigma of my father's early life: why did he decide to give it all up? There is no one left to ask. Perhaps it was because his war service in the ranks meant he was older than most of the other 'snotties' commissioned with him. Did someone tell him that his late start meant he'd never make it to the very top? I have a suspicion that marriage and the fairly rapid arrival of three children made him think he ought to be spending more time at home. It vaguely troubles me, thinking about it, that I cannot imagine him feeling that he *wanted* to be at home more. Whatever the reason, it was a disastrous decision.

Though he continued to play the sailor all his life (the naval cry of 'Two, six – heave' accompanied any manual labour in the family, such as pushing the car), in 1954 he resigned his commission, bought a motor scooter and took a job as a typewriter sales-man. Just about my earliest memory is of being woken by a commotion one night, slipping out of bed and creeping down-stairs to see my father standing in the kitchen in a pool of blood. The back of his pale gabardine coat was stained a dark brown, and Mother was helping him take off his peaked crash helmet. When she succeeded, more gouts of blood fell onto the stone floor. Accidents can happen to anyone, but the contrast between this bloody spectacle and the glamorous wartime figure I had imagined in uniform, sword and even a cape, seemed for years to demon-strate the unhappy consequences of the decision he had made. My abiding feeling is that leaving the navy was the biggest mistake of his life. We cannot pretend to be what we are not, and my father was by no stretch of the imagination a family man. Like many others who never had a chance to enjoy their youth, being a sailor was his *métier*. He should probably never have pretended to be anything else.

Whether or not this was the reason, he had an appalling temper. He was accustomed to chains of command, and the merest sugges-tion of insubordination would send him into a fury, during which he'd grab the nearest hard object with which to beat whoever had provoked him. I was thrashed with sticks, shoes, cricket stumps, cricket bats or the flat of his hand. In the most intense row – or at least the one I recall most intensely – he sent me to my room for disobeying him, and when I stood my ground, he tried to drag me upstairs. Within a minute or so all that was left of the shirt I had been wearing – it was a black-and-white check – was the collar.

It is in the nature of childhood that we only know what we know. The phrase 'dysfunctional family' could certainly be applied to ours. But then, it describes just about every family in the land. Did I love my father? My feelings ranged from resentment to passion-ate hatred. It was not a sophisticated reaction, but I was too young for sophisticated reactions. Now, I see a damaged man. Many years later my younger sister told me that she had once walked in on him lying on the floor of the bathroom, sobbing. He asked her to leave him alone, which she did at once. It was a traumatic moment for both of them, and was never mentioned again.

Ours was perhaps not so different from many other families of the time, with their largely uncomplaining mothers making do and mending, and insisting that if you didn't eat what was put in front of you for supper you'd get it again for breakfast. There were certainly moments of tenderness – the Saturday-morning visits to Woolworths in the local High Street with Dad to buy twisted little greaseproof-paper bags of salted peanuts, the times he'd help us build model warships, or his snorting laughter at *The Goon Show* on the radio. Jenny, his youngest child, seemed to bring out the best in him, and he could arrive home with posies of violets or anemones for her. But he could also change in an instant.

He had lost his own father, to whom, according to his sister, he had been devoted, when he was only eight years old. The death had apparently plunged the family into a financial crisis – an eccentric aunt once told me that even when he was on leave during the darkest days of the war, my father never went home because he had become convinced that his mother had decided to remarry for money. Although he was educated at a school in Bradford established for the sons of Methodist ministers, he had an absurd affectation of pronouncing selected words as he imagined Southern posh people pronounced them – so a waistcoat he always called a 'wiskett', and a hotel 'an 'otel'. In material terms he had 'married well' – although Mum was certainly not posh, her father being a self-made man who spoke with flat Yorkshire vowels and talked of 'having a luke in the buke'. With the marriage came a cushion of prosperity, but I have a strong feeling – though without any evidence to support it – that Dad later came deeply to resent the fact that it was his father-in-law who paid our school fees, and we all believed that the house was in Mum's name.

Certainly, my childhood impression was of a man incapable of expressing affection, concerned with keeping up appearances and permanently on the edge of an explosion which might well be expressed in physical violence. In my late teens he was taken into hospital for some undignified operation on his bum. When I went to visit him I had only been there three minutes when he said, 'You can go now. You've done your duty.' He understood duty a lot better than he understood affection. Perhaps as an adult I might have come to forgive and forget and understand, but by then he had left England for the South Pacific.

It had been a wartime romance. Mum was working as an ambulance driver at Grantley Hall, an enormous seventeenth-century mansion near Ripon in North Yorkshire, requisitioned for use as a convalescent home for wounded servicemen. Dad's sister Margaret was also working there, and it seems to have been through her that Joan and Keith met. It was an on-off courtship which lasted for several years before finally leading, in 1949, to marriage. Shortly before she died Aunt Margaret told me that Dad had said that if he didn't marry Joan he probably wouldn't marry anyone. Joan was twenty-nine when they married, he was twenty-seven, and the relationship seems to have been troubled from the start. Although they did not separate until over twenty years later, there had been some sort of tension on their honeymoon in the Scilly Isles, when, as Mother told us later, she felt Dad paid too much attention to a Wren whom they had met on a ferry between the islands. Children rarely imagine their parents being troubled by sexual feelings, but the incident clearly still rankled with Mum decades later.

Dad's elder sister, our maiden aunt Kathleen, whom we visited many times, remained loyal to him to the end. She lived in a tall Victorian house in a leafy corner of Richmond in south-west London – or, as Richmondites then insisted, 'Richmond, Surrey'. In practice she lived in two rooms on the ground floor, with the rest of the place let out to various slightly desiccated characters, from Sheila, a French teacher who rented the basement, to Mr Lewis, a bald, plummy chap who occupied rooms on the top floor, accompanied at weekends by his younger friend from the Isle of Dogs. Kathleen had bought the house after the war – a bargain, apparently, because of bomb damage. There were ancient Persian rugs on the floors, a payphone in the entrance hall, and extraordinary pieces of furniture she prided herself on having bought from junk shops and then repaired. Some of them were rather beautiful, and others just rather odd.

Long residence in Richmond had stripped Aunty Kathleen's voice of any Yorkshire twang, and she spoke like a duchess slightly perplexed at the way the butler had laid the table. She was one of that great tribe of solitary women, stalwarts of clubs and voluntary organisations, whose representatives you could find in every corner of Britain in those days. I discovered from one of the nurses at the home in which she spent her last couple of years that there had once been a young man called Albert, but he been killed during the war. There were legions of women like her, forced to make their lonely way in the world, acquiring the necessary no-nonsense bustle that made it possible, but somehow always carrying a slight whiff of sadness about them. Several years ago, when I was giving a talk in Cheltenham about the English identity crisis, a middle-aged woman in the audience asked, 'Have you thought about how much the problem of English identity is bound up in the disappearance of the maiden aunt?' I hadn't. But she was definitely on to something. Though they were often sniggered at, these women bereaved in youth carried forward an idea of nationality that is very hard to locate in any other group of individuals. With my mother's unmarried sister Muriel, and Dad's two unmarried sisters Margaret and Kate, I had a total of three maiden aunts.

Aunt Kate was accident-prone. At some point she had broken her right leg, and her injuries never healed properly, so that every time she went outside the shin shone through her hosiery in a lurid shade of purple and black. Once she somehow managed to track down a distant relative in training for the Catholic priesthood and arranged to meet him at the entrance to the coffee shop in Brown Muff, the great department store in the centre of Bradford, the nearest city to his seminary. As the young man shook her hand she felt the elastic in the waistband of her knickers break, and they began to slide down her thighs. She strode towards the table she had her eye on for tea, and with 'Just a minute' to the putative priest at her side, reached up under her skirt, grabbed her pants and stepped out of them. That sort of thing was always happening to her, like the seven attempts she made to pass her driving test at the age of fifty-something, at least one of which included her reversing her primrose-yellow Triumph Herald into a six-foot-deep hole in the road, watched by half a dozen astonished labourers. She was wonderful.

When we were children she often came to stay, taking us all on walks which somehow always ended at an ice-cream parlour. Once a year she would meet us off the train at Paddington and take us to the Boat Show at Earl's Court, where we ogled floating gin palaces and she considered various labour-saving devices she might install on *Kirsty*, her horribly unstable little cabin cruiser moored on the Thames. She usually decided that she really didn't need them, and our excursions on the boat retained their fish-paste-sandwich flavour to the end of our teens. Mercifully, none of us had been on board when her previous boat, *Lorac*, caught fire and sank – an event indelibly linked in my mind to Sir Francis Drake's 'singeing of the King of Spain's beard' at Cádiz in 1587, which we must have just tackled in a history lesson. *Kirsty* met her end one day when Aunt Kate asked me to row across the Thames to the mooring and bale her out after several days of heavy rain – Kate had broken her arm, and couldn't do it herself. On board the boat I lifted the decking and was baling away when a vast pleasure steamer passed by, sending out a great wash. I lost my balance, stuck my foot through the bottom of the hull and unleashed a Buster Keaton-style fountain in the cockpit, after a few minutes of which *Kirsty* settled on the bottom of the river.

None of us quite knew what Aunty Kathleen had done before the war, during which she served as a nurse. Apart from the *Richmond and Twickenham Times*, which she read from cover to cover, mainly for the items of staggering unimportance reported as if they were the invasion of the Sudetenland, the only other publication in the house was the *Draper's Record*. In the 1960s she acquired an old barber's shop which she turned into the 'Kate Paxman Boutique', appealing, she explained, to 'the sort of women who'd like to shop at Harrods, but can't afford to'. (Harrods at the time was still considered a smart shop.) The business seemed to do all right – there must have been some shopkeeping gene on that side of the family, because Aunt Kate's stepsister Margaret kept a haberdashery shop in Selby.

In her last few years poor Aunt Kate developed a brain tumour, which triggered what she tried to laugh off as 'the shakes'. She endured the pointless interventions of brain surgeons with a stoicism which humbles me even now.

In early 1957 – the year that the Prime Minister, Harold Macmillan declared that 'most of our people have never had it so good', my father took a job with a steel company and uprooted the family from Hampshire to the Midlands. With help from Mother's parents we moved into a tall, gloomy house in the Lickey Hills near Bromsgrove in Worcestershire, alongside what had once been a main road to Birmingham. High Lea was an austere brick Victorian building, which must once have dominated the hillside on which it stood – it had the stamp of a man who'd done well in Black Country metal-bashing and would rather like people to know. It still had tumbledown stables, haylofts and garages, a kennel block and a paved yard. There were acres of garden, paddock and orchard, a vile-smelling septic tank at the bottom of the adjoining fields, and an enormous lime tree on the central lawn. Another lawn surrounded a circular ornamental pond which was drained after my infant sister had been discovered one day lying almost drowned among the water lilies. There was also a tennis court, the surface of which had been wrecked by grazing horses.

Suburbia was creeping in upon the metal-basher's mansion, and the land around the big house was increasingly occupied by infill housing. It was a time when living standards were rising, which showed itself in the new religion of do-it-yourself. The Messiah was Barry Bucknell, a dull man in striped tie and cardigan who seemed never to be off television, instructing his disciples how to tear down Victorian cornices or ruin the interesting features of doors by nailing hardboard all over them. Every man aspired to a bench and a vice, and Dad was soon sending away for kits to make glass-fronted bookcases and a not-very-attractive workbox in which Mum could keep her wool, thread, buttons and stuff. Dad was not a very effective devotee – he seemed to hammer his thumb a lot, and he didn't look after his tools particularly well. A corner of our vegetable garden had been sold off to another DIY enthusi-ast who built an entire new house which, although he moved his family in, never seemed to be finished – the man lost interest, and settled for living among piles of bricks and timber with a big black dog called Bimbo which didn't do much except fart.

Like most houses of the time, High Lea had no central heating, and the place rang to constant cries of 'Close the door!' Once we had stopped toddling, all the children were given domestic chores, the worst of which was bringing coal up from the basement. Every few months the coalman would empty jute sacks of coal down a chute which ran from the front garden into the cellar. The task of shovelling it into a scuttle for delivery to the sitting room was unpleasant, not only because the place was cold and damp and lit by a single lightbulb, but because it was infested with frogs. When you struck the shovel into the heap at the bottom of the chute something black and sparkling with coal dust was liable to leap up at you.

That aside, High Lea was a terrific place. There were endless war games among the ruined outbuildings, and den-building and camp-outs in the garden with my closest friends, Paul Davies, who lived with the smelly black dog in the permanently unfinished house in the sold-off corner of the garden, and Gerald Mullen, the son of an Irish assembly-line worker at the Longbridge car plant a few miles away. When, a year or so after our arrival, we recorded a message on the new-fangled reel-to-reel tape recorder Grandpa had bought, my brothers and I sounded as if we had been born and bred in the Black Country.

My mother's mother, who had been born in a Glasgow slum and escaped by joining the Salvation Army, once told me of Mum's insistence that 'Only the best was good enough for you children.' In that belief my brothers and I were sent to different schools from my friends Paul and Gerald. For a couple of years we attended The Mount, a local pre-preparatory school of which I remember little, which probably means it was a happy place. The only clear memories I have are of my youngest brother reciting verse after verse of *Hiawatha* from memory over tea, and an occasion on which he was cornered by a gang of girls who pinned him to the ground so that their leader – now doubtless a highly respectable grandmother – could clamber on top to kiss him. On our first day of term there we returned home to find that Mum had given birth to a baby girl who would be named Genevieve – which, after Jeremy, Giles and James, at least had the advantage that when someone was to be shouted at, there was a reasonable chance that the first syllable might come out right.

The next stage of 1950s private education required ambitious parents to commit their children to the care of a bunch of drunks, pederasts and cashiered army officers at a local preparatory school. There is said to have been a question posed in the *New Statesman* of the time: 'Has anyone ever met a sane prep school master?' I do not know whether any was found, but there were certainly very few at the Lickey Hills Preparatory School.

The place had originally been built as another Victorian mansion for a successful Birmingham businessman, and over the years had had various classrooms added on to the original structure. The headmaster was – or appeared to a small boy – a tall man with straight brown hair swept back from a face which seemed to have been sculpted from sandstone. He wore cavalry twill trousers and tweed jackets, and turned an exceptional shade of violet when angry, which was much of the time. When he was in this state you could see the pulses in his temples throbbing. I imagine something had happened to him in the war.

But then, something had happened to more or less every grown-up in the war. Colonel Collinson, who taught us French (more precisely, he taught us how to make an invisible margin down the middle of the page, on either side of which, at some vague date in the future, we might perhaps write French words and their English counterparts) was missing a finger, and Mr Thomas, our gym master, was minus an eye – if you asked him nicely he'd pop out his glass replacement and let you have a look inside the socket. It was hard to imagine Mr Steer, the classics master, in uniform, since he found it hard enough to puff his way up the three steps into our classroom, pinching out his roll-up at the door with mahogany-brown fingers and slipping the dog-end into a match-box which then went into the pocket of his astonishingly filthy houndstooth jacket. There were a few older masters who might, I suppose, have seen action in the First World War, and the occasional young man about to go to university or seminary – the only thing I learned from them was that the Prayer of Humble Access in the communion service was 'almost certainly blasphemous'.

The sole women in this odd world were the headmaster's long-suffering little wife and the school matron, a thin, beaky figure who bustled about the place in dark-blue uniform and starched nurse's cap, dispensing 'malt' to boys who weren't growing quickly enough, 'tonic' to boys who were growing too fast, and laxatives to anyone who hesitated in answering her questions about their bowel movements. Since the lavatories were housed in an outbuilding which regularly froze up in winter, daily bowel movements were low on the list of priorities. Matron also supervised the compulsory once-a-week bath.

Why did our parents surrender us to the care of such a bizarre institution? The short – and correct – answer is that they thought they were buying us a head-start in life. Neither Paul nor Gerald, my friends at home, seemed to be especially disadvantaged by being spared the experience – though it was hard to tell when we were playing war games or cooking bannocks on the ovens we made in the woods out of old bricks and a sheet of corrugated iron.

Slowly but surely, though, the chasm widened. There were new friends among the fellow inmates of the Lickey Hills Preparatory School, and they were the sons of doctors and architects. Which, I suppose, was one of the things my family was paying for. British class divisions were much deeper then (though the subject is still endlessly written about in newspapers and magazines, as if nothing has changed). The truth is that, for those who can afford it, education has been for generations a way of translating the children of one class into the adolescents of another. The parents made things and generated wealth. Their children emerged from education for careers in the professions. On the way, they have been hived off from the mainstream. Few of us ever recover. The obvious solution is to make the education provided by the state so good that no one but a lunatic would want to go elsewhere.

My parents' pockets weren't deep enough for me to feel entirely at ease with the boys who genuinely belonged to the professional classes. One day, at my friend Philip Kelly's house, I saw the milk delivery. It included yoghurt, a substance which had never darkened the door of High Lea – or 262 Old Birmingham Road, as it was less portentously known – and of which I had indeed never heard. Phil's father was an architect. My own father's sally into sophistication was to bring home an avocado pear one day. We were all rather baffled by it.

Life at High Lea had a predictable routine. In the morning, after a teaspoonful of cod-liver oil followed by another of viscous orange-juice concentrate – both of them provided, I think, by the National Health Service – my brothers and I set off in our grey shorts, blue Aertex shirts, navy blazers and caps to walk the mile to school. Occasionally we were waylaid by other boys, notably the son of the local butcher, who once boasted to us that he could hold a piece of liver in his hand for longer than any of us could imagine. Sometimes the encounters got physical and we had to run for it. On the way home in the evening we might stop by the post office to see if we could extract any forgotten coins by pressing button B in the telephone box, money we would then spend on sweets – the penny chew was particularly popular.

The sixty or so boys in the school ate together in one great dining room. There was tea from an enormous urn, at break there was a small bottle of milk (again provided, I think, by the state) and chunks of bread coated in beef dripping – delicious when heavily sprinkled with salt. Lunch was generally a stew or some variety of shrivelled offal – liver or kidneys or whatever was cheap that week, I suppose. The evening meal was usually something like tinned pilchards in tomato sauce, washed down with soapy-tasting tea from The Urn.

For the last year or so of my time at prep school I was expected to live in as a boarder, the final enrolment into the repressed self-reliance of what the middle classes took to be 'a decent education'. We slept in dormitories of four or five beds apiece, in which the only visible contact with home was the rug we had each been given by our mothers. Mine was in some odd artificial fibre, striped in yellow, grey and white – testament to the family's unfamiliarity with boarding-school life: everyone else had some species of woollen tartan, sometimes claiming it to be that of the family clan. Sunday mornings were spent writing letters home. This was done under the eye of a member of staff, and followed a strict formula:

Dear mother and father,
How are you? I am well.
The first eleven played Abberley yesterday. We lost five–nil.

After that, it was a desperate struggle to creep over onto the back of the piece of paper, as we knew that a letter that was too short would be rejected by the supervising teacher.

Looking back on it, the life we were leading was so utterly separate from our home lives that it was a wonder we found any point of contact at all. A stranger glancing in through the big Victorian window might have guessed that the adult was there to censor what was being written. And indeed, sometimes he did: my brother Giles, who was having an absolutely wretched time, several times wrote letters reading 'I hate it here, please come and take me home,' which were torn up. He managed to smuggle a couple of notes out in the pockets of day boys at the school, but our parents thought he was making a fuss about nothing, and would eventually settle down. When he finally ran away and barricaded himself in his bedroom at home they returned him to the school: it was important to them that you did your duty, and 'putting up with things' was part of that.

By the standards of the time, I suppose the Lickey Hills Preparatory School was no worse than many others. If there were school inspectors in those days, we were unaware of them, and it seemed that anyone could open a school whenever and wherever they liked. At least we had little trouble of the kind which befell a friend enduring a similar education elsewhere. When he eventually plucked up the courage to go to the headmaster to report that the geography master kept putting his hand up his shorts, the head replied with a long-suffering air that 'Mr Jones is what we call a homosexual. Do you know what that means? No? It means he prefers little boys to little girls. You will find that many of the staff are homosexuals. Frankly, on the money I pay them, they're the only people I can get to work here.'

The language betrays the lazy prejudices of the time. As far as I was aware, we had no trouble with paedophiles at Lickey Hills, though one or two of the masters did seem to take a keen interest in supervising communal showers and suddenly switching the water from warm to freezing. In the popular cliché, the prep and public schools of the fifties and early sixties were alive with depraved behaviour. All I can say is that in the whole of my school career I never came across a single paedophile teacher, and very few boys with a taste for much more than the solitary vice.

Lickey Hills was a business, and, it seemed, a not very successful one. Shortage of money was a fact of life at every level. Because the school could not afford a physics laboratory, the elderly science master was reduced to describing the outcome of experiments by drawing the usual results on a blackboard. Since we had to imagine that the line of chalk was a piece of metal, we were not left much the wiser about its powers of conductivity. But if the school was poor, the teachers were much poorer. Colonel Collinson seemed the only one who had any form of car – a Messerschmitt three-wheeler in a shade of paraffin pink. When he had lifted the roof and eased his great frame and moustachioed face behind the steering bar he looked like some crazy life-sized children's toy.

Apart from having a missing finger, Colonel Collinson must also have been bit deaf. One morning while we were at breakfast there was an explosion from the staff area.

'Colonel Collinson, I have asked you three times to pass my wife the marmalade!' roared the headmaster.

The Colonel mumbled some explanation.

'Colonel Collinson,' barked the head, 'you are dismissed!'

There was no going back from such a public sacking, and the Colonel's imminent departure was the only topic of conversation among us in the twenty minutes between the end of breakfast and the first lesson of the day. I cannot now recall who came up with the evil idea which ensured the poor man's final humbling. It required several of us to carry it out, so perhaps it was just one of those things that emerges naturally and collectively. By applying all our strength first to one side of the Messerschmitt bubble car and then to the other, we levered it off the ground, grabbed a few bricks and lowered it back, so that all three wheels were just clear of the surface. A few minutes into the lesson we looked out of the window and saw the Colonel descending the school steps, wearing a British Warm officer's greatcoat and carrying a small brown leather suitcase, which presumably contained all his worldly goods. We watched as the poor man strode to his car, opened the Perspex bubble, tossed his battered suitcase into the back, and started the engine. The wheels spun, but nothing moved. His humiliation was complete.

For schools like Lickey Hills to work their alchemy, there had to be as great a disengagement from the outside world as possible. ('What do you expect of the parents?' one of those paying the bill for this transformation asked my next headmaster. 'Pay the fees and stay away!' he replied succinctly.) Fathers generally seem to have understood this better than mothers. The son of a distinguished lawyer recalled a particular low point when he was gathered with his fellow inmates at the end of term, awaiting the arrival of his father to collect him for the holidays. He watched as his father strode into the room, grabbed another child and dragged him protesting to the car, saying, 'Oh, *do* come on, Stephen.' It was only as he was about to drive off, and the small boy managed to attract his attention by exclaiming, 'But sir, I'm not your son!' that the father turned, and with a cry of 'Oh no, you're not!' realised his mistake.

'Teddy boys', with their long jackets and quiffed hairstyles, were a 1950s phenomenon. Not at Lickey Hills School – or 'Hillscourt', as it had by then been renamed by its bonkers proprietor and headmaster – they weren't. Well into the 1960s they were blamed for anything that went wrong in the school grounds. On one occasion I watched the headmaster's son chucking lighted matches into gorse bushes, and duly setting the hills alight – when the fire brigade arrived he explained that the inferno was the work of the teds, who were blamed for just about everything that went wrong at the school (apart from the hit-and-miss teaching.) Periodically, the teds clambered over a fence and vandalised the wooden huts at the end of the swimming pool. This was a concrete-lined hole in the ground, fed by a stream from the hills and replete with frogs and newts. 'Learning to swim' involved being dropped into the pool and trying to reach the other side before death by drowning or exposure.

The headmaster became obsessed with preventing the teds from sharing this luxury. One Sunday afternoon he decided it was time to act. Fifteen or so of the more senior boys (all aged twelve or thirteen, therefore) were summoned to his study, where, we discovered, he had amassed an arsenal that would have equipped a minor peasants' revolt. Stacked in the corner were scythes, sickles, chisels, hammers, an air rifle and a shotgun.

'Boys,' he said, 'if the teds break in this afternoon, you're to deal with them.'

Since we knew that the local youths were all fifteen, sixteen or older, we were terrified. But we had weaponry and they, we hoped, did not. The headmaster was halfway through his pre-battle briefing when a small boy knocked on the door and entered the room, exclaiming breathlessly, 'Sir, the teds have broken into the swimming pool!' 'Get them, boys!' barked the head. The most eager sprinted for the pool. The rest of us followed at the pace of Russian conscripts being thrown into an assault at Stalingrad. Only when we reached the hole in the ground did we realise that we had left the scythes, knives and guns in the headmaster's study.

By the time we reached the pool, the teds were clambering back over the wooden fence separating the school grounds from the local park. With a great feeling of relief we paused our mission, until in the distance we heard the headmaster bellowing that we were to bring the culprits to justice. With sinking hearts we climbed the fence and followed them into the park. The teds jogged on nonchalantly, turning occasionally to shout obscenities at the posse of much smaller boys pursuing them. Then, to our horror, they stopped and stood their ground. Two or three of them tore planks of wood from the park fence, and brandished them like clubs.

The gang leader beckoned, saying, 'OK. One of us, and one of you.'

Jeremy Clewer, the son of a Quaker family, was one of the quietest and kindest boys in the school. He also had the misfortune to be one of the tallest.

'You,' said the ted, pointing at Clewer. 'You fight.'

Clewer looked out from under his floppy fringe. This was definitely not the way the Society of Friends usually dealt with things. The head ted stepped forward and punched him. Clewer fell to the ground, and the two of them rolled around in the dust for a few minutes. The battle of champions ended inconclusively. One of the other members of the gang pointed at the identical woollen jumpers we all wore – hoops of dark and light blue – and said, 'What is that place then, some sort of approved school?'

The two combatants brushed the dust from their clothes, and the gang sauntered on their way while we gathered around Clewer and told him how brave he'd been, before heading back to describe the battle to the headmaster. He exploded, grabbed the telephone and shouted at the Duty Sergeant in the local police station, threatening him with the Chief Constable and demanding he set off immediately to arrest the teds. An hour later the Sergeant appeared outside the school with half a dozen sheepish teenage boys, and explained that he wasn't sure there was much he could do. The headmaster took this as confirmation that the world truly was going to hell in a handcart.

2

Didn't You Hear the Bell?

As their name suggests, 'preparatory schools' like Lickey Hills were supposed to prepare you for an adolescence to be spent at an independent secondary school. My parents had chosen Malvern College, founded by a group of Midlands businessmen in 1865, at the height of the mid-Victorian belief in educational alchemy. Malvern was an early-nineteenth-century spa town in Worcestershire, and the great stone mock-Gothic buildings testified to the school's ambitions. It had never escaped the Second Division (but then, the First Division was really only Eton, Winchester, Westminster, and sometimes, when the wind was blowing in the right direction, Harrow). It was, though, unquestionably one of the better schools in the Second Division, aping the grander institutions while jealously preserving its own unimaginative slang as if it were Holy Writ. All new boys were examined on their familiarity with this stupid vernacular ('wagger' for wastepaper basket, 'Shaggers' for Shakespeare, 'ducker' for swimming pool, etc., etc.) to determine whether they were fit to enter the school community. You were also expected to know the nicknames for each of the sixty-odd members of staff – all but one of them Oxbridge products.

The school's expansive grounds lay in the lee of the Malvern Hills, replete with a beautifully situated cricket pitch, an enormous stone-clad chapel and a library intended as a memorial to the hundreds of pupils who had died in the First World War. The six hundred teenage boys slept and ate in a series of ten rambling Victorian houses scattered about the grounds, each run by a separate housemaster. Every house had a distinct reputation: boys in Number Eight house were all sex maniacs, those in Number Seven unnaturally athletic, and those in Number Three compulsorily gay. Most of the classrooms were housed in the three-sided neo-Gothic main building, which surrounded a courtyard dominated by a statue of St George, though science lessons tended to be held in a purpose-built modern block beyond the Memorial Library. There was an elaborate cricket pavilion, fives, squash and racket courts, a purpose-built gym, which also housed a shop selling jockstraps and thick woollen games shorts, and a grim swimming-pool building where we were made to practise rescuing victims of drowning while fully dressed. In the tuckshop ('the Grub') Mr Davies, a short, grey-haired Welshman in a white overall, dispensed tea and cheese-and-pickle rolls all day. There were many obscure rules about how many buttons on your jacket you were allowed to have undone at various levels of seniority in the school.

That sort of pettifogging tyranny – another unwritten rule specified the grade of seniority necessary to be permitted to have one hand or two in your trouser pockets – was deemed vital if the school was to achieve its goal of transforming the children of successful Midlands manufacturers into something approximating to gentlemen. I hated the place, though I have to admit that it was very effective in taking boys whose parents had made things or provided services, and turning them into the sort of chaps who would be decent District Officers somewhere in the fast-vanishing Empire, or members of some profession or another. There was much sport, a compulsory afternoon each week in the Combined Cadet Corps, for which we were required to dress up in army, navy or air force uniform (I chose the navy, on the grounds that Malvern is getting on for being as far from the sea as is possible in England), and straw boaters were worn when leaving the school grounds. Our uniform was pinstripe trousers, black jackets, and detachable stiff collars on Sunday. We looked like spotty clerks scurrying to our ledgers in a Victorian counting house, apart from the school prefects, who wore tailcoats, carried silver-topped black canes and affected an ascendancy swagger.

C.S. Lewis had lasted a year as a pupil at the school before the First World War, and described the place (not affectionately) in his account of the spiritual journey he made from atheism to Christianity, *Surprised by Joy*. 'Wyvern', he recounts, was essentially run by the senior boys, or 'Bloods', and characterised by homosexuality, of which, for his time, he took a rather tolerant view. He thought it the least spontaneous, least boyish society he had ever known, in which 'everything was calculated to the great end of advancement. For this games were played; for this clothes, friends, amusements and vices were chosen.'

Unlike the works of old boys who had become generals or county cricketers, Lewis's memoir was constantly being banned from the school library, which only made it all the more alluring. The school had obviously improved a bit since Lewis's day, but the influence of the Bloods – sporty oafs happiest on the games field – was still profound. When I recall these days, I am astonished that they occurred in my lifetime. Can it really be true that only fifty years ago junior boys were expected to act as 'fags' – effectively slaves – to senior boys, and that the eighteen-year-old who had been appointed head of house had the formal right – frequently exercised – to beat boys? I had been beaten by the headmaster of my prep school. Now I was beaten by his son.

The ritual on these occasions was always the same. A few minutes after lights-out at 10.30, the junior prefect would be sent to fetch you from the dormitory where we slept in groups of around a dozen. The form of words was unchanging.

'Put on your dressing gown and come with me downstairs.'

You followed this much larger figure down the cold, dark stair-well and along the corridor to the prefects' common room, where ten or so other eighteen-year-olds sat in a circle, with a single chair in the middle. You were told to stand inside the circle.

'Why did you refuse to get into bed when you were told to do so by Robinson [the prefect on dormitory patrol that night]?' demanded the head of house.

'Because I didn't want to.'

'But you had been told to do so.' He spoke with all the authority of an army subaltern, which within a month or so he might have become.

'But I don't respect Robinson,' I replied.

'The *purpose* of a public-school education, Paxman, is to teach you to respect people you don't respect. Take off your dressing gown and bend over the chair.'

It hurt like hell.

The post-match analysis after these beatings was always the same. You went back to your bed under cover of darkness, trying not to reveal that you were crying. The whole of the rest of the dormitory was lying awake in the darkness, of course. Finally, a voice would whisper, 'How many did you get?'

And then the bragging began. It hadn't hurt much.

Where, you might wonder, were the staff while all this was going on? The answer is that they were always somewhere else. The housemaster lived with his family on the other side of a green baize door. Each house generally had a house tutor, a bachelor who slept somewhere on site, but rarely emerged from his room during daylight. And there was Matron, a woman of about fifty, I suppose, sturdy and ample-bosomed, who wore her hair as I imagined she had worn it ever since she was a teenager. Oddly enough, like Mr Thomas, my old boxing teacher, Matron also had a glass eye.

I don't know whether there was any formal qualification required to become a matron, though I imagine not, since anything more serious than bruises and sprains from the playing fields was referred to the school doctor. Indeed, when I passed out one day Matron seemed to have very little idea what to do, apart from shouting at me. As at my prep school, our house matron supervised the doling out of tonic and a gooey 'malt' to boys who were held to be a bit weedy. But her main role was to bring a little femininity to the testosterone-charged atmosphere in which the boys lived, as a mother substitute. She had a flat in the basement where she would sometimes provide cups of tea to particularly homesick boys, but most of the time, apart from the sessions when she dispensed her malt and witch-hazel, she was to be found in the great linen cupboard, where it was her unhappy job to sort the horrible laundry of sixty boys.

In my last year, Matron conceived a tremendous passion for the house tutor, a bachelor with a wheedling tone of voice and the only natural Mohican hairstyle I have ever seen. Because he had once talked of the nobility of the clerical profession, we called him 'Scribe'. One night Matron took me into her basement flat and wept her eye out as she told me how Scribe seemed to fail to notice her. Unrequited middle-aged love was not the sort of predicament a teenage boy was well suited to give advice upon.

For the rest, with one or two noble exceptions, the staff were largely absent from our lives. Several seemed to have been recruited solely because they had won sporting blues at Oxford or Cambridge. This seemed to be particularly true of the geography department, where George Chesterton, who had played cricket for both Oxford and Worcestershire, taught the subject unspectacularly, but was widely seen as an amiable Mr Chips figure. (Though not by me, after the day he interrupted my reading of Ludovic Kennedy's brilliant investigation into the Christie murders and the subsequent execution of Timothy Evans, *Ten Rillington Place*, picking the book up, jabbing his finger at the author's name and harrumphing, 'That man is a disgrace.' I think he felt that Kennedy – whom I admired, and later came to know and like – was a class traitor for exposing the fact that the state had hanged an innocent man. As an Eton and Oxford man he should have known better.)

Then there was 'Jimmy B', an ancient history teacher who began every lesson with a headcount and then said, 'Who no come?' and was always digressing into tales of British wars with 'the Portugoosey'. 'Zombie' Nicholls moved with great deliberation around the chemistry labs, played the tuba, and was said to have been responsible at his previous school for allowing the main bridge over the Grand Union Canal in Berkhamsted to have been blown up by one of his pupils. The remedial maths set, of which I was inevitably part, was taken by 'Groisy' Shaw, the nickname an acknowledgement of his obvious devotion to Brylcreem, though his main responsibility was not maths but the woodwork workshop.

We were all barbarians, of course, so inevitably called the oeno-phile English master 'Sluice'. Mr Kennedy, who taught Latin, was reputed to belong to the clan of the Victorian author of the immensely tedious *Kennedy's Latin Primer* which we all used (the cover invariably doctored to read *Kennedy's Eating Primer*). Once a term Mr Kennedy supplied his classes with copies of *Acta Diurna*, a spoof Latin newspaper packed with terrible cartoons. As with many Latin teachers, his folly was to assume that he spoke like an ancient Roman, his main gag being to ask, 'When is a yoke not a yoke, boy?' To which the only permitted answer was, 'When it's in *Acta Diurna*, sir.' The music department was the domain of Leonard Blake, who rejoiced in the name 'Charlie Crap', after the way he sat at the upright piano during choir practice. When the school tried to rein back the use of this nickname it was changed to 'Charlie half-past-eight', on the grounds that 'That's what you do at 8.30.'

But the majority of the staff were a huge improvement on the deadbeats I had lived with at prep school. It wasn't until my last year that I had matured enough to appreciate the particular charm of 'Jeezbeez', George Sydney Benedict Sayer, the head of English, who had a habit of turning up to lessons apologising for the fact that one's essay was covered in marmalade, or that 'the cat seems to have walked all over it'. He had been a close friend of both C.S. Lewis and J.R.R. Tolkien.

Other teachers who did their civilising best in the otherwise rather brutal environment included the thoughtful history master, Ralph Blumenau – of whom it was rumoured that the governing body had only allowed him to teach at the school on condition he didn't try to infect the boys with his liberal prejudices – and my housemaster, Tony Leng. We all knew that he had served in the Royal Indian Navy, and had won a DSC (Distinguished Service Cross) in the war. He joked to his fellow masters that he'd been decorated for 'dropping prostitutes with VD behind the Japanese lines'. There may have been a couple of Burmese hookers dropped on the beaches of the Arakan coast, but most of the passengers on his night missions were actually Special Forces soldiers.

Most of life at Malvern revolved around sport, which occurred every afternoon. The high corridor through the main school building was lined with oak-framed noticeboards to which were pinned small sheets of cream-coloured notepaper emblazoned with the school crest and motto ('*Sapiens Qui Prospicit*' – wise is he who looks ahead, which could be a very depressing thought indeed to an unsporty thirteen-year-old) on which were the handwritten names of those who had made it into the teams for forthcoming matches. These were the gilded ones. Anyone who had won a school 'cap' or 'colours' was a sort of demigod.

Apart from a brief interlude in the cross-country team, where determination counted as much as talent, I did not feature on any of these lists. But no one was immune from the general ethos, for the principles upon which the great nineteenth-century schools were run included much chasing of balls around sports fields, in all weathers. My dominant sensory memory of those days is of chafed skin as the afternoon rain made our long woollen shorts grow heavier and heavier, until our thighs were a brilliant scarlet. Housemasters and other members of staff might occasionally turn out to cheer on their team – few of them to quite the effect of Mr Rambridge, who when required to referee a football match in the rain would drive down to the side of the pitch, opening his window occasionally to blow a whistle if he imagined he'd seen a foul.

Initiation into the world of sport came soon after arrival. I was a tall thirteen-year-old, with no spare flesh anywhere. Unfortunately, my weight and age put me into the one under-14 category in the inter-house boxing competition for which there were no other candidates in the house. I had, in theory, learned to box at prep school, under the unblinking supervision of Mr Thomas's glass eye, and reckoned I might just about survive a round or two, owing to the fact that I had long enough arms to keep most opponents at bay. Defeat on points in an early round would be sufficient to see honour satisfied.

To my great anxiety, I got a bye into the final. This must have been because the boxers from other houses had seen the fighter from Number Seven house. I stepped into the ring to find myself facing an enormous human tortoise. My adversary was barely five feet tall, and almost as wide. He looked as if he had been shaving since leaving the womb, and wore a creepy smile, which I have only ever seen replicated in horror films as vampires prepare to sink their teeth into a virgin's neck.

For most of round one I danced around the ring like a badly handled marionette, a blizzard of naked arms and legs, not much caring if I ever connected with the pile of bricks facing me. That didn't happen very often. The human tortoise emerged for round two having obviously been told what to do, or – less likely – worked it out for himself. As I deployed my spindly jab again, a very odd thing happened. My opponent somehow popped up between my arms. Then he proceeded to hit me repeatedly in the stomach. When I doubled up he turned his attention to my face, upon which he rained a torrent of blows. I felt my lip split, and heard my nose crunch. I soon had no idea what the hell was happening, and failed to hear the bell for the end of the round. My opponent broke off hostilities and started to waddle back to his corner. Suddenly aware that the beating had stopped, I pulled back my right arm and let fly. My one punch landed squarely between his kidneys.

The impact didn't seem to register too heavily with him – he just turned and glared at me from beneath his low brows. The referee, however, definitely noticed, grabbed me and pushed me towards my corner, where my seconds did their best to wipe the blood off my face. The referee came over, took one look at the mess, and walked to the enemy corner, where he raised my opponent's arm and declared the 'fight' over. It had not been a glorious exit. But I had at least left the ring properly knocked about. I should like to say that it led to a new respect from my classmates, but if so, I didn't notice it.

Needless to say, being battered in the boxing ring was not the sort of thing you were expected to complain about to your parents. Had I done so, I have no doubt at all that I would have been told it was part of my education, and that I'd just have to put up with it. Because by now the family was in full mimicry of what were presumed to be our betters. Belonging – or appearing to belong – to some period before the Industrial Revolution is one of the very odd ambitions of the British upper-middle class. We were not upper-middle class, as was demonstrated by the listing of High Lea's location at 262 Old Birmingham Road in the termly 'Red Book', which contained the school calendar, the credentials of the staff and the home addresses of all the pupils. Dad had had a pretty swift rise through the management of his steel company, and was now in charge of factories all over the West Midlands and South Wales. High Lea was sold, and we moved well away from anything as urban-sounding as Birmingham Road, to a place in the proper country which had nothing as *déclassé* as a street number.

In fact, Stonebow House, Peopleton, was not especially grand and not especially old. It had been built in the Vale of Evesham by Fred Allsopp, the jockey who had ridden the 40–1 outsider Sir Hugo to victory in the 1892 Derby. He had chosen a curious style which married Victorianism with mock-Tudor. Not surprisingly, there were lots of stables, numerous outbuildings, and a yard. I seem to recall that the asking price was £13,000, but the depth of the previous owner's financial troubles became clear when Dad visited the house during the negotiations to buy and had to step around a pig farrowing in the sitting room.*

The part of Worcestershire to which we had moved was splattered with wonderfully-named villages – Drakes Broughton, Elmley Castle, Flyford Flavell, White Ladies Aston and Wyre Piddle among them. Stonebow House stood imposingly on a corner from which a lane led up to the village of Peopleton, surrounded by paddocks and orchards filled with plum and apple trees. Our grounds ran down to a brook lined with elms, and in summer the air was heavy with pollen: Mother complained it made her perpetually drowsy. By the standards of the area, Stonebow was not an especially grand house – in the heart of the village was a Georgian mansion which, local legend had it, had once been the home of Barbara Cartland's mother.

---

* The house has since been turned into a care home for the elderly. Coincidentally, our previous home, on the Old Birmingham Road, has also now been turned over to medical use, and trades as Tranquil House – 'the leading independent provider of psychological services in the Midlands'. I am not sure that either holds quite enough of a draw to persuade me to move back in.

Father still wore his horrible brass-buttoned blazers, but following the move his voice seemed to undergo a noticeable change. His accent was posher than it had been previously, and the wardroom humour was more evident. Because he now had a much longer journey to and from work, during the holidays when we were at home we saw less of him – he left for the office before we had breakfasted, and when he returned in the evening poured himself a pink gin and retired to his wood-panelled study with the newspaper.

For a couple of years we lived the life of an *ersatz* country family. My sister Jenny had a succession of ponies, there was a bad-tempered donkey in one of the paddocks, and dogs and cats in the house. The local hunt would meet occasionally outside our house, and both Mother and Jenny rode to hounds. The moment I passed my driving test most weekends were spent towing a horse trailer around for my sister to compete at some gymkhana or other. For a while Dad even joined an organisation called the Country Landowners' Association, and sometimes, to our utter embarrassment, wore a monocle or plus fours. Once or twice he even borrowed an enormous horse and turned out at a meet of the hunt. He was not a natural horseman.

'Knowing your place' was a vital component of life in the fifties and sixties, and while institutions like Malvern offered the opportunity to jump a few steps in the gradations of class, the school itself was run as a rigorous hierarchy. At the top were the tailcoated school prefects, and below them the house prefects, whose authority extended only over the sixty or so boys in their house. Below them in each house were the 'inferiors', the longest-serving of whom rejoiced in the title of 'Senior Inferior', or 'SI'. This was a post with no privileges whatsoever, but which had, I felt, a certain cachet. On the two occasions I was promoted to house prefect I never made it to the end of term without being 'de-pre'd' for some offence or other – usually to do with smoking, drinking or meeting girls illicitly – and returned to the ranks of the inferiors. At the bottom of the heap were the 'fags', who would spend most of their first year slaving for their fag-master house prefect.

There was no job too demeaning for a fag to be given. They were expected to keep their fag-master's study tidy, to spit-and-polish his shoes and brush his coat, to make him toast during the break between morning lessons, to blanco the belt and shine the brass fastenings he wore when playing soldiers on Wednesday afternoons. On winter mornings there was the ever-present risk of being sent to the freezing lavatory block with orders to warm up a seat before your boss sat down to empty his bowels.

In addition to this drudgery, all junior boys lived in terror of the shout down the corridor of the single word 'Fag!' This was the equivalent of shouting 'Taxi!' on a London street, and the moment it was heard every junior boy in the house would drop whatever he was doing and tear down the corridor in a flailing mass of thirteen- and fourteen-year-old arms and elbows, in a desperate attempt not to be the last outside the prefects' common room. The last arrival was given whatever task was at hand – often to run over to one of the other houses, perhaps half a mile away, carrying a note, usually about some upcoming interhouse sports match. A friend who had been given a note to deliver to a named prefect in another house once opened it. It read, in its entirety, 'Wait five minutes, and then send a note back with this fag.'

After two years of this skivvying you escaped fagging and won the right – assuming you could ever get to the kettle – to make yourself a cup of tea or coffee in the house. By now, aged fifteen, the tricky subject of girls was beginning to raise its head. Contrary to many stories about these institutions, the school was not a hotbed of sodomy. After dark, every house thrummed to the rhythm of the solitary vice, but the obscure objects of our desire tended to be pupils attending one of the six girls' schools in the area.

There was no universally shared pin-up, but in the minds of a very large proportion of the school there was a small shrine devoted to Amanda Stobbs, the daughter of the housemaster of Number Nine house. Like most of the nineteenth-century public schools Malvern had a Latin anthem, sung at the beginning and end of term by the entire complement of six hundred teenage boys. I sometimes wondered whether, in the Holy of Holies of her bedroom, she could hear all those ignorantly lustful male voices belting out the special emphasis of the chorus:

Age frater, iuxta, fratrem.
Celebremus Almam Matrem.

And then the crashing final lines:

Quae nos ornat, haec ornanda
Quae nos amat, ad AMANDA.

The truth was that if she, or any of the other local beauties, had given any one of us the slightest indication of interest we would probably have run a mile: the sexual revolution of the 1960s took many years to creep into our benighted corridors.

I had learned the facts of life with no thanks to my father or mother. The closest my father ever got to explaining anything like that was his warning when I was well into my teens and about to spend the summer staying with a French family on the Île de Ré that 'They're different to us, you know. If you spend the evening on the beach with a girl, they'll assume the worst.' I could scarcely contain my eagerness to cross the Channel. As for Malvern's contribution to sex education, the headmaster, a short, bald man known as 'the Dome', gathered the eighteen-year-old boys who were moving on to work or university and warned us that if we found ourselves in an intimate situation with a girl we should be very careful, because females found it 'much harder to stop' than we would. Eighteen was a bit late for a sex talk, and his caution made girls even more mysteriously attractive.

The Church of England had by then played an invaluable role in educating us about sex. The assistant chaplain, a former padre in the Royal Navy who spoke in a strange elongated drawl, had one day and with no warning broken off from exegesis of the Book of Zechariah to warn us that 'If you get a boyyyylll the size of a pea on your penis, you have ghonnoray-ah. If it is the size of a kidney beeeean, you have syphilis.'

More comforting was the sermon given by a visiting Canon of Coventry Cathedral. The cathedral had been flattened by German bombs during the war, and recently rebuilt to a visionary design by Basil Spence. The clergy liked to think that their pastoral and theological work was just as modern in idiom, and when the time came for the visiting Canon's sermon he ascended the chancel steps in the school chapel and, instead of going to the pulpit or lectern, stood in plain view and opened his mouth. Already, six hundred boys had consigned the forthcoming fifteen minutes to the bottomless chasm wherein lay the endless hours spent listening to irrelevancies, freezing on sports pitches or attempting to keep step on some fatuous marching exercise.

'Now boys,' began the Canon, 'I don't know what you've been told about …' he paused for moment '… masturbation.' The rustling, fidgeting and whispering stopped at once. Suddenly, you could hear a pin drop.

We had probably been told we would grow out of it, he said. Well, he could tell us from personal experience that we would not. And secondly, and most importantly, there was nothing to be ashamed of – masturbation was a gift from God, and there to be enjoyed. We looked at each other in delighted astonishment. (Not so either the masters attending the service, nor the forty or fifty parents waiting to take their sons out to Sunday lunch. The Dome spent the rest of the morning receiving one after another of them in his study, as they complained that this was not the sort of filth for which they paid the school's hefty fees.)

Chapel attendance was compulsory every day, but of all the many sermons delivered during my five years at the school, this was the only one of which I have the slightest recollection. After lights out that night the familiar rustlings began under the bedclothes. From the end of the dormitory came a voice: 'For what Aubertin is about to receive, may the Lord make him truly grateful.'

According to the company's advertising, Old Spice has '75 years of experience helping guys improve their mansmells with deodorant, antiperspirant and fragrances'. They seem to have forgotten the main advantage of their aftershave. It was the pong of choice for anyone who had taken up smoking.

Once one had finished fagging, it was time to begin with another sort of fags. By the mid-1960s the fact that cigarettes gave you cancer had been pretty well established, though the tobacco companies were doing their best to throw a great deal of dust into the air. Allowed the full run of newspaper and television advertising, they were quite successful in convincing addicts that a product which had turned a very rare cancer into a worldwide epidemic was doing them no harm at all. Some brands even claimed to be doing you good.

Both of my parents were among the many millions of smokers who preferred the blithe deceits of the tobacco firms – my mother's favourite being 'cork-filtered' Craven A from a red packet with a black cat on the front, while my father smoked untipped Senior Service, which came in a white packet illustrated with a three-masted sailing ship, suggesting they were the very essence of a life on the ocean wave and carrying the slogan 'The Perfection of Cigarette Luxury'. When, at the age of thirteen or so, I stole and smoked some, they tore the back out of my throat. The cigarettes that had been stolen by Neil Saunders, my friend living over the road, from his very exotic mother (she was rumoured to have been divorced) were altogether nicer. During school holidays we would take ourselves off to one of our falling-down outbuildings and stand in the cold, earnestly puffing through cocktail cigarettes in astonishingly coloured papers – black, pink or peppermint green. We thought we were rather cool.

Normal teenagers, whose school day ended in the middle of the afternoon, poured out of the school gates and lit up on the way home. At boarding school there was no such opportunity, so life was a series of escape and evasion manoeuvres which, with a little elaboration, could have been used to good effect in an SAS manual. Since the smoking spots tended to be passed on from one generation of boys to the next they must have become tediously familiar to every member of the staff common room, most of whom sensibly went out of their way to avoid going anywhere near them. Furtive pupils made a point of returning to school reeking of Old Spice and peppermints – two smells which, even after all these years, retain their ability to make me swing along the street trying to look as if I couldn't possibly have been up to anything. The holidays were another matter. Free of the necessity to strike an attitude before one's classmates, one only had to smoke when there was a pressing need, like a girl to whom one wanted to look nonchalant and sophisticated. Most of the time you could give your lungs a much-needed rest.

There seemed to be no shortage of holiday jobs to be picked up in order to raise the money for some absurd pair of shoes or a new record. Some of these jobs – for example the couple of weeks I spent as a fifteen-year-old hospital porter, or the two months as a builders' labourer – positively demanded that one smoked. For the most part, a builders' labourer mixes cement or carries bricks up and down ladders in a hod, so the bricklayer can lay them uninterruptedly (brickies were paid 'on the rip' – i.e. by the number of courses they got down in a day). But as far as I was concerned, the most demanding duties were brewing tea on an open brazier and running down to the bookies with the afternoon bets. This last task in particular required much smoking, as well as rather terrifying feats of memory about whether it was number six in the third at Kelso or number three in the sixth. Work as a hospital porter necessitated a similar familiarity with cigarettes during breaks in the porters' duty room, but this led to meeting a pretty red-haired nurse whom I took on the 143 bus to the Essoldo cinema in Edgbaston. We were so keen on the back row of the stalls that she didn't seem to mind sitting through the Beatles in *A Hard Day's Night* twice in a week. There was much furious smoking on the top deck of the bus on the way home.

Smoking at Malvern College was more problematic. However many mints one chewed or gallons of Old Spice one splashed on one's face, there remained the question of where to store the numerous packets of fags that a serious habit required. It was rumoured that Rasmussen, a Swedish boy who came to spend a year at the school, had arrived with a tuckbox packed with cartons of cigarettes, bottles of vodka and a gross of condoms, and that the first thing you saw on lifting the lid was a revolver. About the only part of the story that seems plausible is that the contents of his tuckbox were known to the school authorities, since it was accepted as a fact of life that the boiler room in which the tuckboxes were stored was regularly inspected by Scribe, the house tutor, as he pursued his fervent crusade against tobacco.

One was bound to get caught sooner or later. Because the place was largely run by the prefect corps, most punishments were meted out by them. But beatings became progressively rarer as time passed, and the commonest form of punishment was to be 'dropped lines', which required you to attend the housemaster's study, report that you had been sentenced to fifty or a hundred 'lines', and be given sheets of special crème-coloured foolscap paper on which the housemaster had signed his name in the top right-hand corner. The prefect then prescribed an essay subject on something like 'Why no country can exist without a hierarchy', or 'Describe the inside of a ping-pong ball'.

Smoking, drinking and making night-time assignations with girls were more serious disciplinary matters, and were generally dealt with by housemasters themselves. I managed to be punished for all three. The carpeting for smoking began with the usual 'Have you been smoking?', an accusation I denied. 'Well let me remind you,' my housemaster replied, as he blew clouds of smoke from his pipe. 'On Monday you had three cigarettes, on Tuesday you had two, and on Wednesday you had another two.' I was toast, and although I had no evidence, I immediately concluded that the study patrols by Scribe, the House Tutor, had included monitoring my not-very-secret stash on a daily basis. The punishment was, if I recall, to be 'gated', or not allowed to leave the school grounds, for a few weeks. They soon passed.

Scribe was also the author of my downfall when it came to drinking. The school's Officer Cadet Corps, which over the decades had produced thousands of soldiers, had been formally renamed the Combined Cadet Force, but was still known as 'corps'. In the Royal Naval section Wednesday succeeded Wednesday in tying knots, building rope bridges, and occasional expeditions to try to sail decommissioned 'whalers' on a muddy stretch of the river Avon. On one of these afternoons I somehow managed to capsize not one but three dinghies while they were still moored to a jetty. By the time I was sixteen I had determined that I wasn't a sailor at all, but a conscientious objector. I joined the Peace Pledge Union, swearing to renounce war and inviting two splendid old ladies who led the deeply unfashionable organisation to visit the school and take part in a debate on militarism. Some time after that I approached the headmaster and told him that I really could not reconcile Wednesday afternoons with my conscience. Being a wise man, he merely said that I should find something socially useful to do instead. I discovered a nearby school for what were then known as 'mentally subnormal children', and went along each Wednesday to help teach them to do things like tying their shoelaces. I rather enjoyed it.

The problem came a year or so later. Field Day was the one weekday each term when there were no lessons, and instead the entire school played soldiers. The special-needs school only wanted me for a few hours, which provided a perfect opportunity to meet my friend Stuart at the Blue Bell pub at lunchtime. Because Stuart was an American citizen at the school on an English-Speaking Union scholarship for a year, he was excused military service. The Blue Bell, like all pubs, was seriously out of bounds, but when the entire school was out on map-reading exercises in the hills, it seemed safe enough to risk a leisurely lunchtime drink. We cycled the couple of miles from school quickly, installed ourselves in the back bar and began our first pints of ale.

Well before we had reached the bottom of our glasses we looked through the hatch into the bar at the front of the pub. There, shiny pate gleaming, was Scribe. At that instant he turned to look through the hatch, fixed our eyes and expostulated 'Hmm' in a nasally theatrical fashion. For reasons I have never understood, at that point Stuart and I stood on our chairs, pulled open the casement window, climbed through it into the garden, ran to our bicycles and cycled off, as if it was possible that we hadn't been seen.

I cannot recall what happened to Stuart, but I was rusticated – sent home – for the rest of the term. I begged my father not to make me go back to school next term, and when he asked what, precisely, I would do for a living, came up with some nonsense about 'becoming a photographer'. Fortunately, no one took me at my word, for the family dog had better photographic skills. My father quickly killed the idea anyway, saying that I had to return for another year and sit an exam or two to improve my terrible A Level results (a B in English, a C in History and – how had this happened? – an E in Geography, of all things). Otherwise I'd be 'leaving school under a cloud', an expression usually used of young men who had attempted to seduce a master's wife or to burn the place down. To a teenager a year seems an eternity, but back I went.

If you had asked me then whether I thought it possible that schools like this would survive into the twenty-first century, I should have answered with a resounding 'No.' I was with Bernard Shaw, who believed that the public schools of England should be 'razed to the ground and their foundations sown with salt'. But that never happened. Instead, they not merely survive but flourish, and have somehow retained their charitable status. The schools stand foursquare and confident across the land, an ivy-clad rebuke to the notion that advancement in Britain is based purely on merit. The country has perhaps never been as class-bound as caricature likes to suggest. But for all the high-minded notions of 'a classless society', perhaps 7 per cent of children are still educated privately.

The essential thing to remember about these institutions is that whatever their pretensions, they are all first and foremost businesses, and no school will survive for long if the business is unstable. Though they are not necessarily the most academically rigorous, the public schools consider themselves an elite, and have overcome the *Tom Brown's Schooldays* image problem by what some head teachers call 'getting the mothers' vote' and appearing warm and caring: the improved comfort of the schools is the direct consequence of the increasing importance of the maternal role in families. But what is still striking about many of these schools is the assumptions they feel entitled to make. To take one very small example: of the fifty or so talks I have given to teenagers in the last ten years, only three have been at the invitation of state schools.* I shared my schooldays with the children of doctors, lawyers and professors, but the fees at many of these schools are now becoming so astronomical that they are quite beyond the reach of the ordinary middle class. The empty desks are filled by the children of Chinese billionaires and Russian oligarchs. A high occupancy rate no doubt pleases the governors, but it is quite absurd to suggest that the schools do anything much for social cohesion.

The fact that these institutions are so successful in attracting overseas students testifies to their reputation. It is not surprising that a school like Eton sails on from decade to decade. The remarkable thing is how many of the Second (and Third and Fourth) Division schools also flourish. They do it by a clever combination of fear and flattery, and an insidious moral pressure on domestic parents which goes as follows. Most of us are not going to leave our children anything much when we die. You may be able to give them a sense that they're loved, but don't you think you should do what you can for their education? The key figure in this is the head teacher, who is increasingly a public relations smoothie.

It would be unfair to call 'the Dome', who was headmaster during my time at Malvern, a smoothie. But he was a visionary. Throughout my childhood and adolescence most of the British Empire, for which the school had been churning out young men, was being hastily returned to its rightful owners. Left to its own devices, the school would doubtless have succumbed to irrelevance. But Malvern embraced change in the nick of time, and the place I left at the age of eighteen was not the place I had entered as a thirteen-year-old. It became the first independent school in the country to have a language laboratory, in which we sat, wearing

---

* Don't misunderstand me – I shall be happy if no one ever again asks me to give a talk at a school. But it is striking that the same places send invitations again and again.

Bakelite headphones, in front of great reel-to-reel tape recorders. A few years later, new science courses were introduced. Mr Blumenau was encouraged to teach an art history course. The black jackets and pinstripe trousers were replaced by grey suits. Personal fagging was abolished. A few years after I left, the school went co-educational.

Too late for me, of course. As the Canon of Coventry Cathedral had recognised, all adolescent boys are sex-obsessed. So when my study-mate Richard Atkins and I advertised ourselves in the pen-pals slot on the music station Radio Luxembourg as 'two frustrated schoolboys', it seemed just the small-change of life. We forgot all about it until one morning a furious housemaster came into breakfast with dozens of letters and postcards cascading from his arms to the floor. He had better things to do with his time, he said, than to carry around all these stupid letters (and many of them, in pink envelopes and reeking of cheap perfume, were clearly very stupid indeed). He didn't know what we'd done, but as punishment we were to reply to every single one of the letters tumbling onto the floor. Since this would have taken most of the rest of term, we pulled out the half-dozen that looked most promising and sold off the rest as 'red hot dates' to junior boys at a few pence a time. One or two of the letters – particularly one from a couple of girls which began 'It would be unladylike to commit our feelings about you to paper' – came from local schools, and led on to rather bizarre dates in the hills. How other letter-writers reacted when they received a letter from some thirteen-year-old confessing his passion, one can only guess.

Some months later I managed to make a date with Georgina, the head girl, no less, of one of the local schools. We arranged to meet at midnight in one of her classroom blocks, and on the appointed night I crept out of my boarding house, having stuffed a couple of pillows beneath the stripy rug on my bed. I was undone by Scribe, yet again, who noticed my bed was empty during a late-night tour of the dormitories, and discovered where I had gone from a friend. He immediately telephoned the headmistress of the girls' school. The head girl and I were just getting acquainted when suddenly all the lights came on.

'You again!' shrieked the old crone, as if she was about to throw a bucket of water over some wailing tomcat.

'But I've never even been here before,' I protested, bizarrely outraged at the thought of being considered a repeat offender.

The following morning I was called before the headmaster, who generously explained that he didn't think I was a bad person, but he really couldn't have boys slipping out of the school at night – that way there'd be chaos. I had to be punished, so he was rusticating me for the rest of term. Again.

'Why did you do it?' my mother wailed when I finally reached home that night. She made it sound as if I had murdered someone. There was really no way of satisfactorily explaining what had happened. I was just a teenage boy. My father was, mercifully, away on business, but when he returned there was a curious sense of *déjà vu* about our conversation. Again, he said I should have to return to Malvern for a further term, so as not to 'leave under a cloud'.

A couple of days later a letter arrived from Georgina. 'My headmistress has explained to me that I have ruined your life, that you will never go to university or be employed by anyone respectable,' she wrote, 'and I am very sorry.' As it happened, had it not been for our midnight assignation, I would not have had to return for one final term at Malvern, during which the only thing I could do was to sit the special exam required to get into Cambridge.

Many decades later, my old housemaster's widow showed me a note she had discovered while clearing out her late husband's desk. It was from George Sayer, the head of English. He thought I was 'neither stable nor industrious', and 'would not make a satisfactory university student' because 'his enthusiasms are short-lived, and he is very bad at working when he does not feel emotionally involved with the subject of his study'. It was a fair criticism, though Sayer did believe that in a year or two I might grow out of it, because I had 'a good mind, logical as well as intuitive, with a literary imagination and genuine, if rather narrow, appreciation of great writing'. Reading the note so long after the event made me fondly recall his endless instruction to enjoy life – 'Do it!' – and all the marmalade on the returned essays. I was embarrassed by the contrast between his sensitivity and my own boorishness. He was a model for all teachers.

That last term at school made up for all the years beforehand. There were half a dozen of us taking the Oxford and Cambridge scholarship exams in English. We sat around a big table, arguing about books and ideas. George Sayer encouraged us to spend the rest of the day reading anything at all. It was bliss.

The trick for the entrance exam, I discovered, was to learn a few seemingly profound observations by heart, ready to deploy them in any context – a vital tool in journalism, too, as someone or other has doubtless said. Quite by chance, in the school library I found a copy of Walter Pater's *The Renaissance*, and was seduced at once by his talk of all art aspiring to the condition of music, of the transitory nature of perfection, which, if only one could 'burn with this hard, gem-like flame', one could appreciate. His writing was like a chocolate fondant – too rich to take too much of it, and the sort of thing you can really only enjoy as a teenager. But his ideas blew through my head like organ bellows. He obviously also appealed to someone who read my essays at Cambridge, because St Catharine's College offered me an Exhibition – a minor scholarship worth a grand total of £30 or so a year – provided I passed the universally required Elementary Maths O Level. (I had already made five attempts to master this exam, each one conducted in a slightly more comical frame of mind than the last. Now that it mattered – Cambridge promised freedom – I wasn't going to let some stupid quadratic equations get in my way.) The promise of schools like Malvern was that they offered those who could afford it a chance to alter the odds in what is supposed to be a fair and open race for the glittering prizes. Whatever my feelings about the place, the school had delivered on its promise. But I still left it feeling that when it came to how Britain was run, there was a party going on somewhere to which I had not been invited.

3

What Do You Really Know?

Before I could go to university in the autumn of 1969 there were nine months to kill. For the first few I worked as a waiter in the Angel, a whitewashed, bow-fronted old coaching inn on the High Street in the nearby market town of Pershore. It was very different from my previous jobs as a builders' labourer, Christmas postman, hospital porter or fruit-picker. Catering was something else: when they were sober, most of the rest of the staff seemed to be either fighting or fucking each other. It was only Paddy, the head waiter, a short Irishman in an ancient dinner jacket and with thinning, slicked-back hair, who kept the place functioning.

It takes a moment or two to appreciate how bad – and yet how good – British food used to be. At home, our mothers worked with ingredients which were generally unprocessed, and which certainly hadn't had huge quantities of sugar and salt added to them by multinational corporations with not the faintest care about what they were doing to the nation's health. In my childhood, eggs were stored in a solution of isinglass in a preserving pail. Meat was kept in a pale-green metal meat-safe with a grille on the front to keep the flies out. When refrigeration became widely available it seemed like a work of magic. But how many people could have imagined that the provision of potentially life-saving temperature control would see the triumph of junk food?

In the 1960s it was quite rare to see fat people: the mark of poverty was exaggerated thinness, not obesity, something which is now very often entirely reversed. Those who could afford to eat out did so in dingy rooms with red plush curtains, starched napery and a carpet you didn't want to examine too closely. A posh meal consisted firstly of a prawn cocktail, which was mainly chopped lettuce smothered in pink sauce; followed by a grilled steak; and finally a Black Forest gâteau – a chocolate sponge with cream and cherries – the whole thing accompanied by a bottle of Blue Nun or Chianti in a straw container. Men who were trying to show off to their girlfriends tended to order a Steak Diane, which the waiter had to cook on a spirit burner at the table. The final stage of this process was a nightmare for the novice such as myself, for it involved the addition of a liberal splash of brandy, resulting in a bonfire in the pan which was more or less certain to singe your hair and eyebrows and leave you looking ruefully through the smoke at the smugly grinning diner, now more confident than ever that he was going to get his leg over. You retreated to the kitchen smelling like a blacksmith's forge when a horse is being shod. I considered myself lucky the flames didn't melt the blue jacket I had to wear, which, in keeping with the modern mood of the times, was made of some artificial fibre which promised to 'drip dry' if I ever got around to washing it.

After three months at the Angel I had saved enough money to take myself abroad. My politics at the time were even more incoherent than they became later. Conventional political parties were dull, and like most young people at the time I was much more inter-ested in Bob Dylan, the Who and the Kinks. The early years of the twenty-first century have seen a massive withering of support for mainstream political parties (at the time of the 2015 election I checked the Liberal Democrats' membership statistics and discov-ered there were eight times as many members of the Caravan

Club). Though parliamentary politics was quite as unattractive in the sixties as it is today, mainstream parties still had mass memberships. I knew I certainly wasn't a Tory, but the spectacle night after night on the television news of angry trade union leaders trooping in and out of 10 Downing Street, demanding the settling of grievances, wasn't much of an advertisement for the paradise promised by slippery old Harold Wilson's Labour government either. I decided to take myself off to see what life was like on kibbutzes, the utopian collectives in Israel.

I have never felt more alone than on the night I arrived at Tel Aviv airport, emerging into a crowd of expectant faces awaiting the arrival of friends and relatives and knowing that not a single one of them was waiting for me. I caught a bus into town and spent the night at the local youth hostel. The next day I took another bus into northern Israel, and found the kibbutz I had made contact with from England. I was full of enthusiasm and half-baked ideas about socialism and communal life.

Kibbutz Yif'at, in the great fertile plain below the Sea of Galilee, turned out to be a tremendous disappointment. The kibbutz movement was inspiring in its insistence on the dignity of work and the sharing of earnings. The principles were wonderful: groups would gather, work the land together, and live as small democracies, electing their leaders. Families might have their own modest houses, but children would live separately from their parents for most of their lives. Everyone would eat together from a collective kitchen, and each kibbutz would have a school. Money would not change hands. It was a seductive idea to a young person, and the *kibbutzim* did a remarkable job in establishing the state of Israel. In the (slightly anti-Arab) cliché, they 'made the desert bloom'.

It was hard work all right, out in the fields picking oranges and grapefruit, laying irrigation pipes or mucking out the cowshed. Yif'at was a well-established kibbutz, and there were perhaps a couple of dozen foreign volunteers working there. The only other

British person was Peter, a croupier from Glasgow. The others included earnest Zionists from Eastern Europe, a deserter from the US Navy, a couple of Vietnam veterans (American and Australian), a Czech, and a brace of quiet Latin Americans. Since the number of Jewish pupils at my school could have been ticked off using the fingers of one hand, it took me a little while to work out what they all had in common. The scales fell from my eyes when I signed up to take Hebrew lessons. The great attraction of these was that if you attended the classes you only spent half the day toiling in the fields, and the rest of the time sitting in a classroom. On the first day the teacher pointed to each of us in turn and asked us to introduce ourselves. I was sharing a desk with my friend the croupier, who to my astonishment answered, 'Pinhas.'

'But you're Peter!' I whispered.

'She wants your Jewish name,' he replied.

Mumbling the first thing that came into my head, I said, 'Very unorthodox family. We didn't use Jewish names.'

'Very well, then,' said the teacher, 'we will call you Yeremeyahoo.'

And so I remained for the rest of my education in Hebrew, although the only words of the language I can now recall are those for 'cucumber', 'bus station' and 'Where is the lavatory?' Israeli Ambassadors who later came into the *Newsnight* studio to be cross-examined on their government's foreign policy tended to be slightly nonplussed by my greeting.

Sitting in a classroom was certainly more congenial than sweating in the fields, but it soon began to trouble me. It was not that I was anti-Israel – at school I had been horrified by accounts of Nazi atrocities in Lord Russell's *The Scourge of the Swastika*, and the fact that the country was surrounded by enemy states, its own forces massively outnumbered by their armies, gave it (at the time) the image of the plucky underdog. Most of the British newspaper coverage of the country's remarkable victory in the Six Day War two years earlier had been pretty fiercely pro-Israel. But kibbutz

Hebrew classes were clearly intended for new immigrants to the country, of which I was not, and never could be, one. The fact that our teacher had a number tattooed on her wrist, signifying that she had survived a Nazi concentration camp, made me especially uncomfortable with my dishonesty.

I was, in any case, becoming increasingly disillusioned with the kibbutz. The movement as a whole had made a remarkable contribution to the development of Israel, producing, for example, a disproportionately large number of army officers. But it seemed to me not altogether in the spirit of the movement that local Arabs were employed by the kibbutz to do some of the most menial jobs, which residents felt were beneath them. I really did not like the way they talked about Palestinians, and the nuclear option in any conversation about politics was to be told, 'Well, you're not Jewish, you wouldn't understand.'* There came the inevitable moment in the communal showers when one particularly vehement Zionist with whom I had been laying irrigation pipes looked through the stream of water, eyed up my genitals and walked out. I left a couple of days later.

You rarely hear people in Britain acknowledge that a good share of the blame for the miserable mess in the Middle East belongs with their country, but it is true. The plain fact is that during the First World War, the British – then the greatest imperial power on earth – made contradictory promises to Arabs and Zionists; to say nothing of side deals they did with the French, the other colonial power

---

* Many years later I received a letter which began, 'Dear Mr Paxman, I know you are Jewish. But have you ever considered the virtues of Roman Catholicism?' I replied that I hadn't, and furthermore, I wasn't Jewish. When I made the story public, the author Chaim Bermant wrote a letter to the *Daily Telegraph* in which he argued that I was indeed Jewish because I had a large nose, was successful, had a name which ended in the suffix '–man', and – the clincher – 'he denies it'. You can't win.

in the region, to carve up the Middle East between the two states once the war was over. The Declaration of November 1917 by Arthur 'Pretty Fanny' Balfour, the British Foreign Secretary, of the British government's enthusiasm for 'a national home for the Jewish people' in Palestine is still cited as the source of the war raging there a century later.

On subsequent visits over the past forty years I have shuddered more than once at pathetic scraps of paper from the period of the British Mandate which Palestinians produced from old wooden family chests and said were title deeds to land now built over by Israeli settlements. The plain fact is that, with lavish American aid, Israel has turned itself into the superpower of the region. No one seems to care very much about Palestine, including many of the smug regimes in the region which profess concern. Of course, on many occasions Palestinians have been their own worst enemy: desperation makes for bad judgement.

It is grotesque that refugee camps established in 1948 still exist, yet when I asked a clever young Palestinian why he didn't leave the camp he was living in and get the job elsewhere to which his medical training would surely qualify him, he replied that 'Without the camps we have no cause.' You can see his point, but it is quite something to condemn your children, grandchildren, great-grand-children and unborn generations to a life of squalor. One US administration after another has made grand promises about trying to secure a just and lasting peace, but they ring pretty hollow to Palestinians stopped every day on their way to work by soldiers clothed and armed by the United States. Cowering in a Palestinian refugee camp years later, as American-made Israeli warplanes came in on bombing raids, I found it hard to think of Israel as the underdog of my kibbutz days.

I spent the next few weeks living in Jerusalem, which seemed the most magical city on earth, and then caught a boat from Haifa to Turkey. It was a leisurely journey home – too leisurely, as it turned out, because Harold Wilson's economic miracle had restricted anyone going abroad to £50-worth of foreign currency or travellers' cheques, plus £15 in sterling. I augmented my budget by sleeping rough, selling my blood a couple of times, and getting occasional odd jobs. I was sleeping on a beach in Crete when Neil Armstrong became the first man to walk on the moon: someone else spending the night there had a transistor which picked up the American Forces radio service. There was something astonishing about gazing up at the moon from inside a sleeping bag and know-ing there were fellow humans walking about on its surface.

By the time I had hitch-hiked up through Yugoslavia and arrived in Trieste, the money had finally run out. When I couldn't find even a job washing up in a restaurant I hitch-hiked on to Milan and threw myself on the mercy of the British Consul there, who bought me a train ticket home out of his own pocket.

Back in England, the last few weeks of pre-university life passed by in their undramatic rural way. I dated a girl who lived in the village mill house, and drank good warm beer in the Crown with a farmer who boasted that he still castrated his unwanted male lambs with his teeth. I was as eager to get on with life as any other nineteen-year-old waiting to go to university, though clearly at times I must have seemed an insufferable prig. Why didn't the local newsagent stock the *New Statesman*, *New Society* or the *Spectator*, I moaned. 'I don't suppose many people want to buy them,' was my father's sensible response. 'But they sell lots of copies of *Farmer's Weekly*.' On Sundays Mum still dragged us off to hear the vicar, a bony jeweller who had had a late vocation, preaching on thoughtless texts. 'How odd of God/To choose the Jews,' he began one Sunday. As anti-Semitic doggerel goes I suppose it's mild, but just back from Israel as I was, it seemed especially offensive looking up from the pews to see the vicar's enormous Adam's apple quivering above his dog-collar in the pulpit. I mentioned it at supper, and Dad just said, 'That old nonsense. Why didn't you get up and say, "Not half as odd as those who choose/A Jewish god, yet spurn the Jews"?' I hadn't wanted to make a fuss, I suppose. Plus the fact that it had never occurred to me.

By this time, Dad's business career had taken a decided turn for the worse. As part of its commitment to ensure what Clause Four of the party's constitution called 'the common ownership of the means of production, distribution and exchange', the Labour government had nationalised the steel industry. Father's employers, the pipe company Stewarts & Lloyds, disappeared into an enormous, hugely inefficient corporation owned by the state and chaired by a businessman appointed by Wilson. When, years later, the whole project turned out to be a misconceived shambles, the chairman, Lord Melchett, let it be known that he had harboured serious private reservations all along about whether the state was any good as an employer. Pity he didn't act upon them. But they were anyway not as great as Dad's. He stuck it out for a couple of years, and then decided he'd had enough.

Unfortunately, he quit without really having any idea what he was going to do with his life. The Steel Corporation let him buy what had been his company car from them, but by the time I set off for Cambridge he was unemployed. A farmer neighbour gave him work for a while, driving a tractor, but then he fell victim to a scam – for an apparently sensible businessman, he could be astonishingly naïve. He decided to invest almost everything he had in a company cooked up by a Californian shyster named William Penn Patrick. In theory, 'Holiday Magic' sold cosmetics to customers in their own homes. In fact it was a pyramid scheme in which the only way to recoup your outlay was to recruit other suckers to buy a franchise; they in turn would only see any money by finding more victims. The thing was wrapped up in much mental mumbo-jumbo and some sinister-sounding 'Leadership Dynamics'. Dad bought a mountain of overpriced cosmetic products which he stored under the stairs, and which clearly made Mother feel very uncomfortable – she must have had a sixth sense about the scheme. The mountain never seemed to get much smaller, and the levels of stress in the household became almost tangible. Somehow Dad managed to get out of Holiday Magic with his shirt, and the cosmetics were dumped at the local tip, which was better than the alternative, which was to ruin someone else.

Dad then decided that the future lay in launderettes, and eventually built up an empire of six, in various Midland towns. Who knows where it might have ended, if houses had continued to be built without a place to install washing machines?

Cambridge turned out to be everything I had dared to hope it might be – a beautiful, bountiful feast from which you could pick anything you wanted to taste. No one told you what to do, and the only expectation was that you found something interesting to say or write.

During a speech just before he took his party down to defeat in the 1987 general election, the Labour leader Neil Kinnock made a resounding declaration asking why he was 'the first Kinnock in a thousand generations to be able to get to university'. It was typical Kinnock bluster, and probably true. Had I known my own family's history over a thousand generations, I could almost certainly have made the same claim – but then, so could most of the population: post-war Britain saw an enormous expansion of higher education. Since there was no family memory of university I was forced to rely upon what Dad had gleaned from political and other memoirs. The advice he passed on was that I should join *all* the main political clubs. My direct experience of mainstream politics had been restricted to listening to the local Conservative MP, Gerald Nabarro, a dodgy-looking bombast who had once arrived to talk to the school sixth form wearing an enormous handlebar moustache and a noisy Prince of Wales check double-breasted suit. In the years I spent studying political life after university I concluded that every politician needed a spectrum of qualities, at one end of which lay noble altruism, and at the other naked egotism. In Nabarro the latter was enormously well developed – his contribution to British political culture was the possession of a fleet of cars with the licence plates 'NAB 1', 'NAB 2' and so on. He had even successfully claimed in court that witnesses who had seen him at the wheel of NAB 1 as it went the wrong way around a Hampshire roundabout had mistaken his (female, unmoustached) secretary for him.

There was no way I could bring myself to think of becoming a member of the Cambridge University Conservative Association, which was full of braying young people who probably wore tweed pyjamas. The Liberals seemed wet, well-meaning but irrelevant. So I only joined the Labour Club. An hour's exposure to the scheming and malevolence of the sort of people who took it seriously ensured that I never went to another meeting. For reasons unknown, I then tried to take up with a drama club. My sole acting experience at school had been a walk-on part in *Under Milk Wood*, when my entire performance consisted of crossing my hands on my chest and intoning, 'I am Evans the Death.' Since drama at Cambridge was dominated by people who would go on to direct feature films or run television and theatre companies, I was rejected by every drama society. The Mummers even thought I was unqualified to paint scenery.

I went through the motions of joining the Union Society, where people who fancied themselves as future orators engaged in point-scoring debates on subjects they didn't really care about, but I couldn't take it seriously, and was frightened by the strutting self-confidence and ambition on show. I spoke there once, appallingly. The terrifying Arianna Stassinopoulos – later to marry and divorce a bisexual Texan millionaire, and after that to make the revolutionary discovery that if you don't pay many of your contributors you can run a pretty profitable online media business (the *Huffington Post*, named after the discarded Texan), earned herself the title 'the most upwardly mobile Greek since Icarus' by becoming President of the Union. The BBC judged this sufficiently significant to make a documentary about it. In one scene the Great Greek was filmed reaching out from her bed to pick up a telephone, gushing, 'Oh, hello, Lord Longford! How nice of you to call.' At the time she was probably the only student in Cambridge with a phone in her college bedroom.

Sometime in my first term I wandered into the offices of the university newspaper, *Varsity*, in a dreary brick building next to the public lavatories where Magdalene Bridge crosses the river Cam. Inside was a large room divided into cubicles by unpainted plywood partitions. Two more solid partitions separated off an editor's office and a 'boardroom' – not that the board met more than once a term, and no one was quite sure who was on it anyway. In each of the cubicles was a big typewriter and mountains of cheap paper. Ashtrays overflowed on every surface not already occupied by a cup holding cold coffee. The floor was covered in balls of scrunched-up paper. (It wasn't that there were no waste-paper baskets, just that they were usually brimming over – periodically someone would clamber inside one of them and trample the contents down, as if treading grapes.) You could have wandered into an am-dram production of the reporters' room in *The Front Page*.

In our own way we took ourselves quite as seriously as the putative politicians and theatre people, and were consequently more than slightly ridiculous. I started off by reporting what we took to be news, had an inglorious spell on the diary (I wasn't social enough), and wrote columns of absurd portentousness ('If you don't mind my saying so,' said Dr Gregory, an engineering fellow at St Catharine's, 'I think you're just playing with words.' He was right).

In my last year I was elected editor, and succumbed to many of the usual tropes to try to improve circulation, like sending out questionnaires about people's sex lives. According to an unfriendly witness, I spent much of my tenure sitting in the editor's office wearing an army-surplus-store overcoat and exclaiming, 'Where are all the clever people? I'm surrounded by turds.' The truth was that there were lots of clever people. Veronica Crichton, who went on to become the Labour Party's most trusted media adviser, sat in the news editor's chair. Christopher Frayling, later to become Rector of the Royal College of Art, smuggled endless reviews of Sergio Leone films – possibly the same one – into the paper each week (his interest in the *oeuvre* of Clint Eastwood was no passing phase: when he was awarded a knighthood years later, he chose as his motto a Latin translation of 'Go ahead, punk, make my day'). Peter Robinson, the circulation manager (he stuck up occasional posters) became a professor in computing. And Richard Higginson, who reviewed music and ran a gossip column named, for reasons which doubtless seemed smart at the time, 'Olla Podrida', was ordained and taught theology. There was a strong sports team, dominated by figures like Steve Tongue, who later founded the first football fanzine, and Stan Hey, who also made a career as a national sports journalist and learned the folly of owning a race-horse. David Randall graduated to become (in his words) the 'shooting-fish-in-a-barrel columnist at the *Independent*'. Alan Stewart, killed by a landmine explosion while covering fighting in southern Sudan for Thames Television fifteen years later, wafted around, bringing a dash of glamour to the newsroom. Tony Wilson, best known as the founder of the Hacienda nightclub, Factory Records and the 'Madchester' music scene, sat in the office claiming he had just finished his latest essay on Restoration poetry with the words 'Rochester tried to fuck history. But in the end, history fucked him.' When I showed a photograph of the male-dominated *Varsity* editorial team to a *Newsnight* colleague thirty years later, her only comment was, 'How on earth did any of you get a girlfriend?'

The paper was a venerable institution, with venerable debts. In the early 1960s whoever then made up the editorial board decided to ape the *Sunday Times*'s decision to create a free colour magazine, and to plaster its front cover with photos of Jean Shrimpton wearing Mary Quant dresses. The main colour summoned by the *Varsity* magazine was a deep red running through the accounts – even ten years later we remained in hock to the printers. The paper was still printed on hot-metal machines, and each weekly journey to Peterborough to see the thing through the presses ran the risk of being the last.

Then came another existential threat, in the form of a free newspaper, *Stop Press*. This was the invention of the newly formed Cambridge Students' Union, which was nothing to do with the debating club, but wanted to become the sort of place which existed in the non-Oxbridge universities as a focus for student social life and politics – because the university was an association of colleges, no such institution existed in Cambridge. Charles Clarke, the future Labour Home Secretary, somehow managed to get himself made president of this vestigial organisation, and then to be paid to spend a sabbatical year running the thing. A newspaper would give the student union a virtual existence. Everyone said that *Stop Press*, the freesheet it produced, would put the paid-for *Varsity* out of business. We contacted all our advertisers, offered them special deals, and somehow rode out the storm: within half a dozen weekly issues, the *Stop Press* presses stopped.

But the writing was on the wall. The editorship and appearance of *Varsity* changed constantly – the next term, under the joint editorship of the comic writer Andrew Nickolds and Laura Sparkes, later to become a rather inspirational teacher, the masthead adopted the *Variety* typeface and appeared on pink paper. *Varsity* limped on until eventually it was devoured a few terms later by a revived *Stop Press*. It now appears as a pretty good website plus a free paper edition, and boasts of being 'The only independent student weekly newspaper of the University of Cambridge' – which is possibly true, but isn't much of a slogan.

The fate of *Varsity* was emblematic of what was happening in the university as a whole. Much of what is now generally called the sixties happened in the seventies – it was not until 1972, for example, that the first male undergraduate colleges became accessible to both sexes. In the suite of rooms I shared in the eighteenth-century main court, my room-mate could occasionally be found wearing a tweed thornproof suit, although I was by now in tie-dyed T-shirt and loon trousers. By comparison with the news sheets of the left that were appearing at the time, like the *Shilling Paper*, *Varsity* seemed – was – old-fashioned. In 1970 the military government in Greece spent a week trying to promote tourism in their country. Everyone, naturally, detested the Greek colonels, but when half a dozen students entered a travel agency and threw Greek Tourist Board brochures on the floor, *Varsity*'s report (I think it even appeared under my 'byline') included the sentence 'A Greek tragedy was enacted on the streets of Cambridge,' inserted by some smartarse (possibly me).

But demonstrations were definitely no laughing matter. Later that week protesters disrupted a dinner at the Garden House Hotel, also intended to promote Greek tourism. Eight of the demonstrators were sent to prison or borstal by a gouty old bully of a judge. The university was outraged, but still *Varsity* reported another sit-in at the university Senate House (this time about some urgently-felt, but more trivial, concern than the military takeover of a European government) as an action by 'militants'. It was true that most students simply went about their normal lives during the demo, but the tone of the coverage left the newspaper uncomfortably straddling the fence. In fact the whole university was a bit like that.

There were demonstrations every other week about something or other. Many were led by a placard-waving Charles Clarke, with shoulder-length hair – like some Moses leading his people to a Promised Land whose precise map reference eluded most of us. There was usually a point at which another longhair, Bruce Birchall, would start marching back through the crowd with a chant of 'Anarchy! Anarchy!' A few years ago I read that he had died after a career spent playing chess and directing alternative theatre. He had been diabetic for some time, and there was some argument in chess chatrooms about whether that had been the cause of his personal hygiene problems, which were evidently serious.

Prince Charles had just spent a couple of years apparently studying archaeology and anthropology in the beautiful surroundings of Trinity, but St Catharine's was a long way short of being the most glamorous college. Though it was also in the centre of town, it was unfashionable, built of brick rather than the honeyed stone of Trinity, had only one proper court, was sporty, and seemed to be dominated by geographers and engineers. But it was a friendly, straightforward place, and things were a great deal better than they had once been – there were three years at the start of the nineteenth century when the college had been unable to muster any students at all. In 1861 it had also been the scene of such a huge row between two Fellows, each of whom believed he should be Master of the college, that the university ostracised the successful candidate. Since the Master held his office until he died, the college did not recover until after the First World War. The august *Victoria County History* commented in 1950 that 'the undergraduates shared the general odium, and not unnaturally came to be drawn in great part from an inferior *stratum* and to fall in number … Several of those still alive are gratefully conscious of the beneficial effect upon their characters of this struggle against adversity.'

The dozen of us from the inferior stratum who arrived to study English nearly twenty years after those comments were supposed to be answerable to a taciturn Cornishman who ran the Extramural Board. We realised what we were missing when we were invited to tea on our first Sunday by the great Yeats authority Tom Henn, who had retired from the college the previous term. A brilliant man from a down-on-their-luck Anglo-Irish family, Henn had risen to the rank of Brigadier in the Second World War, during which a bad landing in a military aircraft had left him with a severely arthritic hip. As we sat on the floor around his armchair he recited Yeats's 'Leda and the Swan' from memory, pointed his stick at a pimply youth from Barnsley and asked, 'Can you imagine, boy, can you imagine being fucked by a swan?' He could not.

But then, most of us couldn't imagine being fucked by anybody or anything. Every room had a 'bedder' who came in to clean each day – there were occasional, almost certainly invented, stories about students bedding their bedder. But they were generally matronly middle-aged women: mine was a bustling, motherly figure called Joy, and she lived up to her cheery name. Within the university, men outnumbered women by a ratio of about ten to one. As I discovered when I invited a girl I had met in an English lecture to supper, most of the women were much cleverer than the men. Though I suspect she had been as nervous as I was, there was no second date. Homerton, the Cambridge teacher training college, which was dominated by women, was a better proposition, as were the numerous language schools, which seemed to be full of glamorous Europeans – but then Joy arrived in my rooms one morning, sniffed the air like a questing Labrador and said, 'You've 'ad one of them foreign women up here, 'aven't you?' On another occasion a pair of what were definitely girls' knickers appeared in the sitting room, but neither my room-mate Peter nor I could think how on earth they had got there. One good friend who made occasional sorties to London in his Morris Traveller – generally with a tailor's mannequin in a flat cap in the passenger seat – returned with tales of forbidden fruit, one of his insights being that the skin of a Japanese girl was softer to the touch than anything we could imagine. He later married one. Eventually, in my second year, I fell hopelessly in love with a beautiful girl who worked part-time in the Copper Kettle coffee shop. The relationship with Noel lasted for much of the rest of my time at Cambridge.

The system was quite clearly unsustainable. I had been asked to send in a mugshot for the college records before arriving in Cambridge. It was sent back to me with a letter from St Catharine's saying that some 'tonsorial adjustment' was required, because my hair was too long. But once you were installed in college, there was nothing anyone could do about how you looked. Gowns were still required at college dinners, attendance at a set number of which was compulsory in order to be eligible to graduate. (Other meals were buffets, the most notorious components of which were chunks of mechanically recovered meat known as 'pork nasties', which I rather liked.) All the dons were men, a chaplain lived in college, and students could sign a chit for any number of bottles of gin or whisky – the first thing I did on receipt of my (quite generous) local authority grant was to pay off the previous term's bar bill. We could rely on Wilf, a genial North Country night porter, to tie those of us who'd had too much to drink into an upright chair so we didn't drown in our own puke. But the system only worked as long as everyone agreed on how it should work, and by the late sixties and early seventies fewer and fewer of us were prepared to agree that things were as they were because that was how they were.

To the ordinary undergraduate, the university hardly existed: you had applied to a particular college, and it remained the only place that really mattered. You ate there, slept there, and if you played sports, unless you were quite startlingly good, you played them for the college. The English faculty, to which the dozen of us studying the subject were notionally affiliated, was based in an expanse of concrete a ten-minute walk from the centre of town. It organised lectures on a very random basis (on one occasion my room-mate and I were the only people in the hall – we'd gone along because we felt sorry for the crumbly old figure who was speaking). Some of the lectures, though, were terrific, notably those given by A.C. Spearing, who used to act out *Sir Gawain and the Green Knight* in Middle English. The University Library served superb cheese scones which one could eat with much brighter girls from the women's colleges, like Julia Cleverdon (now a dame, perhaps the best-connected person in the land, and invariably described as 'formidable') and Liz Archibald, who was clearly there for more than the scones, since she subsequently produced *Apollonius of Tyre: Medieval and Renaissance Themes and Variations*, and became head of a college at Durham University.

But the governing body of St Catharine's wasn't entirely sure that English was an academic discipline at all. Perhaps they had a point – it often seemed to me that the main consequence of studying the subject was to remove most of the pleasure of poetry and prose, in order to make whatever point suited the fashionable school of the time, whether ethical, linguistic, philosophical or political. It probably had something to do with the decline of religious belief that English literature could be co-opted into the service of Freudianism, Marxism, Situationism, Structuralism, or almost any other kind of 'ism'. To dullards in the senior common rooms, the schisms that splintered the English faculty did nothing to enhance the academic credibility of the subject. But the opportunities offered by three years in which nothing more was required of you than to read and think and write were wonderful. More supposedly 'respectable' fields of study, like law or engineering, seemed drudgery by comparison.

Inside college, separate societies were expected to encourage a diversity of interests. The literary society was the natural one for me. Trinity had Byron and Tennyson after whom it might name its literary society. King's had Rupert Brooke and E.M. Forster. Queens' had T.H. White. All our college had was James Shirley, a minor seventeenth-century playwright of whom most of us had never heard. True, there was a rather unexpectedly distinguished modern theatrical tradition at the college – Ian McKellen, Howard Brenton and Peter Hall (and later his daughter Rebecca) had all been Cats students. But since we were mainly a sadly unliterary college, the job of organising the talks of the Shirley Society was not sought after. My room-mate, Peter Davies, was driven at one point to invite the General who had just commanded the British Army in Northern Ireland. He arrived unsure where Shirley was, and delivered a recruiting speech to a roomful of truculent longhairs, one of whom exclaimed 'Horseshit' before leading a small walk-out.

We found a better – if much thirstier – speaker in the Scottish poet Norman MacCaig, a lovely man who finished his poetry reading with a suggestion that we all go to the bar. When the bar closed an hour or so later Peter, the poet and I adjourned to our shared sitting room, where we had laid in a bottle of whisky. It did not last very long, and sometime around midnight Peter and I were reduced to breaking into the drinks cabinet of one of the Fellows and helping ourselves to another bottle. We returned to our third-floor rooms to find the great poet standing on the windowsill and pissing into the street far below, periodically shouting at angry passers-by to hold their whisht.

How harmless it all seems now. But the older you get, the harder it is to recapture the intensity of youth. The university was wonderful, but the Black Dog was still around. An email from Peter the other day reminded me of how it often seemed at the time:

> You had discovered Nietzsche and it was very fashionable to be in a semi-permanent state of what was called 'ID crisis'. You managed to marry your 'search for self' and nihilism in

a quite alarming and quietly dramatic way. 'Jeremy's down on Silver Street Bridge, again,' someone would burst in on me. And there you would be perched on the parapet in your long regulation coat like one of Dylan Thomas's forlorn, angst-racked cormorants. You would usually send us all away, but sometimes you would look at me and say, 'It is completely and utterly meaningless, isn't it?' I would nod rhetorically and suggest a final pint of Greene King at The Anchor. You would usually oblige and your cormorants would die as we got sozzled at a 'lock in'.

There is no denying it was a privileged life, and why ordinary tax- and ratepayers should have been expected to fund it was just another absurdity in an already rather preposterous life. The arrangement was hardly sustainable when – as then – just over one school leaver in ten went to university, but it became completely impossible once a political judgement had been made that half of school leavers should have a higher education. The charging of fees was inevitable, even if it is unjustly applied. And since when has a mountain of debt been considered a sound basis for adult life? It is not surprising, perhaps, that many students try to reduce the burden by living at home. But the great skill of the older univer-sities is that the students teach each other – in an ideal world that would be true of all institutions of higher education. There is something about communal living which can encourage thought, tolerance and understanding.

University teachers complain that twenty-first-century student fee arrangements have turned higher education into a business, and students into customers. They are right, of course, and they belong to a trade that has seen its status plummet dramatically. In the late sixties and early seventies the universities still clung to the notion that they were communities of scholars, implying an entirely different relationship between old and young. If universities are to function as businesses, young people are surely entitled to give consumer assessments of what they are getting for their money. Is it acceptable to be charged £9,000 a year simply to hear a not-very-good-lecturer recycle the same talks he has given for the last decade? That was a question which would never have occurred to us. But then, we were getting it free of charge.

4

Why is it Like That?

Towards the end of my last term at university I was summoned for a glass of dark, horribly sweet sherry with my tutor, who was responsible for my 'moral welfare'. Augustus Caesar (really – his father was called Julius) was also the Senior Tutor of the college. He taught geography at Cambridge for thirty years – rather well, apparently – seemed the height and shape of a cruiserweight boxer, spoke with a growling Hampshire burr, smoked a pipe more or less permanently, and wore a series of shapeless tweed jackets. He was also rumoured to be the recruiting officer at the university for MI6.

'Well,' he said, 'you'll soon be gone. Have you got a job yet?'

I hadn't, and he asked what sort of thing I was looking for.

As I had at school, I still had a feeling that somewhere there was a party going on to which I had not been sent an invitation. But the fact that organisations were actively soliciting applications indicated that I might at least get into contention. The problem was what happened next – I had by this time been turned down for every job in the civil service, in commerce, in business and in journalism for which I had applied.

'Well,' I said, 'something with a bit of foreign travel, perhaps. Somewhere I could serve my country. Somewhere I could maybe use my *intelligence*.'

'Oh,' he said idly. 'Like MI6?'

I tried to assume an expression which might be interpreted as either innocence or worldliness. To no effect.

He smiled. 'I don't think so,' he said with a genuinely worldly shake of the head.

Looking back on it, I suppose I should applaud the intelligence services for their selection skills. A couple of friends got much further in the recruitment process, even having meetings at a so-called Liaison Department of the Foreign Office, before dropping out, one of them explaining to Gus Caesar, 'I don't fancy all that cheesewire stuff.' (Which drew the response, 'Oh, don't be so silly, there are people to do that sort of thing for you.') At least one other contemporary went the whole way – when I looked him up years later he was listed as a trade attaché somewhere unlikely. I would have been a useless spy. Curiosity, the thing that gets me out of bed in the morning, is common to both journalism and intelligence-gathering. But a spy finds things out in order to keep them quiet. A journalist finds things out to pass them on.

I have rarely looked at anything – particularly received wisdom on a topic – without asking 'Why is it like that'? Journalism is the trade I have followed for the last forty-odd years, and while I've had occasional urges to do something different, they never lasted long. To think that I once considered trying to run a pub makes me squirm – I would have been so rude to the regulars that the business would have been bankrupt within a year. Instead, I have been amused and amazed, troubled and terrified, and have laughed a great deal. My work has taken me to astonishing places and provided a close-up view of some extraordinary events. I've been very lucky.

At the time I became a journalist, the trade was held in very low esteem, which is probably where it belongs. To judge from the false glamour now sprayed on the media, you'd think that journalists, disc jockeys, reality-show contestants and associated low life performed a useful social function, equivalent in value to the life-saving skills of paramedics or the discoveries of Nobel Prize-winners. They do not. I have suffered all my working life from impostor syndrome, unable to quiet the nagging voice inside asking, 'And what, precisely, do you bring to the party?' I have never walked up Downing Street to interview a Prime Minister, or sat in the Ambassadors' Waiting Room at the Foreign Office, without wondering what on earth I'm doing there.

Please don't misunderstand me. I believe passionately in the importance of free-flowing information. Every journalist has to be convinced that a well-informed democracy is a healthy democracy, and that a great part of the trade's function is to hold to the fire the feet of those who have the nerve to tell us what to do. But we are no more important to a healthy society than the men and women who keep the sewers flowing. In fact, now I come to think about it, we have much in common with them. Too often, journalism is the *cloaca maxima* of the political world.

At the time I entered this trade, journalism's position somewhere below the salt was well understood. It was not a profession, and the image of the reporter had hardly progressed from that of a man in a grubby coat with a press card stuck into his oily hatband. The BBC was considered slightly more respectable. But only slightly: my father's boring golf-club joke when I started work there was to introduce me to his friends as 'one of those communist homosexuals in the BBC'. Real work was making things or managing things, not observing or commenting on them. I have never really lost a nagging sense that he was probably right: if we are ever to establish what has gone wrong with the British economy, we shall have to examine what the educational system has done to the spirit of enterprise.

In retrospect, I can see that whatever I did as an adult was bound to be something to do with words and with finding things out. At

the time I just blundered around, firing off half-hearted job applications here, there and everywhere, and consequently being turned
down by almost everyone – including, I think, a multinational firm
of distillers whose headquarters I had spotted through the rain on
the train from Cambridge to London on an industrial estate, and
which seemed an awful portent of life as a wage-slave. One of the
very many employers who turned me down was the BBC, a
benign-seeming institution – a cross between the Church of
England and the Post Office, as I once heard it described – in which
it was said you could have a lot of fun, as long as you were willing
to sign the Official Secrets Act, be vetted by MI5 and wear the occasional cardigan. I duly applied, and went along for a selection board
in front of four or five grown-ups, chaired by a personnel manager
in pinstripe suit and stockbroker-belt vowels. I was rejected.

The BBC was not alone; I also collected polite rejection letters
from the Diplomatic Service (where the selection process included
an interview with a psychiatrist who seemed to my untutored eye
to be barking mad), from two well-known Hong Kong trading
companies, from independent television, from several manufac-
turing firms, and from every newspaper group hiring graduates
that year. In fact, by the time I left university in the summer of
1972 I had drawn a blank all round. The only employment I could
find was a temporary post as a 'tutor' on a Cambridge summer
course for foreign students. The work was pretty minimal – one
talk on contemporary poetry (the English faculty's view was that
poetry stopped in 1945) and living in one of the colleges where the
students stayed, in case there was a fire in the night. I was rather
smitten by a French girl who attended the end-of-course dance
wearing skin-tight white jeans and nothing on her top but a scarf
attached to her necklace and tucked into her waistband. (I later
made the mistake of going to visit her in Paris and discovering that
she was a great deal more interested in the female English teacher
who had accompanied her from France to the course.)

As the leaves on the trees began to brown I realised that the state of well-breakfasted indolence into which I had fallen for the rest of that summer in Worcestershire couldn't continue when one day my father put down his paper and announced, 'If you think you're going to carry on living here indefinitely, you've got another think coming.' I thought hard and fast. Nope. There was no prospect of a job anywhere.

Then, like a prop in a bad play, the telephone rang. It was a woman with a cut-glass accent from the BBC in London. Although she – of course – never said anything so clumsily explicit, it was clear that the person who had been offered the job that wasn't offered to me had decided to do something else with their life. If I could get myself to London I could start on a training course to learn to be a journalist. Salvation! I bought my first suit – a hideous shade of aubergine purple.

What the BBC really wanted, it turned out, was sub-editors for the radio newsroom. The training was largely carried out by Keith Clarke, a retired sub-editor who seemed to have either a cigarette or an extra-strong mint in his mouth at all times, and Eric Stadlen, a worldly Hampsteadite who had spent many years producing a World Service programme called *Radio Newsreel*, whose theme tune – a military band playing a rousing march called 'Imperial Echoes' – took you straight back to the Britain of Celia Johnson and Trevor Howard in their prime. Eric, who had been born in Vienna and had fled Hitler at the time of the Anschluss, was something of an imperial echo himself, and began most of his comments with, 'When I was on the *Reel* …' He often arrived for work having played poker all night.

The six trainees he was educating were taken on occasional excursions to meet the weather forecasters at the Met Office, to Parliament, and to the Black Museum at Scotland Yard – where an ancient detective showed us assorted murder implements, and the tub in which the Edwardian swindler and bigamist George Smith had drowned one of the brides in the bath. The rest of the time we spent learning shorthand, acquiring a rudimentary knowledge of the law, and having dinned into us useful practices, such as that 'We say Argentina, NOT The Argentine.' After several months we were allowed to help out in the radio newsroom, writing a sentence or two about what were judged to be relatively unimportant events, for inclusion in the HRU (Home News Roundup) or FRU (Foreign News Roundup). These were then read out by a newsreader who looked as if he seriously missed the days when announcers wore evening dress to broadcast the news. Afterwards, for reasons I never understood, the news bulletin was retyped on a rotary duplicator for circulation to dozens of people who never looked at the thing. I eagerly appropriated the roneo'd printout of my first two broadcast sentences – about the latest of the industrial disputes which were then a constant feature of British life – and promptly realised that I had no idea what to do with it. Woodward and Bernstein it was not.

The few months working in the television newsroom were more amusing, but no closer to the cutting edge of journalism. The radio newsroom had been located in Broadcasting House, the magisterial BBC headquarters in central London, its entrance adorned with Eric Gill's sculpture of Prospero and Ariel and the motto 'Nation Shall Speak Peace Unto Nation' looming over the entrance lobby. The television service was based in a strange circular building near the White City dog track in West London, and seemed to promise a less deferential approach to power. Here, trainee journalists came under the tutelage of Dick Ross, a young New Zealander in sneakers, jeans and a hooped sleeveless sweater who didn't seem to take anything very seriously.

But although the journalists at Television Centre wore casual clothes and affected a more cavalier style, again, no one chose to rattle the bars of their cage. The Senior News Editor, wearing a pair of Bakelite headphones, was not to be disturbed at his desk when a Test match was being played. The Chief Sub spent a lot of time on the phone to his broker or his mistress. Everyone smoked, usually cigarettes, but one or two of the writers who fancied themselves philosophers would turn up with pipes and suck noisily. The newsdesk was occupied by an ever-changing array of sub-editors, some of whom worked night shifts in one part of the organisation, immediately followed by day shifts in another. Their skin was the colour of soggy newsprint, and they spent much of the day in a state of barely controlled fury.

Certain corners of the building were no-go areas, for fear of disturbing someone who was sleeping. The most adroit of the vegetating tendency had somehow got keys to dressing rooms in the basement where they passed the day without bothering anyone. There were occasional blow-ins from Australia and New Zealand who turned up on the newsdesk while working their way around the world. One of them told me he was off to France next month. 'That'll be fun,' I said. 'Do you speak any French?' 'Enough,' he replied. '*Ne viens pas la crevette cru avec moi, bleu.*' There was a bar on the fourth floor where you could count on a few pints of beer and a liver-sausage sandwich at lunchtime to help the afternoon along.

There was no guarantee of a job at the end of months of sweating through rewrite after rewrite of copy from the news agencies (a story was only true if it was reported by two separate agencies, even if you'd seen it happen with your own eyes). But we were given the opportunity to spend time working in other parts of the organisation. I found myself at Radio Brighton, sharing a room in a flat with a social worker I'd never met before, and being made aware all the time that there was no more important news outfit in the south of England than Radio Brighton, with its jaunty signature tunes and urgent jingles announcing each bulletin. The news editor had an appalling toupée, but imagined that no one would notice he seemed to be wandering about with a dead weasel on his head.

For all that, it was there that I learned the basics of daily journalism – the calls to local police and fire services for news of recent emergencies, attending council meetings and telephoning local MPs. Most of what we passed on to the public was what vested interests had chosen to tell us, and with the increasing poverty of news organisations, this is a pattern that has since become a great deal worse: much so-called journalism is now nothing but the repetition of press releases, sometimes without even going to the trouble of rewriting. (A young woman proudly told me the other day how many papers had printed her copy. She was a public relations officer.) Court coverage – a terrifying business, since I had not paid proper attention in shorthand class – came later, when I found myself in Belfast. But often – early in the morning or late at night, for example – I was the only person in the newsroom, and could have told the loyal listeners of the south coast that more or less anything had happened, including the outbreak of World War III. Mercifully, there were a few more experienced figures on hand, like Roy Greenslade, a kind and measured man who later became editor of the *Daily Mirror* before achieving eminence in the Society of Distressed Journalists teaching in universities.

After three months or so in Brighton, in early 1974 I pitched up in Belfast, staying in a bed-and-breakfast just off the hardline Loyalist district of Sandy Row, where each day began with a mountainous Ulster Fry breakfast swimming in grease. I knew nothing much about the benighted politics of Northern Ireland, beyond the generally shared belief among thoughtful people that the Catholics had been badly treated – how could there be a corner of the United Kingdom where children of different religious denominations received separate educations, where employers kept Catholics out of jobs, and where the electoral system was so gerrymandered to ensure a Protestant-dominated local parliament that claims to be a 'democracy' were simply laughable? There could be no parity of esteem between the largely Catholic civil rights protesters who marched for change and the reactionaries who cracked their skulls, backed by 'B Special' police reservists who were overwhelmingly Protestant and armed by the state.

Yet things changed very fast, and concern about the origins of the conflict were soon overtaken by alarm at the conflict itself. A friend who was serving with the British Army in Northern Ireland had told sickening tales of firefights with the IRA in which he had lost members of his patrol to snipers, and then had to try to keep control of his men as women poured onto the street to jeer at the body. (He never got over it, and killed himself a few years later.)

The local branch of the BBC seemed ambivalent about its role – did it exist as part of the state, like the courts or the schools, or was its task simply to tell people the truth as far as it could be ascertained? In Belfast, it seemed to me, the BBC had long ago decided that it was part of the Establishment. In the context of a divided island, that meant that it upheld the status quo, reported the processions of drum-banging Protestant supremacists every 12 July as a joyous celebration of a blessed history, and had plenty of members of staff who saw the civil rights marches that had erupted in 1968 as a threat to everything they held dear. Yet even in Ulster, the finer instincts of the organisation – frankness, the better sort of paternalism and a bureaucratically ingrained decency – attempted to assert themselves. The newsroom, which suffered from the handicap of having only one Catholic in a relatively senior position, and one other as a junior sub-editor, did seem to be trying to get to grips with the mayhem that had broken out all around.

Before the explosion of dissent and subsequent sectarian warfare, Northern Ireland had been a dozy place where there was little overt political dissent. If you could stand the fact that there were councils which chained up the swings in public parks on a

Sunday, it was also peaceful: in 1968 there had been only five murders in the entire province of a million and a half or so people. Now there were murders at least every week, and sometimes every day (a total of almost five hundred people had died in political violence in 1972 alone). Reporters – and the police and everyone else – had had to learn fast. I was scared by this squalid little war, and uneasy about more or less everything else to do with Northern Ireland, which had all the machinery of a normal state, with its own odd politics and politicians (most of whom were appalling), a distinct legal system and a separate civil service. I was familiar with none of it.

Unsurprisingly, when a job became available in the BBC newsroom in Belfast there was no surfeit of people clamouring at the door. I applied. The job interview was conducted by three men who sat in easy chairs, firing the sort of questions that BBC managers usually asked on these occasions – what was the most important news story that day?; whose opinion had we not yet heard on a subject?; and what was the internal chain of command, in order that someone could inform me I was wrong. Many years later, I was told that what swung the decision in my favour had been my response to what was considered easily the most testing question of the selection process. Robin Walsh, the tough and talented news editor recently hired from the local commercial television channel, had ruptured his Achilles tendon playing cricket, and sat with his leg stretched out in front of him in a plaster cast.

'Now,' said the Head of Programmes, who was chairing the interview panel, 'I want you to imagine that Robin is Seamus Twomey, the Provisional IRA Chief of Staff, so the man who is top of the army's most-wanted list. You are walking up the Falls Road when you see him in the crowd, coming towards you. What do you say or do?'

The question cut to the heart of the BBC's ambiguity about its role in society. I said, 'You interview him.'

'And what do you ask me?' said Robin. Though I rather doubt that I really had the presence of mind, he claims that I replied, 'Hello Seamus. What happened to the leg?'

They gave me the job.

Much of the routine of my early days in Belfast was similar to that at Radio Brighton, with the difference that the early-morning calls were less about cats up trees than overnight shooting incidents, bodies found on the streets, or bomb explosions. I struck up a good friendship with Martin Dillon, a young journalist from the *Belfast Telegraph* who by the age of twenty-three or so had covered more murders than the average chief crime reporter on a national newspaper could expect to tackle in his entire career. He came from a lower-middle-class Catholic family who lived in a terraced house in West Belfast where his mother seemed always to have a meal on the go, which she expected you to share. A great number of sisters with names like Imelda came and went; the place buzzed with warmth and welcome. The family were related to the artist Gerard Dillon, some of whose works hang in the National Gallery in Dublin, and who was buried, at his own request, in an unmarked grave at Milltown cemetery a few miles from their house. Martin gave me one of Dillon's pen-and-ink drawings, along with a copy of Yeats's collected poems and Dante's *Divine Comedy*. There could hardly have been a more extraordinary contrast to his fascination with the gangs of Loyalist psychopaths who roamed the streets, kidnapping, torturing and murdering random Catholics.

However much the authorities in London or Belfast liked to claim that the violence that engulfed Northern Ireland came from nowhere, it wasn't true. Later, when I had experienced wars from Latin America to the Middle East, I realised that violence was the natural product of injustice: if you deny people free expression and equality, sooner or later there will be an explosion. The statelet the British government carved out of the island of Ireland in 1922 was founded on resistance to rule from Dublin, and became the expression of bigotry. One day, as I walked through the bomb-proof doors into the BBC's Northern Ireland headquarters with the West Belfast journalist Jack Holland, one of the security men exclaimed by way of apology, 'Sure, this'd be a grand wee place if it weren't for the Troubles.' It was the observation of a staunch Loyalist, and as we walked on Jack muttered, 'No it wouldn't. It'd be a bloody awful place.' As a Catholic, he came from the community whose hopes the state had been set up to thwart, and who had suffered generations of discrimination from the Protestant Establishment ever since. Though the violence was horrible, I could see what he meant.

People often forget that the British Army was originally deployed in Northern Ireland to protect Catholic enclaves from rampaging Protestant mobs. But the worm soon turned: the army came to be seen as an occupying force, and the IRA took its weapons from under the floorboards where they had been stashed after the last campaign to drive out the British. The IRA persistently referred to its gunmen as 'soldiers', cloaking themselves in a historical tradition of armed resistance to foreign invasion. They seized and held ground in Londonderry ('Free Derry'), Belfast and a number of other towns. Even after the British government had sent in its massively superior force of troops to extinguish the 'no-go areas', parts of the big cities, to say nothing of country villages – of which Crossmaglen in County Armagh was the most infamous – were never secured for the state, their roads often blocked by hijacked burning buses, street lights disabled and the areas generally dark, dank and eerily quiet but for the sound of howling dogs. To be sent on a winter's night into a West Belfast housing estate like Ballymurphy with an English accent was a very scary experience.

It was Martin Dillon who disclosed in the early 1970s that 'Loyalist' murderers (what, precisely, were they loyal to, if not to

Journalist, conservationist and ambassador.
Brother James is boldly defying the 1950s law that ties
were compulsory on boating trips.

The sea, or a bit of river at least, is in our blood.

Father and sons
about 1959.

Dad as would-be
Magnificent Man, 1940.

Mother always followed
health and safety guidelines
when driving her
ambulance. About 1945.

Training for a Boy Scout Cycling
Proficiency badge on my new bike, 1961.

Doing my duty to God
and the Queen, 1962.

Sunday lunch at the grandparents'. Left to right:
brother Giles, me, Grandma, Mother, sister Jenny,
brother James, Aunty Muriel. Probably 1959–60.

My prep school was not overwhelmed with choice when picking its football team. I am front right, brother Giles 'Pulveriser' Paxman back left.

This is what passed for gender and ethnic diversity in 1972 Cambridge.

Breakfast in an alpine refuge, 1978.

Knees That Tease in the High Pyrenees, 1975.

Though it seems improbable, this sort of haircut was once nearly fashionable.

Accommodating the BBC's pogonophobia. Sri Lanka, 1985.

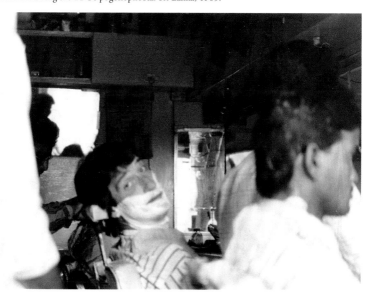

In Iran with Simon Berthon, 1977.

Impersonating Detective Starsky. Nicaragua, early 1980s.

Interviewing a rather better turned-out army officer, Norway, 1985.

Belfast, 1976. I think Gillian Chambers and I were making a programme about segregated education. Either that or we got married.

the laws of the land and the institutions of the state?) killed in quite a different way from the IRA. The IRA was brutal to anyone it believed to be a traitor, and often delivered 'punishment beatings', or shot drug dealers and others it considered criminals through the kneecap. But at least Republican guerrilla fighters had a clear sense of who the enemy was. The Loyalists could put more men on the streets when they needed to do so, but their killers were often content to murder anyone who even looked as if they might be Catholic. Working with Denis Lehane, another reporter from the *Belfast Telegraph*, Martin noticed that the vast majority of Catholic murder victims had no connection with politics. The two reporters soon discovered that almost all of them had just been unlucky enough to be in the wrong place at the wrong time, often walking home from the pub after dark. Because of Belfast's sectarian geography, in which each community lived clustered around churches, Loyalist thugs could assume that a person walking along the road in a particular direction probably belonged to the other tribe.* Some of the most repulsive killers patrolled the streets in black taxis and cars looking for victims who they then abducted and took back into their own enclaves, where they tortured them to death. All violent deaths are disturbing, but there is something especially stomach-turning about slow, sadistic death. For a while one of the Loyalist paramilitary groups conducted its beatings in so-called 'romper rooms', a term appropriated from a television series for pre-school children.

Much of the Ulster middle class could live their lives happily unaware of the epidemic of sectarian killings that had broken out. But they could not be oblivious to the explosions that shook the

---

* Media reporting of the Troubles often talked of 'Catholic ghettoes', summoning up comparisons between the Protestant ascendancy and Nazi Germany. In fact, while some of these enclaves were indeed the product of bigotry in planning decisions, others had been actively promoted by the hierarchy of the Catholic Church, which did not wish to see its flock dispersed.

Province just about every day. A civilised convention, established through intermediaries, meant that most bombs were preceded by a telephone warning. Since all of the devices were home-made, and many of them were charged with unstable mixtures like fertiliser and fuel oil, these warnings were often inadequate, and sometimes failed to get through at all – frequently because the local telephone exchange had already been blown up by the IRA in its campaign of economic warfare against the British state. On these occasions there were often horrific casualties.

As time passed and each side became more familiar with its enemy's approach to what was clearly a war – but which the British government persisted in calling merely 'the Troubles' – they became better at waging it. The army had begun by trying to apply in Northern Ireland the counter-insurgency techniques learned in imperial uprisings in Kenya, Cyprus and Malaya. Almost every one of these, from mass internment to selective assassination, proved to be a mistake. Indeed, it was rather shameful that the British had been able to get away with them overseas – it can only have been on the 'out of sight, out of mind' principle. Faced with a guerrilla war closer to home, the army improved their tactics. Within a few years they had hugely more effective intelligence-gathering, and had developed remote-controlled robots to disarm bombs. The critical political development was the successful presentation of the conflict as a matter of law and order, and therefore the business of the police, rather than as the liberation struggle which the IRA saw themselves fighting. Ultimately, it was only shared war weariness that finally put an end to the conflict. Twenty years after my arrival in the Province, the IRA called a ceasefire.

But that was long into the future, and in 1974 there was no end in sight. That spring, the thousandth victim of the violence was buried. The centre of Belfast was a miserable place, like the inside of a street brawler's mouth, with buildings missing, gashes everywhere, the most prestigious hotel in the Province, the Grand Central, turned into a shabby army barracks and shrouded in metal mesh to prevent rocket attack, while anyone who still had the urge to visit shops or bars had to pass through turnstiles at which soldiers would frisk them. The 'bomb damage sale' sign was ubiquitous.

The BBC newsroom had been fitted with heavy steel shutters on the windows to protect those in the building from flying glass if a bomb went off. Inside, in the usual BBC way – because the words were to be spoken, rather than read – we did not write the news stories ourselves, but dictated them to world-weary touch-typists. One couldn't blame them – they had heard it all a hundred times before, and the Englishman reciting his second-hand digest of an outrage in Augher, Clogher or Broughshane could hardly pronounce the place names, while they might have family living there. One Saturday morning I was dictating away, and looked out through the shutters to see a white van drawing up at the road junction below. The driver – whose family were probably being held hostage somewhere – ran from the vehicle as an olive-coloured 'pig' armoured car pulled up behind him. There was much waving of arms and pointing as the soldiers gingerly climbed out of their vehicle, keeping their rifles trained on the clearly terrified man.

'I think there might be a bomb outside,' I said to the typist.

'You'd better close the shutters then, dear,' she replied matter-of-factly.

Half an hour later, both of us having been evacuated from the building, we watched the bomb explode.

It would be quite wrong to suggest that every day was like that. The most bizarre thing about television and radio in the midst of the mayhem on the streets was the continuation of normality. When, years later, I quit *Newsnight*, someone dug up an early example of my reporting career. It was an interview with a female cobbler, so old-fashioned, buttoned-up and frankly sexist as to look like a parody. And the piece of reporting that caused most legal trouble in my Belfast career was nothing at all to do with the Troubles. It occurred when I was sent to the little fishing village of Ardglass in County Down, where two elderly spinster sisters had had a wall built between their house and that of their next-door neighbour, because, they said, they valued their privacy. It was a cramped terrace, and not unnaturally the neighbour objected to breezeblocks a few inches from his kitchen window, and emerged each day to knock the wall down. I cannot recall who was suing for what, but the lawsuit triggered by my report threatened to eclipse the dispute between Jarndyce and Jarndyce which runs through the first sixty-four chapters of *Bleak House*. I have no idea what happened in the end.

It was only the war that made Northern Ireland more interesting than any other corner of the backwoods. I lived in a series of flats near the university and in East Belfast, while visiting 'fireman' reporters from London, Dublin, Washington and Paris stayed in the Europa Hotel, an ugly modern building which laid claim to being 'the most bombed hotel in the world' (it opened in 1971, and is said to have been hit over thirty times in the next twenty-odd years; you were as likely to see plywood on the windows as plate glass). The ground-floor bar, named for some reason the Whip and Saddle, was a sort of neutral territory where stories were confirmed and confabulated. At the top of the hotel was a discothèque decorated with 'Penthouse Poppets', ersatz *Playboy* girls with bunny ears and East Belfast accents, where the wife of a well-known MP once tried to seduce me. This was *terra incognita* to the Presbyterian worthies of the Unionist Party headquarters next door. During the Loyalist workers' protest strike which brought down a well-meaning initiative by the British government to have Unionists and Nationalists sharing power, electricity was cut off across much of the city. But the Europa somehow kept going – the candlelight did the place many favours. It was all light years from a boyhood in the English shires. The preoccupations of young people are much the same anywhere, but the fear and uncertainty gave an edge to everything. Far too many cigarettes were smoked and far too much whiskey was drunk.

Like most people in most places, most of the population of Northern Ireland just wanted to get on with their lives, to which the nasty little war was an occasionally terrifying intrusion. The violence was pretty localised anyway, generally confined to poorer sections of the big cities and to Republican areas of the country-side. Admittedly, there was always the danger of being caught in a city-centre bombing, but if you ignored the army roadblocks on the way to work, the burned-out buses blocking junctions and the perpetual demagoguery, you could lead your life relatively unaffected.

People just put up with things – the more so since the politics were becoming increasingly incomprehensible. In the early days there had been Catholic and liberal politicians demanding civil rights, facing a Unionist government representing the old order. Then came the resurrection of the IRA, followed by other para-military organisations trying to drive the British out of Ireland to create 'a thirty-two-county socialist republic', despite the fact that twenty-six of those counties were south of the border, secure in one of the most unrevolutionary lands in Europe. Paramilitary organisations styling themselves the Ulster Defence Association, the Ulster Volunteer Force and the like arose, claiming to be poised to protect working-class Protestant districts from the IRA.

In 1972 the British government admitted that the place had become ungovernable, suspended the government of Northern Ireland and imposed direct rule from London. Two years later, moderate Nationalists were persuaded by London to share power in a local administration with some traditional Unionists, in the hope of forming a regime acceptable to all sides. That was brought down by a mass strike of 'Loyalists', backed by the Ulster Defence

Association and others. Despite their brandishing of the Union flag, the Loyalists' loyalty was now explicitly not to the British state but to their own interests. By the mid-seventies the conflict was set in a pattern of assassination and explosion, coupled with stalemated, convoluted politics. It seemed endless. Small wonder that so many despaired, shrugged their shoulders and just got on with their own lives.

At the same time the British government was pouring endless money into Northern Ireland, not merely in security costs, but in funding one business venture after another, convinced that people who had a job, a family and a future didn't go in for civil war. Its desperation was so obvious that any charlatan could turn up with a crackpot plan for a factory and be confident of at least getting a hearing from the government, even if he didn't walk away with the £100 million or so given to John Z. DeLorean, an American who looked like an extra from *Dallas*, to build a few thousand stainless-steel sports cars with gull-wing doors, before going spectacularly bust.* The DeLorean fiasco was only the biggest scheme among many to which public money was given and which failed. For those who didn't have a product to pitch to the British government's ill-starred investment advisers there was plenty of other public money sloshing around, spent on roads and buildings and legal aid. There were even publicly funded attempts to attract foreign tourists to the Province. The middle class grew, and the cash registers in the bars of country golf clubs rang.

As in the model the BBC had adopted nationally, journalism in Belfast was divided between 'news' and 'current affairs'. In theory, news tended to stick to a pretty narrow agenda and relied heavily upon official sources. Current affairs reporters and producers were

---

* It was hardly a surprise. 'Is this sports car really going to save the Northern Ireland economy?' I had asked a senior government official when the plan was announced. 'Put it like this,' he said. 'If I thought it was, I'd put every penny I had into building giant-sized garages.'

supposed to be more freewheeling. For several years, though, *Spotlight*, the local current affairs programme, had been presented by a local teacher and part-time football commentator, and produced by a part-time farmer. The comfortable days had to end, and the programme advertised for a reporter. I got the job. A couple of producers were lured over from London – Simon Berthon, who went on to become one of the country's most formidable editors of television investigations, and Bernard Wiggins, whose extraordinary upbringing as a war baby adopted by a couple who belonged to a religious sect (the Peculiar People) had given him a ferocious antipathy to anyone who claimed to have had Truth revealed to them – as many people in Northern Ireland believed they had. Bernard was always saying he was going to quit television one day and write a series of novels about the Peninsular Wars. Not long afterwards he invented Richard Sharpe, a soldier in the Napoleonic wars, turned himself into Bernard Cornwell, and soon after that, into a millionaire. During the years we worked together the bosses pretty much left us all to ourselves, and before long we were breaking story after story.

When I arrived in the Province the British government's Secretary of State for Northern Ireland had been Merlyn Rees, a kind, thoughtful man too decent for the bigotry with which he was faced: stories that he wept when officials told him of terrorist outrages were almost certainly true. In 1976 the new Prime Minister, James Callaghan, replaced him with Roy Mason, a former miner from South Yorkshire whose intellectual activities seemed to be restricted to designing commemorative ties. Bernard and I decided we would make a profile of him, but Mason told the BBC he would have nothing to do with us, thinking that would kill the project stone dead. Instead, we travelled to England that Friday night and knocked on the front door of his house in Barnsley, where we interrupted Mr and Mrs Mason in what Bernard asserted was a conversation about Mr Mason's Odour Eaters. Mason was understandably incandescent, threw us out and contacted the BBC to have a shout. To their credit, the management explained that there was really nothing much they could do to help him.

Mason took office announcing, 'Ulster has had enough of initiatives' – he would achieve with his boot what his predecessor had failed to manage with his head or heart. Soon after his appointment, at a getting-to-know-you dinner at the five-star Culloden Hotel ten miles outside East Belfast, Mason tore into the BBC. His beef was not with how he had been treated (though it most certainly didn't help), but with how the corporation as a whole dealt with paramilitary organisations. Faced with a war on its own doorstep, the BBC had hugely improved the way that it covered the Troubles, and set out to tell a rounded story as far as it could. That necessarily involved trying to understand and explain as much as it could about the incessant violence. Mason's analysis was that it was a simple matter of law and order. At what inevitably became known as 'the battle of Culloden' he said the BBC's coverage of the Troubles was 'appalling', and that as a public service broadcaster it shouldn't really be reporting IRA activities at all. Indeed, if the IRA managed to assassinate him, he didn't expect that event to be disclosed to the public either. Hearing about this meeting, it was hard to not to laugh. Simply to pretend that there was no one in Northern Ireland ready and willing to kill people to attain their political objectives was stupid. If the government was unable to ban these organisations, it was hard to see how the BBC could.

Things came to something of a head with a story dug up by my friend Jack Holland, one of the great unsung journalists of the Troubles, who had begun working as a researcher on *Spotlight*. Jack had been born and bred in West Belfast, and had superb contacts among the militant Republicans. In the summer of 1977 he told me he was certain that a series of fatal attacks in the south of County Derry were not the work of the Provisional IRA, but of another organisation altogether, calling itself the Irish National

Liberation Army, or INLA. It was a pretentious name for what was clearly a small organisation, but if the story was true, it added a new dimension to the war. I checked with the local police, who confirmed that they too felt there was something different about the murders. What was this organisation, what did it want, and why was it killing people?

Once it was clear that there was no early end in sight to the Troubles in Northern Ireland, the BBC's management in London decided that the cosy relationship between the local bosses and the rest of the Unionist Establishment had to end. They sent Dick Francis, a tough operator who had previously overseen the BBC's space coverage (he was known for wearing three watches, showing 'London time', 'Houston time' and 'Space time') to Belfast as the Controller of broadcasting there. It was an Orwellian title, but he had the guts to stand up to the demands of the British government. We researched and produced a thirty-minute film, during the course of which I went to a Republican safe house to conduct a back-to-camera interview with one of the INLA commanders. When the film was broadcast the government angrily denied that any such organisation existed. It was, they claimed, just a bunch of IRA gangsters with a newly-cooked-up *nom de guerre*. We had been duped, and furthermore, had given publicly funded air time to a man who boasted of planning to destroy the state. I do not know how previous holders of his office would have behaved, but Dick Francis stood firm. It was the duty of publicly funded journalism to tell people frankly what was happening, he said, before going on – in the sort of sinuous reasoning that is somehow bred into senior BBC mandarins – to have his cake while also eating it, by adding that 'The demeanour of our reporter left no doubt as to where we stood.'

Things were in fact much more complicated than the slightly simple-minded conflict between publication and suppression suggested. An organisation funded by tax and enjoying special privileges clearly had different responsibilities from those of a commercial news organisation. The BBC pointed out that broadcasting to a divided society required hearing from organisations which may hold repugnant views. Governments periodically passed laws to try to make it impossible for the public to hear gunmen trying to justify their actions, but the paramilitary organisations were increasingly nimble in getting around them – by, for example, putting up spokesmen for the IRA's political wing, Sinn Féin, which was not illegal. Interviewing some of these figures – Gerry Adams being a good example – was like trying to hold a piece of mercury stationary on top of a golf ball. Yet confrontations between the BBC and the government of the day over Northern Irish coverage were a fairly constant feature of life for the best part of thirty years. In the end, as a journalist you have to find things out, and you have to believe in telling people what you've discovered. Anything else is public relations for someone or other.

Was it dangerous? Danger and fear are different – one an objective reality, the other a state of mind. It is fear which crucifies you. No journalist was killed covering the Troubles in Northern Ireland,* though I knew two who had chilling experiences when cornered by political hoods. Twice I took telephone calls from people who threatened to kill me: I was scared, but had no way of knowing whether the menaces were genuine or just the product of too much Guinness. Once I was put up against a wall by a couple of thugs, which was an objective danger: I was terrified, but mercifully someone more senior in their organisation told them to lay off. Twice I was questioned by the police about reports I had made. And once I was summonsed to a court in Glasgow to testify at the trial of a Loyalist gun-runner. All I was willing to do was to certify

---

* Though Martin O'Hagan, a journalist with the Dublin-based *Sunday World*, was murdered by paramilitaries in the town of Lurgan three years after the 1998 Good Friday peace agreement.

that the film we had taken of an arms shipment had not been doctored, but it took a few weeks to forget the glare I received from the man in the dock.

Almost my last assignment in Northern Ireland was an investigation into the IRA for *Tonight*, a network show. British government after British government had tried to find a solution to the Troubles, sometimes through politics, and sometimes through military pressure. (The Republicans stuck for a long time to a policy of combining both approaches, which flummoxed the British at times.) By late 1977 there was a tortured familiarity to the unrest. An attempt by the Reverend demagogue Ian Paisley and friends to mount another 'Loyalist' strike that year, demanding a return to majority rule and a military offensive against the IRA, fell on its face. How much of a threat, then, did the IRA pose?

My report turned out to be a rather boilerplate piece of work, which would do the job while providing no fresh insights. But we had filmed Gerry Adams addressing the annual gathering of Sinn Féin in Dublin. What he said publicly seemed innocuous enough, but within weeks of the film being shown on television, something awful happened. On 17 February 1978 a group of IRA bombers attached petrol cans to an explosive device they left on the windowsill of the restaurant of the La Mon House hotel at Gransha, County Down. Inside, hundreds of people were dining and dancing. The IRA claimed later that they had tried to telephone a warning to the hotel, but the phone booth they had planned to use had been vandalised, and their warning arrived too late for a proper evacuation. The bomb went off at nine that evening, causing a massive fireball that incinerated all those in its path. Twelve people were burned to death and thirty others injured, some of them very seriously. Half of the victims of this grotesque mass murder were young couples, mainly members of the Irish Collie Club and the Northern Ireland Junior Motor Cycle Club, which were having their annual dinner-dances.

There was inevitable, justified outrage, and an ineffectual police swoop the next day. Three days later, Roy Mason demanded that Gerry Adams, the best-known apologist for the IRA, be arrested. When the Ulster Chief Constable protested that the police needed evidence, Mason replied that he just wanted Adams out of circulation. So he was picked up, and a couple of days later a policeman came to take a statement from me. The only evidence, it turned out, was the footage we had shot of Adams speaking at the Sinn Féin conference. During the course of his speech Adams had used military phrases like 'We rely upon the people to billet us.' The use of the word 'billet', the Northern Ireland Office had told the police, was surely evidence that Adams was speaking as a military commander. He was arrested and remanded in custody.

I was in London a few weeks later when a friend and fellow reporter telephoned. 'I've been told to tell you,' he said, 'that you'd better keep clear of Belfast for a while. You're on a list.' A week later a friendly policeman called with much the same message, and an offer that when the Gerry Adams case came to court, the police would be happy to collect me from the airport in an armoured car, put me up overnight, and deliver me to the courthouse next morning. I knew that if I wanted to retain any credibility as a journalist, I simply could not accept this offer, and arranged to stay with a friend instead.

It took months for the case to reach a hearing, during which time I made sure I avoided Northern Ireland, mainly by volunteering for assignments in other troubled parts of the world. Gerry Adams spent the whole period remanded in prison. When the trial day finally arrived, the case was to be heard before the Lord Chief Justice. The only evidence against Adams was the words of his speech and the testimony of an army intelligence officer that he had seen him organising a parade of IRA prisoners during his internment in Long Kesh. Most of the morning was taken up with legal arguments (which, as a witness, I was bizarrely allowed to sit in on), and finally the Lord Chief Justice ruled that mere language proved nothing, and that military metaphors were just 'the common coin'. They weren't, but he had exposed the thinness of the state's argument, and the case was dismissed. Adams – out of custody for the first time in months – looked across at me expressionlessly, and I skedaddled for the airport.

I let a couple of months pass before venturing into West Belfast, and noticed one day that Sinn Féin was holding a news conference about a local housing crisis. I waited until the questions were over and the camera crews were packing up their gear, then walked up to Gerry Adams as he sat behind a table at the front of the room.

'Ah, it's yer mon,' he said as I approached.

'I heard I was on a list,' I said. 'Am I still on it?'

'I wouldn't have thought so,' he replied.

We met many times after that, though never socially. There will probably never be a satisfactory answer about his real role in the IRA, though one was always being told by people in British intelligence that he was 'on the Army Council', was 'Belfast commander', or even that he ran the whole organisation. He himself has repeatedly denied all sorts of accusations – but then, the IRA being a violent, illegal organisation, he would, wouldn't he, as Mandy Rice-Davies famously said in another context.

What is undeniable is Adams's political skill. In a part of the British Isles notable for the number of second-rate bigots who have risen to eminence, the leadership of Sinn Féin has shown real political adroitness. Republicans will deny until their dying breath that the military movement was defeated. But by the 1990s they had recognised that twenty years of murder and mayhem had got them nowhere, and that they were increasingly plagued – as were other paramilitary organisations – by young men who saw the gun less as a means to a united Ireland than to personal wealth through protection rackets and gangsterism. The truth about the war in Northern Ireland is that eventually everyone realised it was unwinnable. Through almost all of that time, whether as prisoner or politician, Gerry Adams lived at the expense of the British taxpayer.

One Saturday morning, after an interview in Belfast, I told him I had to get going, because we were picking up a puppy that afternoon.

'You should have told me,' he said. 'Our dog's just had pups. You could have had one of them.'

In youth, we are encouraged to see our lives in gobbets of two or three years each – a change of school, some exam or other, time at university or in an apprenticeship, the first job or professional qualification – then you want to move on. It is only with middle age that you appreciate you cannot measure out your life in coffee spoons. But I was only twenty-seven. I had done three years in Northern Ireland, and the place had been good to me: I had even somehow managed to get myself sent on assignments to Beirut, Rhodesia and Iran, though precisely why these missions were relevant to British regional television was sometimes opaque. One or two of my reports had been shown on national television. But Northern Ireland's poisonous politics infected just about every area of life in the Province, and when the question of why on earth Catholic and Protestant children were still being educated separately* came around for the third time, I knew I needed to move on. Sean Hardie, a visiting producer who later went on to create *Not the Nine O'Clock News* with the comedy genius John Lloyd, promised he'd mention my name to the editor of *Tonight*, an old-school BBC figure with a taste for cravats. He gave me a three-month contract.

---

* For the most part, they still are.

5

What is 'the Oxygen of Publicity'?

Once upon a time Charles Dickens and the fabulously wealthy philanthropist Angela Burdett-Coutts bought a house to serve as a home for fallen women. Dickens had discovered Urania Cottage in a road called Lime Grove, just outside the metropolis of London. Here, under the guidance of a matron, prostitutes would be taught 'habits of firmness and self-restraint … order and punctuality, cleanliness, the whole routine of household duties – as washing, mending, cooking', and thereby raise themselves out of streetwalking. The plan was that at the end of their stay at the cottage the women would either join emigrant ships for Australia or begin a more respectable life at home. The scheme was a partial success – in the almost fifteen years before the two philanthropists fell out and the refuge closed, thirty of its fifty-seven residents made new lives for themselves. By the time Dickens died in 1870, London was sprawling west, consuming Shepherd's Bush and Lime Grove. Urania Cottage, its lawn and gardens, were demolished to make space for terraces of semi-detached houses which made Lime Grove indistinguishable from almost any other Shepherd's Bush street.

During the First World War, an ugly great cream-coloured brick building was erected on the street. It was said to contain the most sophisticated film studios in the country: William Pitt's speech to the House of Commons took place in one studio, and the Battle of

Trafalgar was recreated in another. Boris Karloff, Alfred Hitchcock, John Mills and David Lean had all plied their trade in the building by the time the BBC bought it after World War II, slapping a gimcrack front onto it as a temporary base while they waited for architects and builders to get around to constructing a purpose-built television centre up the road in White City. Nearly thirty years later the corporation was still there, though it seemed hardly to have spent a penny on the fabric of the place: it was soon nick-named 'Slime Grove'.

When I arrived there in late 1977, unable to cope with the claustrophobia of Northern Ireland any longer, Lime Grove bustled with clever young men and women in jeans who carried clipboards and parked their Alfa Romeos in the street outside. The security industry had yet to be invented, and the front entrance was attended by members of the Corps of Commissionaires, bluff ex-soldiers in heavy dark-blue uniforms who would occasionally say things like, 'Off to Israel, are you? I remember when I was out there in the Mandate. Sergeant told us one day we weren't to shoot any Jews. Well, I can tell you, no fuckin' Jew ever came in my sights and walked away.' God knows what they thought of the scruffy liberals who came and went at all hours.

As time went by and the BBC grew in numbers, the offices had expanded into several of the two-up, two-down houses in the street, giving the place an even more ramshackle atmosphere. Lime Grove never properly shook off its raffish air, which was deeply at odds with the high moral tone of the BBC's founders. In the early days of the organisation, a manager had once been told of two members of staff caught making love in the office. He reported the outrage to the BBC's boss, John Reith. The craggy Presbyterian winced a little, reflected, and then delivered himself of his judgement. 'Two things must be done,' he said. 'Firstly, the desk is to be *burned*. And secondly' – and this was the mark of his true outrage – 'that man must *never* read the Epilogue again.'

Now, local people asserted, the children's programme *Blue Peter* was being produced from the terraced house that had previously been home to the most notorious prostitute in Shepherd's Bush. Though sex in the workplace remained one of the BBC's two definitely sackable offences (the other being failure to pay the licence fee), *Panorama* occupied another couple of houses in which trysts were still said to take place. One of the sound recordists used the dubbing suite to record a catalogue of mildly pornographic songs under the name 'Ivor Biggun'. There was a bar which opened every lunchtime and evening, and panelled 'hospitality' rooms providing guests – and therefore production staff – with a choice of alcohol worthy of a well-stocked off-licence.

Despite the potential for loucheness, the place thrummed with quiet industry. The biggest group of producers and reporters worked on *Nationwide*, a nightly magazine show on which you could find yourself trying to explain the significance of the Ukraine wheat harvest one night and conducting a search for the country's best singing dog the next; those who did well there tended to have a keen sense of the absurd. Producers and film editors on *Panorama* took themselves more (and often, too) seriously, and worked right through the night cutting films, summoning the programme editor to viewings at five or six in the morning – often they arrived in their pyjamas.

But the best thing about Lime Grove was that it was a healthy distance away from the people who ran the BBC, who had their offices in either the Art Deco respectability of Broadcasting House in central London, or the minimalist 1960s 'doughnut' at Television Centre, half a mile or so distant at White City. Because the studios at Lime Grove were so run-down and ramshackle, the bosses rarely attempted inspection visits, knowing there was a high probability they would get lost. Eventually Lime Grove was shut down and sold – with the organisation's usual incompetence in property deals – to developers, and the staff moved to places where the bosses could keep an eye on them. The move was carried out under the pretext that Lime Grove was 'out of control' – which was true. John Gau, the head of current affairs programmes there, had talked of the 'KTBR' principle of film-making. It stood for 'Kick Them in the Balls and Run'. One editor I worked for began a planning meeting by saying, 'Well, which bit of the Establishment can we irritate this week?' It was an exhilarating place.

The coming of John Birt and his cronies a decade after my arrival in 1977 was like an invasion by the Moonies. Birt had been hired from London Weekend Television as Deputy Director General, with a specific mission to 'sort out' the BBC's journalism, which Margaret Thatcher's government had decided was infested with left-wing bias. (Thatcher was both right and wrong: there certainly were a few lefties at the BBC. But Labour governments before and after her administration also complained of bias. The truth is that any decent journalist should question the status quo, and if you happen to represent the status quo, what you construe as bias is usually just the Fourth Estate doing its job.) With Birt's arrival, out went the tweedy, shiny-bottomed, cardigan-clad management. In came lots of people in unstructured suits and unusual glasses who spent on one haircut what their predecessors lashed out on a season ticket from Borehamwood. The new arrivals all wore black and talked about 'a mission to explain', which was apparently something far more important than telling people what had happened that day. The nimble and ambitious underwent a swift makeover; the rest just waited for the new folly to pass.

When I arrived at Lime Grove the descent of the Thought Police was ten years in the future. The place was bumbling along in the fond belief that if people enjoyed the programmes, and they sometimes provoked questions in Parliament or changes to the law, then they probably weren't a waste of effort. The public mission of the current affairs teams at Lime Grove was to see the world afresh, to uncover stories not reported upon by the news teams, and to tell them entertainingly. News bulletins continued to be read out by former actors, who were hardly allowed to change a comma, while current affairs programmes were 'presented' by journalists, expected to be able to think on their feet. Presenters were the 'face' of the programmes, wrote scripts, conducted the interviews and kept things on the rails. They also introduced films from reporters, who were generally selected for their idiosyncrasies – Jack the Lad, Gentleman Jim, Girl Next Door and so on. Among the teams 'on the road', the general rule was summed up as 'The reporter takes the credit. The cameraman takes the money. The producer takes the blame.'

The formula must have been dreamed up by one of the Lime Grove producers, who were generally the creative force behind a film, so they were entitled to feel a bit aggrieved. The reporters, who conducted the interviews and wrote the scripts, enjoyed the glory; but they had none of the employment benefits accorded to the producers, who were mostly on the BBC staff and enjoyed very generous paid holidays, a compassionate regime (the corporation was exemplary for anyone with a drink or drug problem, for example) and a pension at the end of it all. The BBC insisted that reporters were only employed on contracts of lengths varying from a few weeks to a couple of years – I never understood why, but presumably it was so programme editors could get rid of us when our faces didn't fit. When a serious cull took place a few years after my arrival, one of the sacked reporters set off to sail around the world, making a point of sending a postcard from each port he visited to the executive who had fired him, with the two words 'Thank you!'*

* * *

---

* The first he knew of losing his job was when he arrived home from work and his wife told him that a courier had called earlier with a letter. He opened it to discover that while he had been in the office the courier had been delivering a letter telling him he'd been fired. The people who ran the place had not been hired for their management skills.

When I joined *Tonight*, it turned out that it only had a couple more years to live. Daily current affairs was an unloved creature, and the programme was already being shunted around the schedules. On bad days it might not go on air until almost midnight: we rather revelled in the not-for-public-consumption slogan devised by a fed-up producer: 'Yesterday's News ... Tomorrow!' When the management achieved their aim of pushing daily current affairs off BBC 1 and replacing *Tonight* with something called *Newsnight* on BBC 2, I was one of many to see a victory for the barbarians.

We were wrong. Assumptions about which was a mass channel and which a niche were growing redundant, and at least *Newsnight* was promised a regular start time of 10.30. In the 1970s the BBC was living through the years of plenty, so expansion caused no pain. The corporation was funded by a tax on the ownership of televisions, which was levied at a higher rate on colour sets than on black-and-white, and the growth in ownership of colour televisions meant a steadily increasing income. It was not until 1976 that colour televisions in Britain outnumbered monochrome. For anyone making programmes, there was money to spend.

By comparison with ITV, we did not live particularly high on the hog. Union agreements in the commercial sector decreed enormous crews, lavish meal breaks and no-questions-asked expenses. (Managements were happy to pay the price, because, as Roy Thomson said of his Scottish ITV franchise, it was a 'like having a permit to print your own money', and high production costs shut out potential competitors.) BBC crews were smaller and less flash, though producers were still able to put up ideas and see them executed relatively easily. 'On-go Cyprus. Await instructions' was the telex we longed to receive – and some did, only to be sent another a week later telling them to come home after seven days sitting by a hotel swimming pool. My own first assignment for

Tonight was a month-long tour of the United States, during which we filed stories from San Francisco, Texas and New York. Nice work if you could get it.

By the time *Tonight* had been consigned to history I had been offered a job on *Panorama*, the BBC's rather self-important weekly current affairs programme, so my stint as a reporter at Lime Grove was to continue for a total of seven years.

The time in Belfast had given me a specialism of sorts, and I was repeatedly sent back there on assignment. The Province's violent politics were the running sore in British life which continued to reveal the central tension about reporting: how should the national broadcaster report a threat to the state? A journalist's duty is to inform the citizen. Yet Margaret Thatcher's democratically chosen Conservative government determined to deny the paramilitary organisations what they always called 'the oxygen of publicity', as if this would somehow make the problem go away. (Attempts to silence objectionable views eventually led to a ban on broadcasting the voices of certain individuals – but not pictures of their mouths opening and closing. The broadcasters' solution provided out-of-work Northern Irish actors with a far better standard of living than they could ever have achieved from the local Job Centre.)

Reginald Maudling, Conservative Home Secretary in the early days of the Troubles, had clambered aboard the flight taking him away from Belfast after his first visit with the words, 'For God's sake, bring me a large Scotch. What a bloody awful country.' Most outsiders took a pretty similar view. I had left Northern Ireland because I found it oppressive, but it was the sort of place that entered your soul, for good or ill. The commonest feeling in both Britain and the Irish Republic seemed to be that the conflict was a squalid, violent little tussle over a dreary patch of land; people just didn't want to think about it. Yet British citizens were being killed every month, and the Troubles were costing the taxpayer endless millions. Just ignoring them benefited nobody. Because I had spent three years living there I was able in 1979 (before the lip-synch business took off) to persuade the BBC to let me go to Ireland to investigate the state of the IRA. The project would set off the biggest confrontation between the BBC and the government for years.

My producer, David Darlow, and I began our work with a series of conversations with members of Sinn Féin. Because they were convinced their offices had been bugged by the British Army, these usually took the form of walks around scrubby parks in West Belfast. In one conversation I raised the rumour that the IRA had taken delivery of some shoulder-launched anti-aircraft missiles. If the story was true, it would make life hugely difficult for the army in areas like the 'bandit country' of South Armagh, where the roads were considered too dangerous for land patrols, so troops could only be deployed by helicopter. If the IRA indeed had SAM-7s, I asked, please could we see them? The talk ended with no commitments, but we agreed to keep in touch.

A couple of weeks later we were in Dublin to interview an IRA veteran of earlier campaigns for the historical part of the film, when we received a telephone message at our hotel that if we were to drive north, we would be met by a sympathiser in a bar just over the border. The four of us – myself, producer, cameraman and sound recordist – set off, not sure what we would find, but suspecting that we were going to be shown surface-to-air missiles somewhere. We knew the journey was potentially dangerous, but if we discovered evidence that the story was true, we'd have an important scoop. We drove north, found the bar, were approached by a man we hadn't met before, and were then introduced to a member of Sinn Féin I knew.

Half an hour or so into the drive that followed, with six of us crammed into the vehicle, an unmarked car came screaming towards us. There were four policemen inside. The Northern Irish police carried guns.

'Peelers!' exclaimed one of the Shinners, using the antiquated slang still common in Republican areas.

My stomach was by now turning to liquid. We ought to have assumed we were being watched. They must have followed us all the way from Dublin, or at least from the bar where the two Republicans had got into our car. But common sense should have told us this was unlikely. And if the police were indeed on to us, then why were they careering in the opposite direction? We drove on, enveloped in tension, until finally we were told to stop outside a Catholic church in a village in the middle of nowhere. I hadn't even noticed the name of the place. The two Republicans got out of the car, warning us not to move. We sat and smoked. After ten minutes I was even more nervous than before, and getting decidedly irritated.

'Let's go,' I said.

At that moment, a masked man in a beret appeared over the hill in front of us, carrying a rifle. He was soon joined by others, until eventually a column of a dozen or so men was walking down the street. We grabbed the camera and ran towards them.

They set up a roadblock in the middle of the village, stopping any passing cars. After a few minutes I had concocted a piece-to-camera, stepped into shot and delivered some sentences about how there was a corner of the realm where the Queen's writ did not run. We continued filming as the men in masks leaned into cars and demanded driving licences. Then we walked back to our vehicle. I asked one of the IRA men if it was OK to leave, and he said, 'Got enough then? You'd better wait five minutes so you don't get shot.' He claimed the IRA had positioned machine guns on all the roads in and out of the village.

It had been a stunt, and a not particularly impressive stunt at that. One or two of the guns were modern Armalites, others were ancient-looking sub-machine guns and carbines, some of them pretty rusty. One or two local farmers had watched the whole thing, puffing on their pipes as if it were an everyday occurrence. A child rode by on a bicycle. We even heard the driver of one of the stopped cars say to the masked man who demanded his papers with the words 'IRA roadblock', 'Yer right then, Seamus?'

As we sat in the car waiting until it was safe to leave, an argument broke out amongst us. Seeing surface-to-air missiles would have been a story. Watching a few men ambling about with guns in a village whose name we hadn't even known until we saw 'Carrickmore' on a sign as we drove away proved nothing at all. 'It proves they can do it,' said David, which was true enough. 'Well if we use it, we've been had for suckers,' I said, confident that the footage wouldn't see the light of day. I was right – but not for the reason I expected.

The following day I put in a call to the British Army headquarters in Northern Ireland, asking if it might be possible to get a briefing on its assessment of the current state of the IRA. The army was usually only too willing to pass on sanitised versions of its intelligence to journalists, and briefings with the head of bomb disposal could be entertaining affairs in which he would, with no warning, set off detonators he had concealed around his office. This time, however, the response was unencouraging.

'Does the name Carrickmore mean anything to you?' the head of the press desk asked. There was no point in acting dumb.

'When did you know?'

'Within ten minutes of it happening. People are pretty angry. If I were you, I'd let the dust settle and not ask for anything.'

I decided to do precisely that.

A short time later, *Hibernia*, a Dublin magazine with a reputation for fearless investigations, ran an article claiming that a man in the County Tyrone village of Carrickmore had died of a heart attack after being roughed up during an army search. Perhaps sensing that the stunt they had staged was unlikely to he shown around the world, the IRA/Sinn Féin now had a much more sophisticated weapon. They told the *Hibernia* reporter that the soldiers were furious that the IRA had been able to stage an armed takeover of a County Tyrone village. In this account, the weapons on display weren't rusty old rifles but a great arsenal, including rocket-propelled grenades. Advance copies of the magazine were available on a Wednesday night. One of those who saw an early copy that evening was Stewart Dalby, the *Financial Times* correspondent in Dublin, who filed a piece for his paper which alluded to some of the more Gothic aspects of the supposed 'takeover'. Villagers who had seen the event were said to have talked of 'over a hundred' men armed with machine guns. The *Financial Times* report appeared the following morning, and Margaret Thatcher's tame bulldog, Bernard Ingham, spotted the incendiary initials 'IRA' and 'BBC' as he prepared his morning press digest for the Prime Minister. He was predictably furious.

Three events made the storm which now blew up worse than it might have been. Firstly, Thursday was the morning on which the Cabinet met. According to one of those present, when Willie Whitelaw, the avuncular one-nation Home Secretary, arrived at 10 Downing Street, Thatcher drew him aside and told him to 'Go and sort out the BBC.' By unhappy chance, that same day the governors of the BBC were also meeting. The governors were an amiable enough bunch of Establishment worthies who in strict legal terms *were* the BBC, and therefore could say and do what they liked. Mercifully, they generally only found out what was being done in their name after the event. On this occasion Whitelaw's call to the BBC Director General, Ian Trethowan, came in at the very moment that he was briefing the governors on the latest broadcasting strategies. The ears of the chairman of the governors pricked up as he listened to the Director General's half of the conversation. Even now, the thing might have been smoothed over – the chairman, Sir

Michael Swann, was a distinguished molecular biologist who had been the Principal and Vice Chancellor of Edinburgh University. He had remarked on taking up the job that he thought he'd be able to handle producers, because he was accustomed to dealing with troublesome students. An internal inquiry could have buried the whole affair for months, if not longer.

Unfortunately, that Thursday was also a day for Prime Minister's Questions in the House of Commons. This is always an opportunity for backbench toadies to ingratiate themselves with their leader, and Tim Eggar, the newly elected Conservative MP for Enfield North, leapt to his feet to ask if the Prime Minister would please contact the governors of the BBC to express her 'extreme concern' that the corporation had 'encouraged the IRA to break the law in Northern Ireland'. He was supported by the leader of the Unionist bloc of MPs, who wanted the names of those responsible for this act of treason to be passed to the Director of Public Prosecutions. The leader of the opposition, Jim Callaghan, expressed disgust at the 'stage-management' of the news. Thatcher assured them all that the government had already contacted the BBC, which believed that there had been a clear breach of standing instructions, and the matter was now in the hands of the police. The IRA's original stunt at Carrickmore, which I had considered relatively insignificant, was now blowing up into something weighty. The oxygen of publicity really did exist, and its source was in Westminster.

I listened to Prime Minister's Questions on a long-wave radio as I drove across Ireland to interview an elderly veteran of IRA campaigns in Tipperary in the 1940s. It was a long way. The radio signal was ropey, but it was clear that what had been a rather fatuous little demonstration was now a big event. When I returned to the Europa Hotel in Belfast that evening I found myself surrounded by people whom I had previously considered colleagues, all clutching pencils and notebooks and asking what I had to say about being denounced not just by the Prime Minister but by the BBC, which seemed to have concluded that rules had been broken. I checked out of the hotel next morning.

Despite having apparently already decided that there had been 'a breach of standing instructions', the BBC now began its own investigation. Anyone who has made it any distance up the tree in the organisation knows that if you are at any risk of being compromised by this sort of inquiry, there is one vital task: you have to make sure that you are the person conducting the investigation. So it was that one by one those of us who had been at Carrickmore found ourselves called to an underlit office in Television Centre to be cross-examined by Dick Francis, now the boss of BBC News and Current Affairs, who I knew from his days as Controller of the BBC in Northern Ireland, when he'd rather bravely supported me in the face of denunciations by the British government. Less congenially, seated in a particularly dark corner of the room was a bald man who introduced himself as 'the note-taker'. The man from the corporation's NKVD, I guessed.

'Clearly, what we need to know,' said Dick, 'is how you ended up filming the IRA. You know there are rules about this sort of thing. So, who authorised you to do so?'

'Well, Dick, *you* did,' I replied. 'I put up an idea for a film about the IRA. It went from the editor of *Panorama* to the head of Current Affairs, and then it went to you and you said "Yes."'

The NKVD man's ears pricked up.

'Well, we don't need to go into that right now,' Dick said hastily. 'What did you do afterwards?'

'I mentioned it to the Belfast news editor when I bumped into him.'

'And?'

'And he said, "Here's what you do: you do absolutely fucking nothing." I thought that was pretty conclusive.'

The interrogation continued in similar vein for another twenty minutes or so, after which I was told I could leave. At no point in the following months did we hear another peep out of the investigators. Finally – in the not unusual way of large organisations – the sands ran out on the inquiry.

All this time the footage sat in a tin can inside a grey filing cabinet in the terraced West London house where *Panorama* had its offices. David Darlow had taken up occupancy of a desk there, puffing away on cheap cheroots. (Early in his residency, another producer had passed him a note during one of his interminable phone calls. It read 'This is a no-smoking office'. Darlow scribbled on the bottom of the note, 'Not any more'.) We still hoped that one day we would be able to complete the filming. But it was never to be – we were assigned to other projects, and the footage mouldered away in the filing cabinet. Each time one of us asked when we could resume filming a veil seemed to descend over the eyes of the corporate hierarchy, and they also became unexpectedly deaf.

Several weeks after Thatcher's comments, the Metropolitan Police demanded to see the film, and we were told we had to hand it over (though Darlow saw that a copy was made first). A few weeks after that, two policemen arrived to take statements. It was a mark of the false importance attached to the case that they turned up with a sixty-page set of questions, which were read out by George Churchill-Coleman, soon to become the head of Scotland Yard's Anti-Terrorist Squad. His note-taker was a Sergeant. We were each questioned separately. Some questions I could answer. Others I declined to respond to at all. After perhaps forty minutes I showed the Superintendent and his Sergeant out of the building. I knew that under the Prevention of Terrorism Act, anyone who had information that they believed might be of use to the police was committing an offence punishable by imprisonment if they failed to report it. A bunch of armed IRA men parading about a town was clearly useful to the police. We had not notified them, and so had clearly broken the law.

'Are we going to be prosecuted?' I asked.

'Shouldn't have thought so,' Churchill-Coleman replied with a world-weary air. 'It's all political, isn't it?'

As we walked through the recesses of the old film studios next door – all black metal fire escapes, strange noises and grappling hooks at the ends of hanging chains – towards the exit, he looked around and said, 'You know, if I'd known it was like this, I wouldn't have bothered to put on my best suit.'

Almost a full year passed before we learned our fate. In August 1980, a right-wing backbench Conservative MP demanded to know why there had been no prosecutions for what was clearly a crime. The Attorney General explained that we had definitely breached the Prevention of Terrorism Act, but that for various reasons – including the fear of generating more propaganda for the IRA and the fact that he had warned the BBC off ever repeating the behaviour – we were not to be prosecuted. The announcement meant that he both had his cake and ate it: no effort wasted in trying to get a conviction, but judgement passed nonetheless. Not having a trial saved a lot of potential embarrassment. But by then, needless to say, we were all working on other stories.

The whole experience had shown that very often what matters in propaganda is not what you say or do yourself, but how others react to what you have said or done. It confirmed the BBC management view that the only way to bring the people in Lime Grove under control was to shut the place down and move them somewhere where a closer eye could be kept on them, which indeed happened a few years later. The film (or a copy of the film) which so threatened the state sat in the grey filing cabinet until the offices closed, when someone sneaked it out of the building and slipped some of it onto YouTube twenty years later.

* * *

'Every time the English think they have an answer to the Irish question, the Irish change the question,' goes the old saying. The plain fact was that the British had little or no idea what to do about Northern Ireland. Although in the early stages the British tackled it as they had battled insurgencies throughout the Empire, it was never formally called a war. The biggest mistake had been internment, which merely invited questions about where, precisely, was the rule of law – which the government claimed to be defending – when it was locking people up in places like the foul-smelling disused RAF base at Long Kesh without bothering to put them on trial?

Deciding to treat the Troubles as an issue of law and order, and to hand primary responsibility to the locally recruited police force, must have seemed a sensible change of tack. But attempting to treat what were said to be politically motivated actions as no different from other crimes, and the people who perpetrated them in the same way as thieves, murderers and hoodlums, was to bring its own political problems. Internment was effectively an acknowledgement by the British government that the paramilitary organisations were waging a form of war. Locking up IRA men as if they were 'ODCs' – ordinary decent criminals – was an attempt to demonstrate that there was nothing political about the campaign at all.

But many of the men behind the wire would never have been in prison in a normal society. I have been inside several British jails, and the overwhelming impression is of places filled with losers. Many prisoners are functionally illiterate, some dread being discharged because they have nowhere to live, large numbers have lost their families somewhere along the way. Of course there were petty criminals in the paramilitary organisations in Northern Ireland, but a large number of the irregulars I met were motivated and engaged. Many of the Republican prisoners in particular seemed to emerge from the experience of being detained at Her

Majesty's pleasure trailing exam certificates or degrees. Senior IRA figures from the slums of West Belfast came out of prison with a party trick of seeming to speak Irish as readily as the few remaining residents of the Gaelic-speaking or *Gaeltacht* areas of the west of Ireland – the language of the 'Jailtacht' was particularly useful when they didn't want others to understand what they were saying between themselves. Gerry Adams was always doing it.

Things came to a head with the question of how members of paramilitary organisations sentenced to prison should be treated. In the summer of 1972 the Conservative government in London had recognised that these prisoners were different by granting them 'special category' status. They were to be held in compounds according to their political affiliations. Within these compounds they were free to run their own lives, and to devise timetables, classes and even military parades. The British government had effectively conceded that they were prisoners of war. But under the Labour government's new arrangement of arrest, charge, remand, trial and sentence, introduced four years later, these prisoners would be held in conventional cells, laid out in blocks at Long Kesh (now renamed the Maze prison), which when seen from the air formed the shape of a capital letter 'H'.

Republican protests against this undermining of their cause began with newly sentenced prisoners refusing to wear prison clothes. When the British government would not compromise, the protests intensified. In 1978 Republican prisoners began refusing to wash or to leave their cells, and then started daubing their cell walls with their own faeces. Two years after that, as the British government again refused to budge, seven prisoners began a hunger strike, called off fifty-three days later, when they believed that Margaret Thatcher's new government had met their demands.

They were mistaken, and in March 1981 a second hunger strike began, led by Bobby Sands, the IRA commander in the Maze prison. The demands were the same as ever – the right not to wear prison uniform or do prison work, free association, the right to a weekly letter, parcel and visit, and a restoration of any lost remission of sentence. Sands planned the hunger strike cleverly, with one additional prisoner refusing food each week, thereby turning the screw on the British government. When a parliamentary seat in Fermanagh fell vacant, the imprisoned Sands found himself elected to Westminster, which increased the pressure still further. On the streets of nationalist areas of Northern Irish cities the atmosphere was now very menacing – the H-Block protests raised feelings to a pitch almost as high as it had ever been.

Then, on 5 May 1981, Sands died of starvation. Through the spring and summer nine others followed him. In July a mass protest of ten thousand people or so was planned outside the British Embassy in Dublin. It was less than a decade since another protest in Dublin – at the killing by British paratroopers of thirteen civilians on Bloody Sunday – had left the Embassy a smoking, abandoned ruin. This time the Irish police decided to protect the new building by stopping the march several hundred yards away.

I arrived at the police barricade ahead of the protesters. Normally, on occasions such as this the mainstream media tended to shelter behind police lines. Now I found myself standing on the pavement in front of the police barrier when the first protesters arrived, carrying wreaths in memory of the dead hunger strikers. As they pleaded with the police to be allowed through, an irresistible torrent of people pushed forward behind them. It was obvious what was going to happen. The cameraman and I ran, and knocked on the front door of a nearby house. Mercifully, they let us in.

Within minutes bricks were being torn from walls and stones unearthed from front gardens to be thrown at the police. From a first-floor balcony I watched as the barrage of missiles intensified. Even from a distance of fifty yards, I could feel that the country boys of the Garda Síochána were at the end of their tether. Now, as part of the crowd tried to wrestle the barriers out of the hands of the police, while others pelted the reserve lines with rocks, a flatbed truck appeared at the back of the procession of demonstrators. There were three young men in the cab, and it pushed slowly forward. Anyone who had come for a peaceful protest found themselves with a choice of being crushed against the police barrier or being crushed by the lorry.

Police patience snapped. Officers leaped over the barrier and waded into the crowd, truncheons swinging. Protesters fled where they could. From the balcony I could hear as one of the police seized a young man and hit him repeatedly with his stick. As the Northern Irish protester lay on the ground the officer grunted, 'And don't' – thwack – 'you' – thwack – 'ever' – thwack – 'come' – thwack – 'down' – thwack – 'here' – thwack – 'again.' So much for Republican dreams of a united Ireland.

By that time, clandestine indirect negotiations had already begun between the British government and the hunger strikers. Though the government never granted them the political status they sought – how could they? 'British Government Admits it Holds Political Prisoners' would be some headline – the protest achieved most of the rest of its aims.

It was hard to find other stories in Britain where the issues seemed so urgent and the stakes so high as in Northern Ireland. But the atmosphere in the *Panorama* office in the eighties was unambiguously troublemaking. David Darlow, Robert Harris – later a world-renowned writer, but then a researcher – and I decided to have a crack at the ultimate catastrophe: what would happen if the country was caught up in a nuclear war.

The undoubted star of the show turned out to be a retired Major in east Devon. Although there was supposed to be an organised group of human beings who would put an emergency plan into operation in the event of a nuclear conflict, they were (rightly) suspicious of the media. But then Robert Harris heard of Major Tony Hibbert, a gentleman farmer living in the village of Branscombe, near Lyme Regis. Hibbert, we subsequently discovered, had had what was then called 'a good war', including having captured the German port of Kiel, despite his forces being outnumbered by perhaps a hundred to one. By the end of the war he had won a Military Cross and been mentioned in despatches. Like many men who survived similar hazards, he found peacetime life running his family's wine, spirits and soft drinks business unutterably dull, even though he was credited with being the man who introduced the ring-pull can to Britain.

Robert contacted him, and the Major confirmed that he did indeed have a fully functioning civil defence programme in operation in his village. In fact, he'd very shortly be having an exercise. Would we like to film it?

We spent the night before the exercise in a comfortable pub looking out over the sea, and arrived at the Major's beautiful castellated manor house at about nine. He had everything organised – gasmasks, tin helmets, evacuation plans for the village. He had even written a script, culminating in a speech in which he shouted to a woman making her urgent way up the hill to shelter, 'Good luck, Amanda! Good luck to the two of you! (She's pregnant, you see.)' At this point, Robert took himself off behind a tree to collapse in laughter.

For several hours the Major kept us rapt with accounts of how the few hundred inhabitants of his beautiful village on the Jurassic Coast would survive a worldwide nuclear holocaust. This was where the chosen villagers would hide in their bunker. This was where food would be stored. This was where the resistance would be organised. In the afternoon we drove wildly around the village in the Major's Land Rover, as nonplussed locals went about their daily business. We eventually passed a heavily pregnant woman. 'Good luck, Amanda!' the Major shouted at the astonished woman from behind his gasmask. 'Good luck to the two of you! (She's pregnant, you see.)'

The Major clearly enjoyed having a television crew filming his preparations for nuclear holocaust, though I got the distinct impression that his wife was less impressed. At one point, during a break in the triage planning for coffee, I asked him if he really thought nuclear war was likely.

'Well, you know,' he said seriously, 'the Russians have hundreds of nuclear warheads aimed at us.'

'And they're all pointed at the village of Branscombe,' added his wife in a stage whisper.

There was, I now see, something distasteful in the children of peace laughing at one of those who had bought us our freedoms. The Major's preparations may have been absurd and comical, but there was something impressive about a generation which still believed it could control its own destiny. We younger people, who had grown up in the Cold War, knew that if it came to a nuclear exchange it would be all over for us. It made for a certain fatalistic sneering.

'I hope you've handled this responsibly,' the editor said when he came to the cutting room in the middle of the night to watch the rough cut of the film. David, Robert and I glanced at each other apprehensively, and flicked the switch. The screen filled with scenes of rubble, and the soundtrack was thick with groans and screams. God knows how, but David had laid his hands on some footage from an untransmitted drama about nuclear war which had been deemed too terrifying to broadcast. My weasel words in the commentary about 'Is this really what we can look forward to?' did little to sugar the pill, and 'responsibly' was not the first word that came to mind.

The highlight of our report was the screening of a series of short animated public information films called *Protect and Survive*, which had been sitting in locked government vaults for years, awaiting a nuclear holocaust. David had somehow managed to 'borrow' them for long enough to have copies made. They took the form of stark cartoons with a spooky radiophonic soundtrack, suggesting that you might shield yourself from the effects of nuclear attack by leaning a couple of doors against a wall and living beneath them for days. They were absurd. But their unnerving signature tune, bald style and gravel-voiced commentary by Patrick Allen ('Start collecting now items for your emergency toilet room. First, buckets or containers ...') were chilling. Intended as they were to be broadcast when all hope of averting nuclear war was gone, you could not watch them without being distressed.

We also discovered that the country's most energetic Emergency Planning Officer – every county was supposed to have one – had organised a training exercise to prepare the people of Humberside for nuclear attack. Keen to promote his work, he invited us to watch as, ensconced in an underground bunker (from which their families had been excluded), local government officials rehearsed the decisions they would make about fighting fires, treating the wounded and burying the dead if Cleethorpes was incinerated. The man who would decide who lived and who died turned out to be the council's Chief Executive, an accountant by background. We fed a scenario into the plan in which a group of several hundred starving Humbersiders had discovered the whereabouts of the bunker and were advancing on the place to ransack it for food. What would the Controller do?

'I'm afraid,' he said, 'I might have to employ the ultimate sanction.'

'What, shoot them?'

'I'm afraid so.'

Not surprisingly, when it was broadcast the film caused something of a sensation, spurring Raymond Briggs to create his cartoon book *When the Wind Blows*, about an elderly couple dying from radiation sickness after a nuclear attack. I'm not sure our film had any great lasting impact, though. Doubtless even now there are generals and strategists devising *Dr Strangelove*-like 'nuclear-war-fighting' theories. But if deterrence does not deter, the game is up.

Probably because I was younger than *Panorama*'s other reporters, I got sent to war zones around the world. Somehow I construed the fact that I found Lebanon, Uganda and Zimbabwe distressing as a reason to volunteer for more assignments. I cannot properly explain my enthusiasm, for I regarded the relish of many of the war addicts I met on the road as callous and shallow. It was just that matters of life and death seemed starker and more urgent than figuring out taxation and health policies.

At Christmas 1979 I found myself on the Afghan–Pakistan border with Robert Harris, on his first assignment as a producer. The difference in our expectations was obvious the moment we unpacked our bags in Peshawar. I pulled out a sleeping bag, water-purification tablets and an assortment of over-epauletted shirts. Robert brought forth pyjamas, slippers and silk dressing gown. He is the one who has since gone on to become a multi-millionaire, and all of it by living on his wits.

War reporting is a strange business. An anxious newspaper reporter can file his copy from anywhere (I once saw a senior reporter on the *Sunday Express* go to a telephone in the arrivals hall at Tel Aviv airport as soon as he got off the plane from London, to send back a 'front-line despatch' about a Palestinian attack on a civilian bus). The photographer, the cameraman and the television reporter, by contrast, have to be near the action: the fighting does not exist unless it can be *seen*. But the most gutsy role of all was that of the freelance photographer who lived for the picture that might make the front cover of *Time* or *Newsweek*, and thereby pay his rent for the next six months. All of us lived in a state of moral ambiguity, in which we sought out the risky, the distressing or the horrifying in order, as I persuaded myself, that exposure to the reality of war might make people in comfortable old Britain think differently about it. It might even make them rise up and demand that their government take some sort of action. (This was a naïve and fruitless belief, for most of us have become inured to the fact that, in the eloquent American expression, 'Shit happens.' As long as it's happening somewhere else, we may shed a tear, but rarely do we do much more.) With the occasional honourable exception, reporters in the field therefore tried to capture as much suffering as possible, without doing a great deal personally to alleviate it.

In the early 1980s Ronald Reagan decided he would stop the worldwide spread of communism by fighting it in what his supporters insisted upon calling 'America's own backyard'. It was a vague term which included his country's southern neighbour Mexico ('Poor Mexico. So far from God. So close to the United States'), the whole of the Caribbean, and the sovereign nations of Central America. Very few of the remnants of the Spanish Empire were a great advertisement for democracy, and in 1979 a group of kids in Nicaragua had risen up against the dictator Anastasio Somoza and driven him into exile in that refuge of tyrants, Paraguay. The Sandinistas – they named themselves after the 1920s revolutionary Augusto César Sandino – promised a new regime including decent health care and literacy. They captured the imagination of the European left, but to Washington they represented contamination.

Nicaragua was an exhilarating place to be, if you happened to be a liberal Westerner. The air was charged, the aims were high-minded, the revolutionary songs were catchy, the weather was sunny, the girls in fatigues were pretty, and the 'Nica Libres' (cola, lime and Flor de Caña rum) were plentiful. We didn't see the dark cells where the Sandinistas interrogated ideological enemies with the help of the Stasi and the KGB. The Sandinista anthem actually contained the lines:

Luchamos contra el Yanqui –
Enemigo de la humanidad.

(We fight against the Yankee –
Enemy of humanity.)

The schools were full of Cuban teachers and the hospitals awash
with Cuban doctors and nurses, sent by Fidel Castro to aid a fellow
revolutionary state. Within a few years the United States had
organised a force of counter-revolutionaries ('Contras') on the
border with Honduras, and that, combined with stringent trade
sanctions, eventually brought down the Sandinistas.

There was a long and not especially glorious tradition of
American interference in the states of the region, up to and
including organising *coups d'état*, and after the Nicaraguan
revolution the Reagan administration decided that nearby El
Salvador should be next. The country was an almost comic-book
version of a place ripe for revolution: most of its wealth was in the
hands of a tiny minority, often said to be a mere fourteen families,
many of them descended from the owners of vast coffee estates.
But what appeared a relatively straightforward matter of social
injustice looked in Washington to be the new front line between
capitalism and communism.

The memorable El Salvadorean counterpart to the Sandinistas'
catchy refrain about fighting the Yanquis was the sinister song
sung at gatherings of the right: *'Tiemblen, tiemblen, communistas!'*
('Tremble, tremble, communists!') Growled out by a few hundred
plump neo-fascists in Ray-Ban sunglasses, it was chilling.

I had already visited several wars, but El Salvador was especially
squalid, because so many of the killings took place not in combat
but as murders. In March 1980 Oscar Romero, the Archbishop of
the capital San Salvador, preached a sermon begging soldiers in
the army to examine their consciences and to disobey orders to kill

civilians. The next day he was shot dead while celebrating Mass. At his funeral upwards of thirty people were murdered by gunmen. Three American Catholic nuns and a lay missionary travelling from the airport to the capital were abducted, raped, killed and buried in shallow graves by the roadside. The government tried to pass the killings off as a robbery, but everyone – including the US Ambassador, who told Washington of his belief and was then sacked for doing so – knew the culprits were members of the American-trained National Guard.

Most of the thousands of murders during the war were blamed on strangely unidentifiable civilian 'death squads' which were never brought to account. Yet a significant number of those murdered were said by their families to have been arrested by uniformed men beforehand. The most terrifying of the several police forces in El Salvador were the Treasury Police, who wore grey uniforms, close-fitting helmets and jackboots. Their march was a goosestep, and many hid their eyes behind mirror sunglasses: en masse they looked like a sinister giant insect.

As the nightly curfew began, the policemen and their accomplices changed into civilian clothes, and the death squads began their work. When the curfew lifted next morning, the first task of the press corps was the 'body run', driving to the various places – rubbish tips, bridges, roadside verges – around the capital where the death squads dumped the bodies of those they had murdered in the night. The best you could hope for was a victim who had been shot cleanly. Often they had been grotesquely tortured. Worst of all were those who had suffered multiple wounds some time previously, for their bodies turned grey, swelled in the sun and stank. It was a filthy, frightening war, and the clearest evidence I had ever seen of Big Power willingness to disregard human rights in pursuit of a political objective. Doubtless Moscow was meddling too, and it probably marked a degree of bias to see the involvement of an ally as especially bothersome. We are all products of our time

and place, and none of us can see things free of unconscious prejudice: true neutrality is almost unattainable, and is not necessarily
even desirable. It would have been easy to dismiss Ronald Reagan
as an avuncular, slightly comical character, a clapped-out actor
whose hair, Gerald Ford said, had turned 'prematurely orange'. But
he was presiding over something grotesque.

My reporting made no difference to what happened in El
Salvador, except perhaps as part of the great accumulated mass of
media coverage, all of which essentially told the same story of a
ruthless military in the service of a small coterie of landowners. I
spent nights with both some of the bravest people I have ever met
– a group of Irish Franciscan monks on a mission station out in the
killing fields – and some of the most sinister, like the landowner
who explained that there was no need to improve the conditions
of the poor, because 'However much you beat a dog, it always
comes home at night.' One day I followed an army column as they
sweated their way up the side of an extinct volcano. After twenty
minutes' march the rebels opened fire on the column, hitting the
soldier next to me in the chest. One minute the poor boy looked
about fifteen, and the next like a grandfather.

In Mexico City I sought out one of the rebel commanders, a
charming former student of the University of Essex (university
officials periodically still sent him a letter asking if he could take
time off from running a revolution to complete his PhD thesis),
and one day, in the ruins of a destroyed farmstead in the east of the
country, I encountered five of his footsoldiers – thin young men,
boys really, in tattered shirts and jeans, carrying an assortment of
rifles which seemed too big for them. At a press conference I met
the President – a short, pomaded man in a white *guayabera*. When
I asked why he wasn't doing anything to stop the death squads he
took me out of the press room and into his office, where he opened
the drawer of his desk. The ludicrous thought flashed through my
mind that there was a gun in it, and perhaps he was going to shoot

me. But instead of a gun he drew out two sheets of paper which seemed to be reports from senior army commanders saying they had thoroughly investigated a series of killings and could find no evidence at all of military involvement. 'You see what I'm up against?' he said.

Few people in Britain gave a damn about what happened in Central America. For historical reasons, our foreign news largely concerned itself with what occurred in India, Pakistan, Anglophone Africa and the former Imperial possessions the United States, Australia and New Zealand (though very rarely Canada, which found itself rewarded for being a sensible democracy and for solidarity, courage and sacrifice by being considered dull, dull, dull). South America was a vast continent, but it had had the misfortune to be largely colonised by the Spanish and Portuguese, and so, as far as London news editors were concerned, hardly existed.

The contrast was starkly illustrated by the massacres that occurred in Zimbabwe in the mid-1980s, when Robert Mugabe, the country's half-mad President, sent part of his army on a rampage through Matabeleland in the south of the country. Zimbabwe was deemed to matter to the British public because it had once been a British colony, named after the great imperial monster Cecil Rhodes. Transferring Rhodesia to black majority rule in the 1970s was first stalled when the white minority staged what amounted to a *coup*. Once the British government had got all sides into negotiations, London's misreading of the political situation led it to back a well-meaning moderate nationalist, a tiny Methodist Bishop, Abel Muzorewa, who was roundly defeated in the first full elections in the country's history and never heard of again. Robert Mugabe, one of the leaders of the liberation movement, emerged from the elections as Prime Minister and, following sorry African precedent, set about trying to turn the country into a one-party state. Of all the nations on earth he might have asked, Mugabe invited North Korea to train an elite Fifth Brigade of his army, which he then ordered to Matabeleland to suppress dissent.

One corpse swelling in the sun on an African roadside looks pretty much the same as another, whatever its ethnicity. But Mike Dutfield, a witty and particularly brave producer who had begun his working life selling lavatories in Bulawayo, the biggest city in Matabeleland,* and I established that Mugabe's forces were perpetrating something akin to genocide – the President's power lay with the Shona people, while the thousands of victims were Ndebele people. The Zimbabwean government, furious that we had evaded their news blackout, banned us from the country (oddly enough, one of the flunkeys who carried out the ruling was the same man who had banned me when Ian Smith was running the place as a white supremacist).

Zimbabwe had been a difficult and upsetting job, and I began to lose all appetite for 'go anywhere, do anything' reporting. My most terrifying moment had come during the Lebanese civil war, when I and my producer tried to escape from the centre of the northern city of Tripoli crouched inside an ambulance being driven by local Boy Scouts. As we rounded a corner, bullets flew through the vehicle. Ironically, Mike Dutfield, who was the most accomplished man I knew at negotiating with armed thugs,† would be killed in a motorbike accident in England. But I lost three friends on assignments abroad, and discovered that as time went by, instead of becoming more blasé I grew more conscious of how incredibly

---

* Though an expertise in porcelain might seem more than adequate for a career in journalism, by the time he arrived in Lime Grove Mike had also spent several years as a reporter on the *Rand Daily Mail*, a heroically liberal South African paper in the days of the apartheid regime.

† His secret was a big smile and an outstretched hand. I found it was also helpful to have a carton of Marlboro cigarettes readily available.

narrow is the line between getting away with it and not doing so. I couldn't sleep properly, and when I eventually did manage to drop off, I awoke not even knowing what country I was in. In my dreams, men with guns in Africa, Ireland, Latin America and the Middle East got all muddled up in my head. I didn't exactly have a breakdown. But it was pretty like one.

I knew I had to find something else to do quite soon. I was thirty-five, and had hardly covered British domestic politics at all. I had by then co-authored, with Robert Harris, a book about the unattractive subject of chemical and biological warfare, which we titled *A Higher Form of Killing* – the phrase used by the German professor who had been instrumental in his country's develop-ment of poison gas in World War I. Central America had got under my skin, and a book about the place could hardly be any more uncommercial, so in 1985 I set off to travel by public transport from Belize to Panama.

Through the Volcanoes – an awful title which managed to be both derivative and platitudinous – was the result. That Christmas I was invited to a charity book signing one Saturday morning at the London University bookshop in Gower Street. I arrived to discover that I was sharing a table with the Beverley Sisters, three now rather past-it blondes from Bethnal Green whose close-harmony hits had included 'How Much is that Doggie in the Window?' and 'I Saw Mommy Kissing Santa Claus'. We were on the first floor, and although the sisters didn't seem very familiar with the contents of their joint autobiography, their queue of eager buyers stretched down the stairs and out of the front door of the shop. I sat in awkward silence as one happy customer after another asked Joy, Teddie and Babs to sign their reminiscences of life in showbiz. Eventually an elderly woman stopped and said, 'What you doin' 'ere, love?'

'I've written a book.'

'What's it about?'

'Central America.'

'Sold many copies?'

'None.'

'Ah, bless,' she said. 'I'll take one. I suppose I might find some-one I can give it to.'

6

Remembered that Question Yet?

Why does anyone bother to write a book? The newspapers delight in stories of how writing made Jeffrey Archer, Jo Rowling or Ken Follett into millionaires. But most people who write books cannot make a living from doing so. The real reason people write is that they feel they must. Everyone loves a story – fiction or non-fiction – and a story unfolding in your own mind is the most intoxicating story of all. Then there is the joy of the sheer mechanics of the thing, choosing which is the right word and where it should go. On days when it goes well it is like surfing. On bad days, it is like trying to swim in treacle.

Journalists are particularly prone to the book-writing bug, because they already live in a world of words. But the media of their trade – newspapers and television – are fleeting and superficial. Books – words within covers, with a title on the front and, for a little while at least, space on the shelves of a bookshop, promise a sort of permanence, a sense that your efforts haven't been in vain. It is an illusion, of course: the sheer volume of titles decrees that nothing much can last for long, and like most businesses, publishers are constantly seeking new 'product'. They know we all grow sick of seeing the same thing on the retailer's shelf. Half a dozen people have been credited with the remark that 'Every journalist believes they have a book inside them. That's probably where it ought to stay.' It is sound advice.

While writing my non-best-seller about Central America, the small question had arisen of how to pay the mortgage. Yet again, as in a bad play, the telephone rang. It was Ron Neil, a legendary television producer who had begun his journalistic career covering 'unusual deaths' chosen by his news editor from the death notices of Scottish local papers. Now he had great plans for the BBC to recover its former dominance of the early-evening TV schedules, which it had lost to ITV with the culling of *Nationwide*, the early-evening show combining comfy seriousness with features on yodelling dogs. Would I like to join the presenting team on his new show for a couple of days a week?

One of Ron's ideas was that on the new programme (which was to go by the staggeringly inventive name of *The Six O'Clock News*) the presenters would have an editorial voice – unlike the usual BBC practice, which was for producers to tell them to read out whatever was put in front of them, and if they didn't like it, there were plenty of others – or a family pet – who could be hired in their place. The new show was going to be groundbreaking in acknowledging that the faces of a news bulletin might have a brain, which was something rather unusual in the 1980s BBC.

Reading the news is slightly reminiscent of being an undertaker. Both trades deal in sonorousness and require a suit that doesn't fit too badly. A vaguely plausible manner is essential. A talent for appearing sadly shocked is a bonus. For what is newsreading? It is what in primary school is called 'reading aloud' – which is why, for a long time, broadcasters employed unsuccessful actors in the role. In the early days of radio they were anonymous, but the spread of television made that impossible. Now, instead of being actors, every newsreader pretends they're a journalist. With a few honourable exceptions, of whom Jon Snow at Channel 4 is a good example, they are not. In itself, newsreading is not particularly interesting. Some sort of gravitas is essential. You must not squeak or drone too much. A dark-brown voice is a help to males, and a certain bridesmaidly presentableness to females. The news itself – whatever that may be – is the rather frumpy bride. Nevertheless, numbers of the Ken or Barbie figures acting as a conduit for the news come to believe that they are interesting in their own right. They are usually wrong.

What is this thing called 'news'? My favourite explanation of the role of a newspaper editor is that given by the self-important columnist, editor and table-knocker Hannen Swaffer when called before a parliamentary inquiry and asked to define an editor's job. He answered that it was his responsibility to print as many of the proprietor's prejudices as the advertisers would allow.* Broader definitions of 'news' are legion: that 'Dog Bites Man' isn't news, but 'Man Bites Dog' is; that it largely consists of telling people Lord Jones is dead when they didn't know he was alive; that an editor's job is to sift the wheat from the chaff, and then to print the chaff; that it is the first rough draft of history – and so on.

In its most admirable form, 'news' is surely something that someone, somewhere, would rather you didn't know (and I can't recall where I first stole that from). The problem with most contemporary news is that it is nothing of the sort, being instead barely rewritten press releases from commercial companies, political organisations or other loudmouths. Finding things out takes time and money, and there is no guarantee that at the end of an investigation you will have unearthed anything much new. It is much easier simply to fill the pages or the programmes with what vested interests most definitely *do* want you to know. In addition to that, the media's days of plenty are gone, and as commercial pressures on news organisations have grown in the last fifty years they have reduced their staff, to the point where there are now

---

* Swaffer died in 1962. The *British Journalism Review* later commented that he would be remembered for little more than this observation and 'the mixture of dandruff and cigarette ash on his velvet collar'.

some publications which survive only on a mass of unpaid Tarquins and Amelias sweating away as interns in the questionable belief that there is a career to be had in reporting.

There are some important distinctions between 'news' in print and on television, the most obvious of which is that television abhors an absence of pictures. The number of pages printed by a newspaper is generally the consequence of a commercial judgement: print and paper cost money. The BBC, being enviably free from commercial pressures, can afford to set aside defined periods of time, like the thirty minutes dedicated to *The Six O'Clock News*. A decision to dedicate substantial air time to bringing the world to the viewers is an admirable ambition. But it can have slightly odd consequences for those involved. For, whatever has happened in the world, news bulletins usually retain the same urgent musical opening, the same duration and the same portentous style. There are some days when there is simply not enough material to fill them. At times, the most honest thing a newsreader could say would be, 'Not much has happened today – I'd go to bed if I were you.' But you never hear it.

Studio presenting, I discovered on *The Six O'Clock News*, was a very different job from being a reporter, where you were usually earnestly hectoring the camera from somewhere more or less unappealing. The studio presenter – the face of the programme – had to be the sort of person viewers would be happy to have sitting at the supper table with them – confident yet personable; earnest but reassuring; simultaneously mechanical and intimate. No wonder so many presenters were half-mad. Ron Neil had already invited Sue Lawley, a queen of live television at the time, and Nicholas Witchell, a rather buttoned-up reporter who had written a book about the Loch Ness Monster, to front the show. I was to fill in on their days off. (I had left the programme for less glamorous pastures by the time the studio was invaded in 1988 by gay rights protesters. Sue Lawley continued majestically reading the news while her co-presenter Nicholas Witchell sat on a lesbian off-camera, a wrestling victory for which he was soon rewarded by being appointed the BBC's chief cheerleader for the monarchy.)

The job was good news for my building society, but I did not feel that I distinguished myself. This was mainly because I had not much idea what 'news' was. It eventually became clear that it consists of what the collective subconscious of a small group of mortgage-battered middle-aged commuters in newsrooms scattered across the capital consider to be Significant. Identifying it takes a little while to pick up. At that time, news agency reports were still being printed onto paper which spewed out of a teleprinter machine in a corner of the newsroom, and two days running I 'spiked' (shoved onto a spike mounted on a piece of wood) what turned out to be the lead story: my news judgement had some way to go. Luckily, I was not to be tested for much longer, because after six months the BBC's Head of Current Affairs, Peter Pagnamenta, invited me in for a cup of tea.

To describe Pagnamenta as enigmatic is to do a disservice to opacity. A very clever man of few words, he was known for chewing paperclips. (A BBC selection board once asked him how he would communicate with his staff if he got the promotion he was seeking. 'Telepathy?' he was said to have replied.) That afternoon, he said he had a problem and he had an idea. His problem was the regional programme supposedly serving London and the south-east of England. It was no good. In Manchester or Newcastle, which had strong regional identities, the problem did not exist: Mancunians and Geordies felt an emotional unity, enjoyed local news, and often regarded their local newscasters as the authentic face of their city or region. London, which was dominated by incomers from elsewhere, felt no such identity, while the Home Counties had precious little in common either with each other or with the capital. Additionally, because of the concentration of national news media in London, big stories were broadcast across the country, which meant that the local news programme was generally regarded as a dustbin for unconsidered trifles. In an effort to convince viewers that the south-east of England had some coherence as a region, the BBC offering had been given the name *London Plus*, and a title sequence which was intended to indicate inclusiveness, in the form a 'plus' symbol scattering across the screen. The result looked rather like an enormous municipal cemetery. Those who worked on the show were less than convinced that the whole area was one happy family, and called the programme 'Sod Off, Kent'. Pagnamenta's solution was to re-engineer the whole thing. Would I like to front it?

'I'm not sure it's really for me,' I said.

'Oh, think of all the benefits,' he replied. 'In no time they'll be asking you to open supermarkets.'

Opening supermarkets (a height I have not yet scaled) was not really why I'd decided to become a journalist. There are all sorts of acts of prostitution to which television journalists may succumb – voicing advertisements, being the 'face' of products, training corporate criminals to appear plausible when being interviewed. On the whole, all are best avoided. Yet reading the news, even on a successful show like *The Six O'Clock News*, had turned out to be something of an occupation for animated suits. Of course, you need a skill or two to be a successful newsreader on television – mainly the ability to knot your tie, put your trousers on the right way round, and to sound as if you vaguely know what you're talk-ing about. In the end, even if you write as much of the news bulle-tin as you can – and you can never write every word of it – the newsreader is an empty vessel. No wonder one household name is known behind his back as 'the news bunny' (as in, 'Do stick a fresh battery in the news bunny'). 'Sod Off Kent', though, would offer me the chance to do interviews, and perhaps to get out on the road again. Even if only to Pinner.

* * *

It turned out to be rather fun. There is much to be said for being at the bottom of the food chain. At the very least, you have no illusions. But it can also enforce creativity. And there was, I think, something quite helpful about my being utterly ignorant of British politics. Apart from a few days spent in the Durham coalfields during the miners' strike of 1984–85, I had done hardly any domestic reporting for years. I may have had no idea where Penge was – none of us did – but that ignorance gave a fresh perspective on British domestic affairs. I approached the political class as a Victorian explorer might have confronted a new tribe in darkest Africa.

One of the worst things that has happened to the reporting of British politics in the last forty years has been the proliferation of political specialists. There are now men and women interpreting the posturings of our political class who have spent their entire career among that class. The BBC, ITV, Sky and others have filled much of an office block on Victoria Embankment with teams of people whose only function is to pay attention to what happens in Westminster. There is even an entire television channel devoted to proceedings in Parliament. No one doubts that in a democracy people need to know what is being said and done in their name. But it is corrupting for that to be anyone's exclusive focus. '*Tout comprendre, c'est tout pardonner*,' as Madame de Staël or someone put it. It is not the journalist's job to forgive, but to enquire and to hold to account. The reporter is there to speak for the governed, and a journalist who has spent all their working life in the company of politicians loses that perspective.

Much responsibility for the creation of this weird breed lies with an infamous series of articles for *The Times* by John Birt and Peter Jay in 1972. At the time, Birt was running a worthy but dull Sunday lunchtime analysis programme on ITV, and Jay (cursed forever by the epithet earlier bestowed on him as 'the cleverest young man in England') was presenting it. They believed that there existed 'a bias against understanding' in television news. The proposition that what was needed was 'a mission to explain' might have slowly gathered dust on the bookshelves of those shuffling oxymorons, media academics, had it not been for Birt's recruitment fifteen years later to the management of the BBC. He in turn appointed kindred spirits to senior posts (Jay was made Economics Editor) and set about bringing the organisation to heel.

A fair-minded assessment of Birt's influence would have to acknowledge that at the time of his arrival the BBC badly needed a kick, that some of the reforms he introduced generated savings which could be spent on programmes, and that he was alive to the potential of the internet long before most of the old guard. But he also hired in consultants, only a few of whom knew what they were talking about, but all of whom had to be paid – lavishly – who recommended that harmless producers and editors should be sent on bizarre management courses and 'team-building' exercises, on which they were supposed to work out how to get eight people across a river using only a packet of processed cheese and a length of string.* Birt also closed down the Lime Grove studios, where all the nasty current affairs came from, and cultivated teams of specialists, some of whom understood broadcast journalism. The result was that reporting became increasingly dominated by a form of intellectual 'old-boy network' as pernicious in its way as its class counterpart: economics was left to economists, politics to political types. Just as no one should be allowed to stand for election to Parliament until they have done a proper job outside politics, so no one should be allowed to cover politics until they have spent a long time reporting on real life.

---

* On one of these sessions my friend Tom Fort, at the time a sub-editor in the radio newsroom, whose only crime was a weakness for serial anecdotalism, was made team leader of a group charged with reviving the fortunes of a struggling Italian restaurant. When asked to reveal his business plan after a strenuous afternoon's brainstorming in the pub, he disclosed that 'We've accepted a takeover bid from a chain of themed Irish bars. It's now to be called O'Luigi's.' He was not promoted.

Arriving at the job of confronting politicians fresh and ignorant in the 1980s – before the specialist supremacy – was a decided asset. Though we were a mixed bunch on *London Plus*, most had come to the same conclusion I had reached: that live television could only work if it was fun, no matter how big or small the audience. Mark Thompson, later to occupy the BBC Director General's office, was one of the daily producers, and seemed to get the message at the time. Other members of the team had been drafted in because they were said to know something about television production, or, like the recently cashiered local-radio manager who had run off with a vicar's wife, understood regional news-gathering. Others, like the sports presenter – a former jockey known in the office as 'Basil Brush' for his resemblance to the glove puppet – were enigmas. At one point he so took against football, the most popular sport in the country, that he refused to cover it, leading to something of a glut of reports on women's golf. He claimed to telephone the BBC complaints line from home under the name 'Colonel Box from Maidenhead', solely to praise the quality of the *London Plus* sports coverage.

The programme never escaped from the fact that it was catering to a market that did not really exist. The figures showed that – by twenty-first-century standards – a very large number of televisions were tuned to BBC 1 during our time slot. But one never got the sense that anyone was really watching. We probably deserved the public's indifference: one of the senior producers was a Liverpudlian who was perpetually sending Basil Brush off to report on Everton Football Club, to the bafflement of the millions of Arsenal, Chelsea and Tottenham fans in London. Other reporters found themselves shuttling between the pavements outside criminal courts in a relentless attempt to reach the bottom of the pit of human depravity. There were some events which forced their way into public attention, like the Broadwater Farm riots in October 1985, triggered by a heavy-handed police raid during which a black woman collapsed and died. It was striking that it was the brutal murder of a policeman during the riots which gave moral force to the reporting – those who work in the media are overwhelmingly middle-class, and have little first-hand experience of the lives of many of those they report upon. (I plead guilty.) In truth, in a city of nearly seven million – to say nothing of the surrounding suburbanites – most judgements about what is newsworthy can be pretty arbitrary.

London provided, however, the biggest laboratory for Margaret Thatcher to conduct her experiments upon local government, which became her target after she had defeated the miners' strike in 1985. The Militant deputy leader of Liverpool council, Derek Hatton (later to reinvent himself as a male model, property developer and Range Rover driver), was her noisiest opponent until he was finally slapped down by the leader of the Labour Party, Neil Kinnock, in June 1986. Ken Livingstone was Hatton's much more adroit southern counterpart. 'Red Ken' had become leader of the Greater London Council after staging a putsch within the ruling Labour group two years after Thatcher's election to Downing Street. He and his friends on the GLC acted as if they were the country's main opposition to Thatcherism (as, in many ways, they were), and she was determined to abolish the council and its counterparts in six other metropolitan areas. It took several years before she managed it and – to make sure she had driven a spike through its heart – sold off its headquarters, County Hall, to an American hotel chain, an aquarium and a Chinese restaurant.

We repeatedly asked to interview Thatcher about her plans for London's local government, but she declined every invitation. Livingstone was another matter, and would appear at the drop of a hat. Political animosity, even the cordial loathing of thousands of Londoners, seemed to give him energy. And since he usually prefaced every intervention with a knowing smirk, he got away for years with presenting Mrs Thatcher as an enemy of democracy for wishing to abolish extravagant municipal socialism. The fact that his game of chicken didn't save the GLC is perhaps an argument against those who say the media has power. Governments have power. The media may, at most, have influence.

But joy was unconfined in the *London Plus* office when the *News of the World* exclusively revealed in 1987 that the epicentre of English Satanism was in Hastings. At last, a reason to explore the 'Plus' in *London Plus*! Reporter Richard Bath – later to become Mr Plymouth, as the face of *Westcountry Live* – was sent to investigate. In a basement flat he found half a dozen whiffy old wrinklies about to celebrate a Black Mass. They explained that since one of them was teetotal, they were using Ribena instead of wine. If Richard would provide the bread, he could observe the event. The corner shop was unfortunately out of loaves, so, using the skill at improvising that would later lead him to such eminence in Plymouth, he bought a packet of biscuits, which was deemed sufficient. A naked woman was draped across the kitchen table, and what the future Face of Plymouth witnessed that afternoon no pastry chef had ever intended. He returned to the office unable ever again to look a Custard Cream in the face.

Three a.m. is a very ambiguous time. At two o'clock, you might still be on a night out. Four is always 'four in the morning', a very, very early start. But three belongs in that no-man's land when your body cries for a warm bed. For three years that was, though, the time I got up.

Breakfast television is a very strange creature, which British broadcasters ignored for years. The ruling and chattering classes listened – and, having very conservative tastes, continue to listen – to Radio Four over their breakfasts. People with jobs to get to or children to feed listen to music. It took nearly thirty years before the British abandoned their disdain for breakfast television and followed the Americans, who had introduced it in the 1950s. It often struck me that the great misunderstanding about morning television was that British broadcasting executives had only been exposed to it while eating room-service breakfasts in transatlantic hotels, without realising that most people do not live in hotel rooms, and have to make their own breakfast. Unsurprisingly, when they introduced it to the British Isles, it had a very bumpy start.

The worthies regulating ITV decided that the way to make early-morning television work was to abandon their previous belief in regional broadcasters, and to have a single company cover the whole nation. Unfortunately, TV-am, the company which got the contract in December 1980, completely misunderstood what people wanted to watch over their cornflakes. They hired five of the biggest egos in Britain, under the leadership of the one-time 'cleverest young man in England', Peter Jay. After the channel's launch in February 1983, these five – chat-show hosts Michael Parkinson and David Frost, newsreaders Angela Rippon and Anna Ford, and author Robert Kee – swiftly discovered that while the public would tolerate self-importance and seriousness in the evenings, they definitely did not want it curdling their breakfast milk. The company – in which the 'Famous Five' were shareholders as well as presenters – had commissioned expensive architects to build eye-catching offices adorned with giant egg-cups on the site of a derelict car showroom in Camden Town. But that was as far as TV-am's *joie-de-vivre* went. Whatever the nature of the company's self-proclaimed 'mission', it wasn't to acquire audiences.

TV-am failed because it had misunderstood not only public taste, but the nature of the competition. The BBC – as ever in the grip of its obsession with being in every area of broadcasting – had decided that it too must have breakfast television. TV-am had expected the corporation to produce something that chimed with its usual po-faced output. Instead the corporation gave the job of editing its new show to Ron Neil, who from January 1983 produced a programme with the homely name of *Breakfast Time*, which turned out to be the antithesis of the starchy worthiness the bigheads in the commercial sector had expected.

For a start, it was presented not from behind a desk, but from a sofa by people in knitwear. The lead presenter was Frank Bough, an accomplished broadcaster who could cope with anything that happened live on air, even – as he said happened later – Edwina Curry fondling his thigh while he interviewed her. He was paired with Selina Scott, who had been lured across from ITV.* They were accompanied by a laconic weatherman, Francis Wilson, who had also worked in commercial television; a tame doctor to dispense medical advice; a fitness instructor known as 'the Green Goddess' for the colour of her leotard; a cook; and – something previously unheard of – an astrologer, Russell Grant, who spouted gibberish about the influence of the planets whenever called upon. There was also a sports presenter, David Icke, who a few years later announced that he was 'the son of the Godhead', stood for Parliament, began uttering prophecies and declared that the world was controlled by a bunch of giant lizards inhabiting the bodies of people like the Queen, Mick Jagger, and assorted Presidents of the USA. Working those hours did funny things to you.

Crucially, the BBC managed to get its show on air before the erstwhile cleverest young man in England could marshal the Famous Five. It was a catastrophic delay, and the BBC's downmarket line-up punctured the good ship TV-am below the waterline. The Famous Five and their leader were soon thrown overboard,

---

* She was chummy with ex-King Constantine of Greece, then living in exile in Hampstead Garden Suburb, and invited him to come onto the sofa one morning for an interview. When the car collecting him arrived at the security barrier, the driver explained that he had the King of Greece in the back. The guard examined his clipboard, looked baffled, sucked his pencil, then stuck his head through the window. 'Where'd ya say you're the king of, mate?'

and a puppet with oversized ears called Roland Rat and a mission to amuse clambered aboard – as everyone said, the first rat in history to join a sinking ship.

Roland Rat may have been a stage idiot, but he saved the company, and three years later the BBC decided the only way to fight him was to turn its breakfast offering into something more serious. The sofa was consigned to the skip, and replaced by a curved desk. Uncle Frank shed his cardigan and wore a tie. Kirsty Wark flew down from Glasgow several days a week to torture hapless politicians. A pretty newsreader called Jill Dando was brought in from the West Country to deliver the quarter-hourly news bulletins. We teased her endlessly about her devotion to Cliff Richard, but she was so good that soon she was fronting *Holiday*, *Songs of Praise* and *Crimewatch*, until she was cruelly and mysteriously shot dead on her doorstep in Fulham one morning in April 1999. Sally Magnusson, a woman of breathtaking wholesomeness, joined the presenting team. David Icke spiralled into outer space, to be replaced as sports reporter by the former Arsenal goalkeeper Bob Wilson – one of the nicest men you could meet – and then by Sally Jones, a very proper former tennis champion and quintuple Oxford Blue. And, after a year of *London Plus*, I was asked if I'd also like to start getting up in the middle of the night. By this time I had hired an agent, Anita Land.* Should I do it? Her response? 'Go for it.'

Like every other programme I worked on at the BBC, *Breakfast Time* was characterised by the staff's high ambitions, hard work and creativity. For decades the BBC has been an organisation which attracts some of the best and brightest. The problem, then as ever, was the management – though by and large, since most of

---

* 'Let me give you a piece of advice,' Michael Grade, a natural impresario, had said when I was first asked to present television programmes from the studio. 'You need a tough Jewish agent. Like my sister.'

Breakfast Time's broadcasting was carried out while they were still in bed (a normal office day in broadcasting is generally reckoned to be from ten in the morning to six in the evening), they left us alone. But there was no getting away from the fact that we were broadcasting at a godawful time of day. The central illusion – of being bright-eyed and bushy-tailed – was hard to pull off when everyone was really half-asleep. If *London Plus* came at the bottom of the editorial food chain, working on breakfast television was hardly more than one notch up.

Knowing how unimportant we were considered did at least build a great sense of team spirit. I suppose it was that, and the production team's social leprosy as a result of working all night, which led to the weekly knees-up in Albertine's, a wine bar a few hundred yards from Television Centre. These affairs always began innocently enough, with many of us saying, 'Oh yes, I'll come down, just for one.' By 10 a.m. were on our third. By midday, one of the producers – an apparently saturnine Welshman – had launched into 'Solitaire'. It wasn't quite Andy Williams, but it was terrific to sing along with. By 12.30 the first proper customers were arriving at the wine bar for a nice quiet lunch. They were soon deciding to go elsewhere. By one o'clock a Glaswegian producer had clambered onto the circular table around which we all sat and launched into 'New York, New York', kicking her legs into the air at each chorus. By three minutes past one the table had toppled over, bathing everyone in Spanish sparkling wine, and covering the floor in broken glass. There were one or two members of the team, like the weatherman Francis Wilson, who managed to sleep through it all. But by about two in the afternoon we had been asked to leave – everyone was ready for bed anyway – and headed off home. The man who sang 'Solitaire' lived in Kingston upon Thames, and frequently managed to make it onto a train at Waterloo station, only to wake up in Exeter.

* * *

In October 1987 one of the biggest domestic stories of the 1980s entirely passed me by. I had set my alarm for the usual 3 a.m. wake-up, and pulled back the curtains to see the normally well-lit street in total darkness. The bedside light was dead. But outside, a taxi was waiting as usual, and we passed through deserted streets scattered with the branches of trees. Clearly, something astonishing had happened. It was only much later that someone recalled that the previous evening the BBC weather forecaster Michael Fish had said in so many words that there was 'no danger of Britain being hit by a hurricane'.* Now, as the taxi driver slalomed his way towards Lime Grove, 'hurricane' was precisely the word being used.

We arrived at the *Breakfast Time* office just as it too was plunged into darkness. After several minutes of cursing and candle-lighting by the producers, one of the engineers said, 'There's an emergency generator, you know.' 'Could we perhaps switch it on?' I asked. The man disappeared, and five minutes later the lights flickered into life. Ten seconds later they died again. Two minutes after that the engineer reappeared. 'What happened with the emergency generator?' I asked him. 'Well, the thing is, it's not really designed for emergencies,' he replied.

The BBC did produce a *Breakfast Time* of sorts that morning, because up the road, deep in the bowels of the circular 1960s building at Television Centre in White City, there was an emergency news studio with a working generator. So those parts of the country not struck down by power cuts could enjoy the spectacle of Nicholas Witchell sitting in what looked like a nuclear bunker. He made rather a good job of explaining what had happened.

---

* Fish, a man previously best known for delivering the weather forecast dressed like a 1970s Open University lecturer, later claimed he'd *invented* the story about a telephone call from a viewer worried because she'd heard there was a hurricane coming, which enabled him to deliver the patronising, 'Don't worry. There isn't.' There is a moral in there somewhere.

Once dawn had properly broken, we set off to see whether, by any chance, Albertine's had survived the power cuts.

A couple of years after that, *Breakfast Time* was renamed *Breakfast News*, and then it moved to Television Centre. In the next-but-one 'rationalisation', in 2012, the programme would be shunted up to the banks of the Manchester Ship Canal in Salford, a decision which was hugely popular with Lancashire estate agents helping BBC staff to spend their relocation expenses, and – since some of the producers attempted a form of commuting – the shareholders of Virgin trains, if not particularly with either the staff or their families. Or with viewers. It was, of course, pure coincidence that Salford was represented in Parliament by the Chairman of the Labour Party, which had been in power when the decision was taken. *Breakfast* (the *News* was lost on the journey) was joined in its exile by the BBC Sports Department, which arrived in Salford in good time for the 2012 Olympic Games. Which were in London. Meanwhile, it was announced that *Question Time*, a political discussion programme whose staple fare was Westminster politicians, would have its offices moved to Glasgow. In 2013 the one-time state-of-the-art studios in White City were sold off to another bunch of property developers and their occupants transferred to a newly built office block in central London where coathooks and wastepaper baskets were banned. The relocation was justified on the improbable grounds that moving from offices opposite an Express Dairies distribution centre in West London to the heart of a world city was 'economical'. The economies included there being no studios suitable for anything but news programmes, and working space for only a fraction of the producers to be accommodated. 'Starbucks has wi-fi,' the unlucky ones were told.

At the time I had joined *Breakfast Time* a quarter of a century earlier, the *News of the World* boasted on its front-page masthead that 'All human life is there'. Much the same was true of *Breakfast*

Time, where, for all their lofty ambitions, producers were still incapable of resisting the lure of a parrot which could whistle the National Anthem or a gerbil which looked a bit like the Pope. So I was as likely to be interviewing a dog (seriously) as talking to the Chancellor of the Exchequer (which also happened, once). Given the resonance of each of those interviews, the balance was probably about right.

The real problem with *Breakfast Time* was as obvious as it was inescapable. It was broadcast at a quite horrible time of day. Make-up could sometimes hide the ravages of the night before. But nothing could conceal the crushing tedium of the format, which rested on the entirely reasonable assumption that no one with a job to go to, or children to get to school, was going to sit and watch television for any length of time in the morning. It therefore followed that the news – or at least the headlines – had to be repeated about every fifteen minutes, so that anyone dashing out of the house might have some idea of what was going on in the world.* To break the tedium of repetition we were soon playing parlour games in between the news summaries. How many states of the Unites States could you remember? Who could think up the most unusual way of throwing to local newscasters across the country without saying, 'And now the news where *you* live.' I used to challenge friends at home to bet that I couldn't get a word they nominated into a specified link – oddly, the easiest ones were terms like 'machairodont' (sabre-toothed) or 'widdershins' (anti-clockwise), because no one ever did the obvious thing of asking, 'Er, what?' The tricky thing was to get a word like 'gumboil' or 'barracuda' into a weather forecast.

In between the news summaries came the interesting stuff, when you got to interview people. During the couple of hours

---

* The same repetitive philosophy underpins today's twenty-four-hour news channels, which is why so many of their poor presenters look dead behind the eyes.

between 7 and 9 a.m. there appeared – as if on some conveyor belt of possible prizes on a game show – a succession of politicians, inventors, writers, get-rich-quick charlatans, sports stars, philanthropists, entertainers, bullies and weirdoes. Though the public relations industry was slightly less brutal then than it is today, invariably the nicest people were those who controlled their own lives and diaries, and the nastiest were those who were contractually obliged to appear for their three or four minutes selling something – it didn't much matter whether it was a new film or a possible new government. Interviews are the bricks out of which current affairs programmes are built: they are cheap, and can be trimmed to any length. Unfortunately, since live television programmes are frequently unpredictable, interviewees can find themselves invited to expatiate at length on the subject of their choice, only for them to have uttered a single sentence when they suddenly hear their interviewer saying, 'Well, thank you. I'm afraid that's all we've got time for.' Occasionally guests are booked to appear, and then unbooked, which can be pretty embarrassing when they have told all their friends and family of their imminent stardom.

The key to being a successful guest is an ability to say things authoritatively and comprehensibly. But that is convincingly trumped by the mere fact of being available. University professors, ambulance-chasing lawyers and spokesmen for vested interests know that appearing on television or radio translates into kudos or cash. Indeed, a number of charities, 'think tanks' and pressure groups seem to have virtually no existence outside broadcast studios. All you need to do to feed your ego, publicise your charity or guarantee a bonus at the end of the year is to be available. You may not be the perfect guest, but you will at least be a bum on a seat.

Just about the lowest of the low in showbusiness is the 'same-day booking' – the z-lister with so little going on in their life that you can guarantee that, firstly, they won't be offended by a last-minute invitation, and secondly, that they will turn up for the gig. Famously, modern politics is 'showbusiness for ugly people', a comment so close to the mark that at least half a dozen people have claimed to have said it first. Anyone who stands for elected office requires a good quotient of naked egotism – it cannot be otherwise. But what could have persuaded Jerry Hayes, the young MP for Harlow at the time, that he could advance the Conservative cause by allowing himself to be put in the stocks and pelted with custard pies? Every iteration of Parliament has a Jerry Hayes, Peter Bruinvels, Anthony Beaumont-Dark, George Galloway or Simon Danczuk in whom self-centredness seems so much more obvious than usefulness. But sooner or later their hour may come. For the needs of the producer change the closer it comes to transmission time. Several hours ago you didn't book the woman from the local chamber of commerce because you were hoping to get a Nobel Prize-winning economist. With half an hour to transmission, the Chamber of Commerce woman suddenly looks like an authoritative commentator.

The central illusion in all interviews is that they are conversations, which – apart from the fact that each participant has done some homework in preparation for the conversation – is true. The difficulty is that the two people involved may often be talking about entirely different things. This is why it is essential for the interviewer to get control of the exchange at the start. It is especially important at seven-thirty in the morning. Over the course of three years presenting breakfast television I must have taken part in perhaps a thousand of these interviews, and I remember very few of them indeed: they were the journalistic equivalent of the novelty breakfast food, Pop Tarts. Any presenter ought to be able to talk to anyone at any time about anything, but since they may make a slightly better job of it if they know little about the subject they're discussing, they tend to be given briefs beforehand. These have usually been cobbled together by a researcher or producer who has spent an hour on the phone with the guest – a process which sent many potential commentators so far up the wall that they either refused to disclose what they were going to say, or told the producer whatever it was they judged he or she wanted to hear, and often then said precisely the reverse on air. At other times, producers simply got the wrong end of the stick. I once conducted an early-morning interview with Michael Palin by reciting some alleged 'facts' from the brief I had been given and asking him whether by any chance they were true. Most of them weren't.

It was the political interviews on *Breakfast Time* that seemed to make the most noise – mainly, I suspect, because so much of the news is made by, and reported by, a small circle who pay excessive attention to each other, and ensure the merry-go-round keeps turning: someone says something mildly controversial, the newspapers write it up, someone else comments on the reported remarks, and pretty soon everyone is passing Go and collecting £200. The truth is that most news doesn't matter, and most political controversies are neither controversial nor even, sometimes, truly political.

The time of day helped, of course: first thing in the morning most of us are either grumpy or half-asleep, or both. Margaret Thatcher's favourite Cabinet Minister, Lord (David) Young, appeared one morning and got shirty at suggestions that his party had done nothing to moderate rising levels of crime. Her Home Secretary, Douglas Hurd, appeared on another occasion and was rather thoughtful about how no one seemed to understand why the crime rate rose and fell. There were dozens of other politicians who came and went, talking sense and nonsense (though none of them spoke nonsense as insistently as the leader of the National Union of Mineworkers, Arthur Scargill, who seemed to believe that if he said something emphatically enough, it must be true). After a year or so, the programme began to build a reputation as a place where interesting things might be said. We became aware that party headquarters and political journalists were paying attention, after which it became ever easier to persuade significant players to risk ruining their day before it was even 9 a.m.

Every autumn, along with just about everyone who either makes or pays attention to speeches in the Palace of Westminster, the programme decamped to wherever the political parties were holding their annual conferences. For many years these took place in end-of-season seaside resorts, where there were enough hotels and bed-and-breakfasts to put up the thousands of members of the political baggage train – worthy local delegates, beery trade union representatives, wheedling PR men, lovers, ambitious dogsbodies, arrogant political researchers in overbuttoned suits, duck-squawk party spokesmen and the rest of the self-important gallimaufry of our democracy.

The grandeur or otherwise of your lodgings told everyone precisely how important you were. The party leaders, Cabinet, Shadow Cabinet and moneybags stayed in the best hotels, and everyone else wherever they or their employers could afford. At my first party conference for *Breakfast Time*, half a dozen of us found ourselves in a Blackpool boarding house where your feet stuck to the dark-red lino flooring each time you got out of bed to visit the bathroom at the end of the corridor. The sea was grey, the sky was grey, and the grey streets were filled with grey-faced people. The promenade was lined with shops selling plastic rubbish from behind big plastic counters staffed by blowsy girls and young men with terrible skin smoking through cupped hands, the air full of tinny music. Once Tony Blair and his gentrifying friends got control of the Labour Party, Blackpool was struck off the list of venues.

For years the party conferences have been a fraud on the public. In the days when Labour Party policy was made at annual confer-

ence, reporting the decisions of the members was a clear democratic duty. Although I was still in short trousers when Aneurin
Bevan made his speech about unilateral nuclear disarmament
being no more than 'an emotional spasm' which 'would send a
British Foreign Secretary naked into the conference chamber', it
was still resonating thirty years later. But once Tony Blair had
given control of party policy to a National Policy Forum in the
1990s, the speeches at the annual gathering became little more
than exercises in gong-bashing.

The leadership of the Conservative Party had regarded their
annual conference as an inconvenience for decades, and knew
better than to take it too seriously. These gatherings were, for them,
a chance to discharge social obligations to the shopkeepers, estate
agents and sensibly shod local members who ran the constituency
barbecues and knocked on doors at election time. For many of
democracy's footsoldiers a trip to conference can be a bit of a treat.
I have no doubt that my father's mother, Dolly, who achieved
eminence as Chairman of Sewers and Drains on the council in
Selby, would have thought it quite an outing (though she'd have
been scandalised by the way hoteliers rip off the delegates).

Stripped of any great political significance, the annual conferences have become commercial ventures at which the parties sell
space for lobbyists, companies and pressure groups, who set up
stands in the anterooms – effectively buying access to those who
make, or want to make, policy. The sweeter the price, the better
your chances of having the party leader photographed at your
stand. For great numbers of others, conference is merely an opportunity to eat and drink too much. It is to their shame that broadcasters and the rest of the British media Establishment have tried
to pretend to the public that the conferences matter in the way
they used to.

Things became even worse after the IRA perpetrated their
outrage at the Conservative Party conference in Brighton in 1984,

murdering five people – but not, as they had planned, Margaret Thatcher – with a time-delay bomb. Their chilling statement afterwards that 'Today we were unlucky, but remember we only have to be lucky once. You will have to be lucky always' has meant that security demands necessitate conferences' even greater withdrawal from everyday life. You open your hotel room curtains first thing in the morning to find a policeman on the roof opposite staring at you through binoculars. The police are everywhere, in high-vis jackets, in boilersuits, in flak jackets, in plain clothes, on horses, with dogs, sitting in cars with their engines idling for hours, crammed by the dozen into vans.

The timetable of conferences was less than ideal for those of us who worked in the early morning. Jeffrey Archer's champagne-and-shepherd's-pie parties at the Conservative conference rarely got going before about midnight – they were very vulgar ('Krug '62 all right for you?' he'd ask as you arrived) and very crowded, but you could often corner a Minister. At Labour conferences the *Breakfast Time* team would often arrive at 6 a.m. or so for that morning's broadcast from the makeshift 'studio' rigged up in one of the public rooms of the conference hotel to find loyal party workers still sitting about expatiating at length on what This Great Movement Of Ours ought to be doing. The one thing to be said in favour of party conferences, apart from the unusual access they provided to Ministers who the rest of the year hid behind their civil servants and obstructive departmental press offices, was the chance it gave to judge the mood of the party. Whatever was said in the speeches, the body language of the members did not lie.

One morning at the 1988 Labour conference John Prescott arrived for interview saying, 'If you ask me about the leadership, you might get an interesting answer,' accompanied by a wink. At the time the party was undergoing its dark night of the soul, and there was fevered speculation about whether Prescott would challenge the right-wing Roy Hattersley for the position of Deputy

Leader. Prescott had evidently decided he would run for the job, and was offering a scoop. Unfortunately, it completely slipped my mind, the question remained unasked, the programme remained scoopless, and Prescott had to find another opportunity to make his announcement later that day. Every time I met him for the next three years he always asked, 'Remembered that question yet?'

This was, however, some way short of my greatest act of incompetence on *Breakfast Time*, which occurred when I was to interview two middle-aged men, one after the other, in the studio. One of them was there to talk about transport policy, and the other about care in the community for the mentally ill. Unfortunately, the man seated on my left was called Quigg, and the man on my right Quinn. I turned to the first of them and asked, 'So, how serious is the lack of facilities for the mentally ill?'

'I've no idea,' he replied. 'I'm here to talk about the M25.'

I was about to ask, 'And how long have you been mentally ill?' when a voice in my ear said, 'It's the man on the other side.'

It was a punishing time of day at which to work, and Frank Bough, who everyone agreed was one of the most accomplished broadcasters of his generation, capable of handling anything live on air – and from whom I learned much – decided by the end of 1987 that he had had enough of the early mornings, and moved on. He wasn't short of work, and was doubtless invited to open lots of supermarkets. Then there were the *Holiday* jaunts, in which he was seen driving around France with his loyal wife Nesta. Before leaving *Breakfast Time* he had been given broadcasting's equivalent of a knighthood by being invited to appear on *Desert Island Discs*, on which he was interviewed by his friend Michael Parkinson. (He chose a comfy selection of music ranging from Sinatra and the Beatles to Elgar and Beethoven, together with *Barclays World of Cricket* as his one book.) But his world of comforting geniality was about to explode.

For it turned out that as well as the cardigans, Frank had a taste for wearing women's underwear and visiting what the self-appointed bishops of the tabloid press invariably call 'vice dens' in Mayfair, where he took cocaine. In 1988 one of the 'vice girls' sold her story to the *News of the World*. Confronted by a reporter, Frank made the mistake of believing he could cut a deal with the press. Bernard Falk, one of the small army of entertaining reporters then appearing on the BBC, encouraged him to believe that if he confessed to some of the less embarrassing aspects – claiming that stress had driven him to drugs, for example – he would be able to hide the other business about dressing in women's underwear and so on. Bernard, a rotund, jovial Jack-the-Lad Liverpudlian, told Frank he understood how the tabloids worked. This is never a clever claim to make, but Frank took his advice.

Unfortunately for the nation's most famous knitwear model, while his confession did appear, so did the other stuff – trying to cut a deal merely ensured that the exposé got a second chapter. Nesta immediately got the true measure of the revelations, and stood by him. Though Frank has maintained a polite silence on the story ever since, it is repeated in all its humiliating detail each time the middlebrow press mentions his name.

It takes little imagination to appreciate the sickening feeling with which a victim of a tabloid disclosure must read their doom. Those guilty of crime, abuse of position or corruption deserve everything they get, but sex is an immensely powerful drive, and one should never be surprised by the scrapes it gets people into. But being ridiculous is quite different from being evil. Those threatened with exposure find it hard to appreciate that, firstly, most people won't read the newspaper concerned; and secondly, of those who do, very large numbers won't necessarily believe it all; and thirdly, even if they have both heard about the story and believed it, the chances are that in a couple of weeks' time they'll have forgotten all about it. By the time the rector of Stiffkey was mauled to death by a lion at a seaside entertainment, much of the public had long forgotten what he had been defrocked for.*

I heard about the 'scandal' while in Moscow preparing for a live broadcast, in a telephone call from the then editor of *Breakfast Time*. I had the usual reaction – 'Uncle Frank?!' Weeks later, Frank described to me what had happened when the story broke. He had immediately been suspended from work and told to stay at home, while the corporation took its customary eternity to decide what to do. He was then called at home by the man who was about to become the BBC's Managing Director of Television.

'This is serious. We have to discuss it, Frank.'

'Right. When shall I come in?'

A note of panic entered the executive's voice. 'Oh, no! Don't set foot in here,' he blustered, as if one of the best-known faces in the land had been identified as Patient Zero in some looming pandemic. 'Meet me at the Halcyon Hotel – a room will be booked.'

The Halcyon was much favoured by senior BBC figures for expense-account lunches, though the food was never quite as sublime as the name promised. Frank arrived ten minutes early, conscious that his livelihood hung in the balance, and was directed to a room in which there were a few chairs and an enormous drinks cabinet. He helped himself. The manager arrived on time, declined a drink, and told him it was all over: the BBC could simply not have a man like him on its screens. The entire sacking was finished within minutes. The manager left, inviting Frank to

---

* Stiffkey, the village of which Harold Davidson was rector, is on the north coast of Norfolk, but the rector spent much of his time in Soho, trying to save the souls of prostitutes; there were suggestions that his interest was more than merely pastoral. After being found guilty by a Church court he earned a living as a seaside entertainer until, during a performance of 'Daniel in the Lions' Den' at Skegness in 1937 one of the big cats decided the clergyman was invading his space. Davidson never recovered from his mauling.

fix himself another drink. Which he did. Several times. A steady, likeable man who was unflappable on screen, Frank went on to work for various commercial radio and television stations which worried less about the silly things that human beings get up to.

MR PAXMAN - THE LEAN YEARS.

"COME ONN!! COME ONN!!

7

What Sort of Pizza Topping Would You Be?

At the time I joined it, *Newsnight* liked to consider itself the thinking person's alternative to the news. Most of the news team thought we were wankers. Sometimes they were right. The show had been on air for nine years, during which time it had established a stolid, worthy reputation for trying to go beyond the mere reporting of events, aiming to give their context too. It had something of the feel of a senior common room at one of the more self-important Oxbridge colleges.

Not only was *Newsnight* broadcast at the other end of the day to breakfast television, it was its virtual antithesis in content and style. I liked and admired its readiness to treat viewers as grown-ups, and had been badgering the then editor to give me a chance at presenting it for a year or so. In the autumn of 1989, when I believed I was beginning to feel at home in television, he agreed.

By unfortunate coincidence, a few weeks earlier I had been invited to appear as a guest on an ITV quiz show. Much though they affect an air of superiority over the song-and-sequin end of the business, news people really feel slightly inadequate by comparison with it.* But here was an opportunity to be involved in *real*

---

* This perhaps explains those grisly annual appearances on the Children in Need telethon, when people we know as newsreaders demonstrate why they should stick to that.

television. If I would allow a chauffeur to drive me to some studios in outer West London, I could join some people who were household names in recording a show 'like *Call My Bluff*, but funnier', as the producer put it. ITV would be happy to pay £300 for the pleasure of my company. What was not to like? On a sunny July afternoon I sallied off to Teddington, ready to banter with Patricia Hodge and other sophisticates.

'I know, I know! Just like shitting a giant greased grapefruit!' were the first words I heard on walking through the door. The agony aunt Anna Raeburn was empathising about the trials of childbirth. What followed over the next three or four hours was definitely not *Call My Bluff*. Divided into two teams, 'The Boys' (Kenny Everett, 'Bungalow' Bill Wiggins* and myself) and 'The Girls' (Ms Raeburn, the wine writer Jilly Goolden and an actress I had never seen before) were invited by our chairman, Chris Tarrant, to try to identify people or things by asking which sort of object – model of car, building, type of pizza topping and so on – they most resembled. In case we ran out of ideas, suggestions of useful categories – 'household implements', 'vegetables', 'breeds of dog' – had been helpfully taped to the top of our desks. Of Patricia Hodge there was no sign. But it was difficult enough. What sort of pizza topping *was* Margaret Thatcher? Or Mussolini? Or, come to that, the Archbishop of Canterbury? More revealing might have been to wonder what sort of disease they might be. In exasperation I asked at one point, 'If this person were a disability, what sort of disability would they be?'

Chris Tarrant banged his desk, stopped the recording, and boomed in exasperation, 'Will you please take this *seriously*?' Which I suppose was fair enough. As soon as I could, I trousered the £300 and made for the door. I consoled myself that since the

---

* A property developer and gossip-column regular, so named because there was nothing much upstairs but plenty below.

show was due to be transmitted on ITV in the middle of the afternoon, no one I knew would ever see it.

My complacency was unfounded. Apart from the electronics showroom in John Lewis, the one place where you can guarantee that there are televisions tuned to every station all day long is a newsroom. On my very first day on *Newsnight* I was sitting with the editor and the economics correspondent as they discussed what was likely to happen to interest rates in view of the latest figures on GDP growth. I nodded gravely to indicate that while I might have come from the bargain basement end of news, underneath it all I was really a serious person. Suddenly I became aware of producers sitting at the desks in front of me nudging one another and pointing to the screens. 'That's *him*, isn't?' they mouthed, rolling their eyes incredulously before returning to the article in *Foreign Affairs* on peace in Mesopotamia written by Henry Kissinger.

Newsnight was full of clever young people who, if they didn't know about it already, could master any subject in a matter of minutes. Most of all, they were good company. The relationships you form are surely what makes work either tolerable or intolerable, and I was lucky enough to make good friendships with colleagues I would have been glad to have bumped into socially. We laughed a lot. Some of the things we laughed about came back to me the other day, as I rifled through a box of paper containing summaries of the programmes we produced together. The cast of characters on screen changed, of course. Some (Tony Benn, Benazir Bhutto, Denis Healey, John Smith) have died. Some are discredited (Jeffrey Archer, Tony Blair). Some (Mikhail Gorbachev, John Major, Peter Mandelson), once garlanded, are now digging their gardens or dispensing the lessons of public office for a fee. Others reappear time after time in the chronology, like Chris Patten, first as a Minister, then as Chairman of the Conservative Party, next as the last Governor of Hong Kong, then as European

Commissioner, subsequently as Chairman of the BBC – a full house which would have satisfied even Lord Curzon. He finally emptied the dressing-up box by becoming Chancellor of Oxford University. Some one-time interviewees one just wonders about: whatever became of little Jacques Delors, the French President of the European Commission – and what had he done to provoke the *Sun*'s front page, 'UP YOURS, DELORS!' Is that ghastly war criminal Radovan Karadžić still alive? What was the name of the strange spokesman for Saddam Hussein who appeared night after night, swearing black was white? There is nothing like a roll-call of the once-important to prove that the preacher in Ecclesiastes was right – all is vanity.

Some themes remain pretty constant, like the narrowing of real political choice, economic decline, and a refusal by politicians to acknowledge the need to reimagine the National Health Service. After a while, every government, however bold its promises or high its hopes, begins to decay, with Ministers burned out or disillusioned. Looking back, one can see a series of leadership battles in the Labour Party, all of which were really about what it was for, and one crisis after another in the Conservative Party over Europe. There have been twenty years of handwringing about uncontrolled immigration, international squabbling over action on climate change, bad relations between the police and the black community and between Palestine and Israel, and little real change on many things. Like most of the British media, we saw events in the European Union with one eye closed and the other clamped to a telescope provided by the Foreign Office – we were provincial and partisan. We consistently paid too little attention to Germany while being virtually obsessed with the United States, where we generally spoiled whatever we were trying to say with the usual European attitude of 'What a strange place it is.' Some reporters, like Charles Wheeler and Sue Lloyd-Roberts (both sadly now dead), were consistently independent, brave and uncompromising.

There is an undeniable herd mentality to news. Because no one wants to miss a story and potentially look silly, everyone talks about the same things. The written records suggest that occasionally *Newsnight* did break free, doubtless much to the contempt of the mainstream news teams. There were reports which changed government policy and interviews which resonated. But did we really once lead the show on the implications of the discovery of the alleged bones of Haile Selassie? What on earth induced us to spend ages discussing the decline of Received Pronunciation? What possessed an avowedly serious programme to focus on the engagement of Prince Edward to a PR executive, an event of zero constitutional significance? We even discussed cannibalism one night, using a clip from *Carry On Up the Jungle*. What can A.S. Byatt have made of being invited to discuss the lure of the cad from Jane Austen onwards, only to discover that the pretext for her presence was the state of the marriage of the pneumatic *Baywatch* actor Pamela Anderson to a drummer in a heavy-metal band?

It is certainly true that the editor of the time once insisted that a studio be booked so that a deputy in the Russian Duma could be interviewed, merely on the grounds that his name was Rasputin. It was only when the line from Vladivostok came up that we discovered that he didn't speak English. We joined the Gadarene swine in the hullabaloo about dogs attacking children, which resulted in the one of the silliest pieces of legislation of the last forty years, the 1991 Dangerous Dogs Act: not one but two cars had to be sent to Essex to collect an extraordinary woman who owned a pair of Japanese Tosa fighting dogs (neither the dogs nor the owner even got out of the cars when they arrived at Television Centre, because she had apparently become convinced we were going to put them down on air – our ambitions were, sadly, more modest). We sucked our teeth with the rest of Middle England when the Director of Public Prosecutions was caught kerb-crawling, and wondered why successful men felt compelled to take risks. One editor despatched me to New York on Concorde, swearing that President Bill Clinton was certain to have resigned by the time I arrived because of his weird ideas about what constituted 'sexual relations with that woman, Miss Lewinsky'. Another sent me to ask a crowd of drunk Glaswegian football fans in Trafalgar Square for their views on 'Britishness', where a man in a kilt and a singlet stole my wallet.

I had discovered while working the early-morning shift on breakfast television that British politics, which I had avoided for the early years of my career, were really rather fascinating. What is a government for, if not to create a country happy in its own skin, feeling it has a purpose and confident of its place in the world? One after another, political parties came along claiming to be able to provide all these things, and one after another they failed. Other European nations were facing similar problems of relative decline in wealth and influence, but the questions seemed more acute in Britain because the country found it so hard to escape its imperial past – it is further to fall to the ground from the top of the tree than it is from a lower branch. We no longer seemed to be producing things that the rest of the world wanted to buy. And a harmonious relationship with Continental Europe was perpetually elusive.

These were all profound problems demanding strategic thought, which the press of daily events often made impossible. Understanding wasn't helped by the constant preoccupation with who was up and who was down: what was gained from the ambitious political reporter's membership of 'the lobby' was probably less useful than the understanding that might have come from a better historical perspective. An exclusive focus on the comings and goings in Westminster also had the effect of removing political reporters from the nervous system of the news organisations for which they worked. The 'What would you like to say to the nation tonight, Minister?' approach of the 1950s might have gone, but there was an understandable reluctance by political reporters to rock the boat – when you depend upon sources to feed you information, you can become reluctant to embarrass them with difficult questions. The interviewer at one remove is freer to crash in with whatever he likes. It is not the journalist's job to do the politicians' explaining for them, but to ask the questions the average, reasonably intelligent voter might want to ask, if given the chance. While the reporter enjoys some privileges of access, he or she has no constitutional position. Though some of them took themselves absurdly seriously, they were really just armed civilians. Why not use the opportunity?

This was hardly a revolutionary idea, and some, like Robin Day, had already used similar freedoms similarly, for all the chumminess between him and his interviewees. By the 1980s society was well into a change, which has continued at ever greater speed, away from unchanging affiliations, tribal loyalty and mass organisations to a pattern of individual preferences. In the early 1950s the Conservative Party alone claimed to have nearly three million members. In the early 1970s, approximately 5 per cent of the population belonged to the three main political parties. By 2015 the proportion claiming allegiance to them had fallen to under 1 per cent. Though it was much less easy to measure, the fall in party membership had been matched by a rise in cynicism about politicians. Television was attractive to politicians because it seemed to promise an opportunity to talk directly to these more elusive electors, who in return often made personal judgements based less on the arguments that fell from the politicians' lips than how they seemed as human beings – it's a sort of emotional inkblot test.

I arrived on *Newsnight* while the Labour Party was reinventing itself under the leadership of Neil Kinnock, and replacing the red flag with the red rose. Redefining the party's goals and trying to suppress the left wing were accompanied by a recognition of the

Beirut, 1976. I cannot explain the jacket.

El Salvador, 1982. Cameraman Alan 'Bulletproof' Stevens was less scared than I was.

Dinner to mark leaving *The Six O'Clock News*, 1986.
Left to right: Nick Witchell, Tony Hall, self, Bob Wheaton,
Sue Lawley.

Breakfast Time, 1987, with Frank Bough and Sally Magnusson.
It's sometimes forgotten that mullets were unisex.

Radio studio, 1989.

Newsnight, about 1994. World maps – even stuck onto cardboard in Shepherd's Bush – give an impression of omniscience.

Before the embrace of the tie, early 1980s.

Newsnight faces. Standing, left to right: Kirsty Wark, Emily Maitlis, Olivia O'Leary, me, Gavin Esler, Francine Stock, John Tusa, Sue Cameron. Squatting, Martha Kearney and Peter Snow. The appropriate collective noun for such a gathering is 'a preen of presenters'.

How suits and ties grind you down, 2010.

1992 general election, with John Major.

Michael Howard: 'Don't you dare use the word "threaten" again.'

2010 election, with Gordon Brown.

2015 election, with David Cameron.

2005, with Tony Blair in 10 Downing Street.

importance of image and an acknowledgement of the influence of the mass media. The Labour leadership had understood how the rules of engagement were shifting, and most of the next twenty years would belong to them. In this context the interviewer was there to represent the viewer, to challenge rather than to explain. People had straightforward questions – why not put them directly?

One of the stickiest moments of Margaret Thatcher's prime ministership had come when she was confronted on television in May 1983 by Diana Gould, a heroically dogged Gloucestershire teacher, about the decision to sink the Argentine cruiser the *General Belgrano* during the Falklands War, which had cost over three hundred lives. But such confrontations were – and are – rare: most people are innately polite. Interviewers occupy an intermediary role, which is a privileged position. It seemed to me that if you had that privilege, you should use it on behalf not of the governors but the governed. It is a position that is easily abused, and the accusation of abuse is often made by people who don't like having their feet held to the fire. Robin Day, who in a previous life had briefly been a barrister, is said on more than one occasion to have asked a colleague what they thought of an interview, and upon receiving the reply, 'I thought X made quite a good case,' exploding with, 'Not the answers, you fool! The questions!' Quite apart from vanity, interviewers are more generally accused of being responsible for the collapse in public respect for politicians. We must take some of the blame, though it does not keep me awake at night.

One day, on a filming trip in Texas, a man with a large belt across his even larger stomach asked me, 'What exactly is a producer's job?' I told him that a producer had twin responsibilities – to get you to do things you don't want to do, and which are not in your own best interests. The joke was slightly lost on both the questioner and the producer, who at the time was indeed trying to persuade him effectively to confess to fraud. It was also a bit hard on producers as a species. The correct answer is that a good producer makes the baffling clear and the invisible entertaining.

For some reason, the industry persists in referring to those who appear on screen as 'the talent'. In fact, most of the responsibility for how things appear on television rests with the talents of the producers. There are dozens of different aspects to their jobs. Some of them enjoy the research most. Others find satisfaction in describing to a gnarled cameraman in tedious detail the *film noir* effect they're after, at the end of which the cameraman generally says, 'So it's another interview, is it – shall I put the camera where I put it last time?'* Most producers love being in the cutting room. On some shows their job is not much more than to hold the nervous presenter's hand: many of the braggarts you see on screen are feeble inside. Most of all, producers have to find a way of making facts come alive. The best of them have astonishing visual flair. The humdrum ones are responsible for the decree that every television report about education is accompanied by a graphic in the style of a blackboard – television news is the one place where the march of technology in classrooms has been resisted. They also insist that any item about the cost of water supply will be accompanied by a graphic representation of a dripping tap.

Journalism used to be divided into fact and comment. In some more high-minded corners of the world the distinction is said, slightly implausibly, still to exist, although the decision about which facts you choose to hunt for is the product of political judgement. The printed word – either on a computer screen or on paper – is well-suited to both comment and fact. But the inherent difficulty with television is that while it is easy enough to carry

---

* For years I believed that when, after some producer request, a cameraman shrugged his shoulders and said 'DFI' to the sound recordist he was asking for a special lens or microphone. In fact it stands for 'Different Fucking Idea'.

comment, moving pictures are very bad indeed with facts. Television is, above all, a medium of impressions. The first, obvious difference between print and broadcast is that the consumer can take print at his or her own speed, reread or skim sentences, paragraphs or pages, begin on the sports pages and then turn to the gossip or comment or cartoons, and take the information in a sequence to suit their personal taste. Technology promises something similar with television, but there is still a long way to go. Live television demands that viewers absorb information at the speed and in the order in which it is delivered. In our efforts to provide greater understanding, for a couple of decades no war could take place without Peter Snow appearing in the *Newsnight* studio with a *papier-mâché* relief map scattered with plastic soldiers and model tanks. As he excitedly swept his arm across the battlefield explaining deployments, there was usually a producer lying on the floor underneath the map pulling on bits of fishing nylon. The occasion when an Airfix helicopter 'flew' across the battlefield, with rotors turning, was a day for trebles all round.

That sort of visual aid could be justified as a help to understanding. Others were just silly. It became a matter of fashion or professional pride that every subject be illustrated. We could not discuss penal policy without doing so sitting on beds in a prison cell in the studio, or talk about footballers' transfer fees without being inside some manager's 'dugout' looking as if it came from a semi-professional ground in Grimsby but which had in fact been knocked up that afternoon by the props department. When climate change became a subject of political debate Francine Stock was made to perform from the middle of a supposed tropical rainforest, made from plastic plants, in W12. When Mad Cow Disease struck Britain, a producer was instructed to get a cow into the studio. It was only after several hours of pleading with baffled farmers that she discovered there was *a BBC cow*, which was brought in and introduced to Peter Snow. As one of the critics observed, he is not one of nature's farmers. Had Daisy been put to sleep and a forensic veterinary surgeon then performed an autopsy to demonstrate the difference between an infected brain and a healthy one, there might perhaps have been some reason to have a cow in the studio. As it was, she merely demonstrated television's insatiable craving for decoration.

The difficulty of explanation is particularly acute when dealing with economics – not for nothing is it known as 'the dismal science', and most of us are economically illiterate. So it happened that producers had to dream up ever more elaborate ways of telling a story. Graham Ingham, a thoroughly competent economist who grew up to become a senior official at the International Monetary Fund in Washington, spent his years as *Newsnight*'s Economics Correspondent dressed in an increasingly bizarre variety of outfits: wearing the pale blue overall of a supermarket checkout operator to explain the annual budget; as a croupier in bow tie and shiny waistcoat calling '*Faites vos jeux. Neuf à la banque*' to make blindingly clear the mechanics of the so-called casino national economy; and trying to ascertain the likely balance of trade by consulting a fortune-teller with a crystal ball on Blackpool Promenade. His career culminated in a sequence in which he was made to report from what was said to be the 'clean room' of an electronics company. This required him to wear white overalls, white cap and facemask. Since no one could see his lips, he might as well have been reciting the *Rubaiyat* of Omar Khayyam. Neither he nor the then editor knew that I had instituted a monthly prize of a bottle of champagne for the producer who dreamed up the most idiotic bit of stagecraft. It was first won by the woman who went on to become the BBC's Head of Visual Journalism (seriously).

Graham's successors as Economics Editor – Evan Davis, Stephanie Flanders and Paul Mason – managed to avoid some of the buffoonery, partly because each of them was such a distinctive figure in their own right, and partly because there was simply nowhere more ridiculous to go.

The great privilege of journalism is the access it gives you to events which most people only experience through the mass media. Though one of the more important lessons of life is that there is nothing particularly unusual about the people who occupy unusual roles – politicians, bishops, generals or trade union bosses* – I had to pinch myself, despite the fact that over the years I spoke to every senior politician, religious or cultural figure in the land, a cast list that ran from the Crown Prince of Jordan to, well, Jordan (Katie Price, in an interview about plastic surgery).

I never interviewed Margaret Thatcher, and to be frank, I was glad to be spared. After she had quit Downing Street I was once invited, for reasons I never understood, to sit next to her at a lunch. Apart from myself and a couple of other journalists, including Trevor McDonald, it was a gathering of a dozen or so Eurosceptics. Unsurprisingly, the conversation soon turned to the European Union, and Thatcher began a lengthy tirade against the way Brussels was interfering in what ought to have been purely domestic affairs. 'But Margaret,' came a voice from the bottom of the table, 'you were the one who signed the Single European Act' – referring to the law which created the single market and ensured that Brussels could meddle in great new swathes of British life.

'Yes!' she turned on him, eyes blazing. '*I was betrayed.*' It was chilling.

John Major, who succeeded her in November 1990, I interviewed many times. Of course his verbal mannerisms were comical ('I was not inconsiderably annoyed') and his manner

---

* Indeed, the most striking thing about some of them is how spectacularly unimpressive they are.

uncharismatic. But he was a decent man, with a surprising talent for off-the-cuff and witty speeches,* and one only has to look at the mess that is the Euro to recognise that his idea of an extra currency for use in international trade perhaps wasn't such a bad idea.

John Major provided plenty of entertainment for the metropolitan elite. How comical that his father had a garden ornament business! How hilarious that he was in hospital, unable to speak, getting a wisdom tooth fixed when he might have had to declare his support for Margaret Thatcher as the conspirators plotted her demise! But he delivered his party victory in the 1992 general election. The opinion polls had been predicting a hung Parliament, or a possible small Labour majority, so I spent the night of the election at the local community hall in the South Wales coalfields where Neil Kinnock was inevitably returned as MP for Islwyn – doubtless his dog would have been elected had it bothered to stand for Labour. My job was to get a comment from the putative Prime Minister on the national picture. Charles Clarke, my Cambridge contemporary, was now his Chief of Staff, and – was it because he wanted to keep everyone's spirits up? – soon after the polls closed he gave me a steer that Kinnock's inner circle were feeling quietly confident.

I passed this on to my colleagues in London, who seemed to find it very reassuring: they had just published the results of an exit poll which showed the result as 'too close to call'. This exit poll, depicted by the perpetrators of opinion polls as 'reliable', soon turned out to be utterly wrong (though that did not stop broadcasters commissioning them again). It soon became clear that we

---

* His description of a meeting with Boris Yeltsin:
  Major: 'Well, Boris, in a word, how is Russia?'
  Yeltsin: 'Good.'
  Major: 'And in more than one word?'
  Yeltsin: 'Not good.'

were all living in an echo chamber, and politicians and journalists were simply parroting each other. By the time Kinnock and his claque left the community centre after the declaration of his result they had discovered from their teams on the ground that the poll findings were rubbish. They piled into cars to head for London, knowing that the game was nearly up. I was now part of the baying mob of reporters shouting 'Are you going to concede?' and 'Why have you failed?', and discovered what a nasty job that sort of monstering is: the man was clearly distressed. He resigned as party leader soon afterwards.

John Major's victory in the 1992 election showed the importance of being careful what you wish for – his prime ministership was ultimately unedifying, and ended in disaster for his party. 'Black Wednesday', the day in September 1992 when the Conservatives – the party which claimed to understand how the market works – battled the market, struggling to keep sterling inside the European Exchange Rate Mechanism, produced a catastrophic image of British decline which did incalculable damage to the Tories' chances of re-election. When speculators decided to challenge the Bank of England and the German central bank failed to offer the expected assistance, the only weapon left to the Treasury was to raise interest rates. As the speculators feasted (George Soros later claimed to have made £1 billion that day), interest rates went higher and higher. By late afternoon they stood at an utterly unsustainable 15 per cent, but still the value of the pound continued to plummet.

That evening a pasty-faced Chancellor of the Exchequer, Norman Lamont, accompanied by his young special adviser David Cameron, emerged blinking into the glare of the television lights outside the Treasury and read a brief (under)statement: 'Today has been an extremely difficult day.' He confessed that the government had thrown in the towel: sterling would leave the ERM, and would be devalued. Only a few hours earlier he had sworn that there was no chance of Britain leaving the Mechanism, or of the pound being devalued.

The *Newsnight* team watched the unedifying spectacle on television feeds, and later that night the Conservative Vice Chairman came into the studio to explain how the party of economic competence had become the party of economic incompetence. He blamed the French and the Germans. The affair put an end to the chance of another fully Conservative government for over twenty years, by which time Norman Lamont's bag carrier standing in the shadows outside the Treasury that dusk would have worked his way to the top of the greasy pole. Labour and Liberal Democrat leaders uttered hubristic half-truths about the débâcle being the result of Conservative folly. They kept quiet about the fact that both of them had been in favour of membership of the ERM, as if it were some sort of magic wand to fix the economy (mind you, most of the supposedly wise figures in the Treasury and the Foreign Office had also wanted to join the Mechanism).

By the time of the next general election, in 1997, Labour had a grinning, well-scrubbed minor public schoolboy as its leader, had crushed or jettisoned its left wing, and was about to embark upon thirteen years of government. Had John Major lost the 1992 election, the Labour Party, with Neil Kinnock as Prime Minister, would have faced the European Exchange Rate crisis, and it is very hard indeed to imagine it surviving it well enough to win a second term.

Consistently, the biggest challenge for programmes like *Newsnight* was just to get people to agree to sit down for interviews. There is no constitutional requirement for politicians or anyone else to submit themselves to an interrogation. Most potential interviewees make a calculated judgement – 'Is this going to do me any good?' To which I usually thought to myself, 'Not if I have anything to do with it.'

There were many occasions on which it seemed to me that if I were a programme editor I would conclude that my attitude was counterproductive. Assuming you have a journalist on hand to carry it out, the essential prerequisite for an interview is a guest, and there are dozens of other places where politicians can go and have their tummies rubbed on screen. As David Cameron once told me, '*Newsnight* is trouble,' and therefore best avoided. He was, however, happy to cooperate with an interminable ITV documentary billed as 'a look at the Camerons as you've never seen them before', in which his loving wife disclosed that he had changed their babies' nappies, and that he still occasionally did some cooking. Show me a man who has never done at least one of those things and I will show you a weirdo. But the difference between prominent politicians and the rest of society is that most of us don't want to make laws telling everyone else how to behave. There is no reason why voters should not know what sort of people are asking for their votes.* But what they're like with the Sudocrem is low down on the list of qualities necessary in a Prime Minister.

More subordinate figures have less choice about what they do. We usually asked to interview the most senior responsible figure we could find, but understandably, perhaps, they tended to be cautious about putting themselves up for what might (if the programme had any luck) turn out to be a no-holds-barred cross-examination. The only lever we could pull was to suggest that in a democracy, appearing before the voters was a moral obligation.

Rather than have your evening ruined by the looming prospect of interrogation, why not give the impression of discharging your democratic duty by sending along a minion to be mauled? As time passed, this problem became worse and worse. So quite what

---

* Making your private life public is a dangerous game, though. Even putting a photograph of yourself, along with doting family and dog, on election campaign literature invites the media to crash about in your personal business.

Chloe Smith – a thirty-year-old very junior Treasury Minister – said when told she would have to appear on *Newsnight* to justify a last-minute policy volte-face on the tax payable on vehicle fuel in the 2012 Budget we do not know. Perhaps the Prime Minister, the Chancellor of the Exchequer or the Chief Secretary to the Treasury forced her to do it. Perhaps she thought she'd earn Brownie points for trying to explain a policy change she knew nothing about. Either way, it was a disaster, and her flailing around trying to appear competent finished her ministerial career – for several years at least.

My initial reaction on being told that the Treasury had decided that neither the Chancellor nor the second Minister, the Chief Secretary, would be justifying the Budget had been irritation: taxation is the confiscation of money that people have had to earn, and they are surely entitled to hear why they're being impoverished. Not only had most people never heard of Chloe Smith, the politician who was obliged to take the flak, it would have been very surprising if she had been instrumental in forming the policy. The interview turned out to be a car crash. Admittedly, she did not handle her predicament well, but she had been put in an impossible position. Within little more than a minute I was asking whether she had been told of the change of policy before or after lunch. What made her position even more difficult was the fact that if she admitted to not being involved in the decision (which she clearly was not), the obvious next question was why on earth she had been put up to defend it.

How does one feel when a Minister makes a complete shambles of something? There is the initial thrill of discovery, followed by incredulity, and then outrage: how dare they try to pull the wool over the eyes of the public? It would be dishonest to deny an element of pleasure, too – not so much at the damage done, but at the realisation that you've been involved in a terrific piece of theatre. The interview ended with my asking, 'Do you ever think you're incompetent?' – a question which was both unanswerable and unkind. In terms of information, we had learned nothing much. But once you start to worry too much about that sort of thing, you risk changing sides – we could well have learned plenty about the policy change if she had chosen to answer the earlier questions. Interviews like that are unusual. But they are not, in intent, any different to what all of them ought to be about.

Though Chloe Smith did not complain (perhaps she realised that the people she should have complained to were her bosses at the Treasury), it was often the poor producers who had to pick up the pieces after any robust interchange. There was one interview with US Secretary of State Colin Powell after his notorious presentation to the United Nations in February 2003, in which he had dressed up inadequate intelligence to claim that Saddam Hussein had weapons of mass destruction, but there was never a second. Lucy Crystal, the Washington producer who inveigled a US Senator on the Intelligence Committee into doing an interview with me, watched as he tore out his earpiece at the end of the interview. She politely said how much she hoped to see him take part in another interview. 'Not with that jerk,' replied the Senator. But complaining that interviews have been insufficiently deferential is always a mistake. After one session with Condoleezza Rice, Colin Powell's successor as Secretary of State, an official rang to complain that I had been 'very rude'. I hadn't – I generally know when I'm being rude. The real issue is the obsequious manner in which most such exchanges take place. A more senior official called a little later to apologise for the complaint. The public will make their own minds up.

In Britain, persuading people that they really want to spend the evening without having a drink, in order that they can drag themselves to a television studio to be put through the wringer at 10.30, will always be a hard ask. 'Why should I trail out at that time of night, to be treated like a criminal when I get there?' was the way one reluctant Minister put it. From the perspective of personal convenience, he had a point. The only leverage a journalist has in those circumstances is an appeal to some sense of accountability. This can be a rather theoretical weapon when you attempt to wield it against a confident Minister. The problem is most acute at election time, when the political parties and the broadcasters end up playing a game of chicken. The broadcasters know that they are expected to treat the major party leaders even-handedly, and so if they interview one of them, they should extend the same opportunity to all. But the politicians know that if they refuse to take part, such an offer will be impossible, which might therefore scupper the whole project. Generally the political parties come round, although the stand-off demands that the broadcasters hold their nerve. Before the 2010 election the Conservatives took things down to the wire, with David Cameron repeatedly refusing a *Newsnight* interview on the grounds (according to the *Daily Telegraph*) that 'If I want to be shouted at by an overpaid prima donna, I'll join a Premier League football club'. In the end, since his two main rivals agreed to be interviewed, the party calculated that he stood to lose more by appearing scared than by being hectored.

Elections are just about the only time when broadcasters have that sort of leverage. A month after the 2010 election Andy Coulson, the former editor of the *News of the World* who had been hired by Cameron as his Director of Communications, offered the BBC a studio debate in which Cameron and his coalition deputy, Nick Clegg, would be in conversation with voters. One of the main conditions was that I wouldn't act as chairman. In conversation with mutual acquaintances, Cameron made no secret of his dislike for me. I was slightly hurt at first, until I realised that it wasn't my job to be liked. He wasn't the first Prime Minister to dislike me – Gordon Brown had beaten him to that place, and refused an interview for the whole of his premiership, until the general election forced him into it. The reputation of Brown's predecessor, Tony

Blair, may have been sullied since he left office, but both he and his communications bully, Alastair Campbell, understood that the unwritten duties of public office included trying to keep straight with the electorate: Blair even agreed to take part in a debate we staged in Gateshead before the 2003 invasion of Iraq, at which one of the audience lampooned his relationship with George W. Bush by referring to him as 'the Right Honourable Member for Texas North'.

When these exchanges worked, they could lead to informative and entertaining television. Of course there were rows with the politicians and with the people who looked after their interests. But in all the years of dealing with politicians, I never heard a member of the public say, 'I do wish you'd treat them more kindly.' It is not necessarily that people believe them all to be crooks, so much as that they like to see them earn the right to lead.

So all interviews are freighted with risk for guests. Opposition parties are much easier to persuade into doing them, for the simple reason that they have nothing to answer for, and they know that they have to get their message out somehow. Once they get elected to government, though, that readiness dies like a lit match dropped into a bucket of water. Suddenly there are Whitehall press officers to hide behind. The way through the shrubbery is to contact the SpAds, or special advisers – the army of ambitious young men and women (like Ollie from *The Thick of It*) following, they hope, David Cameron's route from dogsbody to top dog. The SpAd and the Minister are in it together.

But you may still fail time and again to get them to appear. The only weapon the journalist has is embarrassment. If it becomes known that a Minister is ducking an interview, after a while he or she can seem what Margaret Thatcher called 'frit'. There may be perfectly sensible reasons for a Minister to decide that an issue is far too complicated to be subjected to a lot of 'yes or no' badgering, but at some point a decision will have to be made and be explained.

Who wants the fate of the nation to be entrusted to someone who's frightened by a mere reporter? But for a broadcaster to brief a newspaper that a Minister seems to be afraid of publicly justifying his or her decisions is a risky strategy, because it leaves the politician able to say, 'Why should I waste my time on such an insignificant outlet and with such a pointless interviewer?' Come election time, though, the boot is on the other foot, because every politician knows that their fate is in the hands of the voters.

Because television is so much a medium of impressions, absurd amounts of energy can be devoted to arguing about the setting for an interview. In the 1992 election campaign, John Major's advisers chose a room in a hotel in Edinburgh. The start was delayed for several minutes while his team – including several apparently important government Ministers – debated whether he needed to be sitting on more cushions to look authoritative. Paddy Ashdown once insisted that he be interviewed behind a great Victorian partners' desk in Westminster. He managed his usual hooded-eyes, man-of-destiny look, unconcerned that his head of communications had crawled underneath a side table next to him.

On one occasion when Ashdown's successor Charles Kennedy was to be interviewed, his office decided that it should take place in the library of what is left of Gladstone's National Liberal Club (much of the place has been sold off to a hotel chain). This turned out to be a tricky confrontation. I had known Kennedy – in a work capacity – for many years, and everyone understood that he liked a drink or two. At the previous election I had interviewed him in Liverpool, where he had arrived jolly and smelling of alcohol. So what? I enjoy a drink myself. But by now it was common gossip that Kennedy was hitting the bottle so hard that it was affecting his ability to do his job. His staff and colleagues covered up the unexplained absences and shambolic performances by talking of diary clashes and stomach bugs. Shamefully, those political journalists who knew the facts kept them to themselves.

In the days before the interview I called a number of Liberal Democrat sources, all of whom said, 'I hope he's sober.' Kennedy arrived for the interview with three or four staff, his usual affable self: he was a friendly soul. It was early afternoon, and we sat down in a couple of armchairs to play the fantasy politics that is the staple of most Liberal Democrat interviews. After several minutes of listening to what the Lib Dems would do if pigs flew and they formed a government, the question of Kennedy's drinking was still in the back of my mind, like a bad dream you can't shake. Eventually it seemed dishonest not to ask.

'Does it bother you that everyone I've talked to in preparing for this interview has said, "I hope he's sober"? Kennedy tried to brush this aside as a 'Westminster hothouse' slur. 'How much do you drink?' I asked, to which he replied, 'Moderately, socially, as you well know.'

'You don't drink privately?' I asked. 'By yourself, a bottle of whisky late at night?' 'No, I do not, no.' I left it there.

I hadn't liked asking the question. Why shouldn't he do as he pleased? But I could justify it, because if – as subsequently became clear – he had a drink problem, then as party leader it had public policy implications.

I was frankly relieved when at the end of the interview I asked him if he was happy with how it had gone and he replied, 'Yes, yes, it was fine.' Off camera, his press officer was gesturing to him with a thumbs up and mouthing what looked to be 'You were great!' That afternoon the film was viewed by various BBC executives before transmission, and no one raised an eyebrow.

But the morning after broadcast, all hell broke loose. A backbench Labour MP asked the Leader of the House of Commons, Robin Cook, if he would take up with the BBC an outrageous smearing of a Member of Parliament. Never one to let an opportunity to score points off an opponent slip, Cook then repeated the thrust of my questioning, and agreed with his colleague that it was indeed outrageous.

I had never intended to suggest to Kennedy that he got through a bottle of whisky a night. But that was what the accusation now became. One after another that afternoon, BBC executives – some of them the very people who had OK'd the interview for transmission – turned up, shook their heads and demanded that I issue an apology. I refused. We soon reached a point where they were saying that if I didn't apologise publicly, then they would. At which point I agreed to add a sentence to their statement, to the effect that I was sorry if anyone was offended, and that maybe there had been a question too many on drink. This was predictably reported by the newspapers (and the BBC) as 'Paxman Sorry for Grilling Kennedy on his Drinking.'

It did nothing to ease Charles Kennedy's drink problem, and three and half years later, with ITN about to report that he had undergone treatment for it, he resigned the leadership, to be replaced by Menzies Campbell, one of the nicest men in politics. Kennedy died soon after the 2015 election, from a haemorrhage attributed to alcoholism.

If one was categorising interviews, then those about politics were the most numerous, those about beliefs the most interesting, and those about performance some of the most comical. By and large the British media give business leaders a shockingly easy ride, allowing the men and women who make decisions about the lives of millions to dictate the rules of engagement – an occasional interview with a house-trained specialist correspondent when the company publishes its annual report may be all there is. The most thoughtful utterances came from religious leaders, and the most precious from people in the arts world. Great numbers of political interviews were a complete waste of time, either because the individual concerned had decided it would be inconvenient or potentially damaging to be frank, or because they chose the soft option of talking not about what they planned to do, but about what they claimed their opponents might do.

Invariably, the most entertaining conversations were with men and women unafraid to speak their own minds. Kenneth Clarke, the Conservative Cabinet Minister, was happy to confess that he hadn't read the Maastricht Treaty which created the European Union, even though he was being interviewed about it – he knew what he thought. John Reid, his nearest counterpart in the Labour Party, was willing to take more or less any question on any subject. Menzies Campbell, who had been seriously ill with cancer in 2002–03, used to claim that his regular appearances on *Newsnight* had been one of the things that kept him alive, because they meant he had to drag himself from his sickbed and appear cogent. I suspect the doctors and nurses actually had more to do with it.

The best use of gamesmanship was by Peter Mandelson, who as we were sitting down to talk, remarked, 'Interesting suit. Did you really buy it yourself?' Which immediately made me wonder what on earth was wrong with it. The most enjoyable person to interview was Boris Johnson, mainly because his brain is quite the opposite of his body – nimble and sinewy. Who else would answer a challenge to name his own party's spokesman on International Development with the remark, 'What a girlie-swot question'? You could ask Boris anything, and be sure of getting an entertaining answer, whether he addressed the question or not. Like many people, I was astonished when Theresa May chose him as her Foreign Secretary. He is, of course, a chancer. But he makes no bones about it, and at least he makes people laugh. I think I can claim the credit (or take the blame) for being the first person to put Boris on television. *Newsnight* was planning some discussion about how relatively uncorrupt British politics were by comparison with the rest of Europe. 'Why don't we get that bloke who's the *Daily Telegraph* man in Brussels?' I suggested. 'The one who's always writing about directives defining what a banana is.' (Some of Boris's stories were true.) He arrived in the studio before the programme began, and I introduced him to one of the other guests, the Italian journalist Gaia Servadio. 'Do you know Boris Johnson?' I asked, to which she gave the most nonplussing response I have ever heard. 'Oh yes!' she exclaimed. 'He used to be my son-in-law.'

A few years after that, Boris embarked on his political career, becoming the MP for Henley-on-Thames. By that time I was living in the area, and although our house was outside the constituency (the boundary ran through the garden), our septic tank was in Henley. Boris never did a damn thing about enabling a connection to mains drainage. I forgave him, because there was something hugely engaging about a man who would turn up for the recording of an interview, grab your notes out of your hand and say, 'This is all, piffle, you know,' and as you were wondering what the protocol was for wrestling with an elected politician to get your notes back, declare, 'Right, let's do it.'

Like the biblical parable of the seed scattered on stony ground, most attempts to lure someone into appearing on television fail. During the long-running pantomime that was Mohammed Al-Fayed's attempt to get a British passport, word came though one day that the owner of Harrods would be staging a photo call. There would be no interviews, though. 'Get down there and see if you can get an interview,' said a producer in that state of desperate optimism which overtakes anyone contemplating a blank screen at 10.30 that night.

I found the great retailer strutting about one of the Harrods shop windows wearing a strange grey shirt with a white collar and trailing an enormous Union Jack, like a UKIP wedding dress. He was accompanied by a man dressed as Father Christmas. Press photographers snapped away energetically, capturing the great weight of the event. When the photocall drew to a close I asked if he could spare a moment to talk.

'Come to the office,' he barked, and we began riding escalators up floor after floor. Once inside his office, I sat in an armchair and he behind his desk. I told him I was hoping he might give me an interview. There was no question of it, he said – lawyers' advice – though for my benefit he was willing to disclose the whole sorry story. With that he embarked upon a forty-minute rant about the arrant ingratitude of 'dis fuggin country' after all the favours he had done it. He had given money to public figures. He had restored the nation's most famous shop. He had lost his son in the car crash in which Princess Diana died. And one fuggin Home Secretary after another had denied him British citizenship. Suddenly he stopped, mid-sentence, and hit a bell on his desk.

The door opened, and in walked a young blonde in very high heels and a very short skirt.

'Teddy bear!' he screamed at her. The woman left the room, returning a few seconds later with a teddy bear.

'Your children got 'Arrods teddy bear?'

I replied that they did not have a Harrods teddy bear.

'You take teddy bear!' he barked.

'I really can't,' I burbled, nostrils twitching at the faint stench of corruption.

'You TAKE teddy bear,' he insisted. I wavered. Ali, the producer I had come with, was waiting outside, and his wife had just had a baby girl. I was confident she'd like a teddy bear.

'That's very kind of you,' I said. Al-Fayed resumed his Byzantine conspiracy theories before suddenly stopping, as if a new idea had come to him, and hitting the bell again. In tottered the blonde in the very short skirt.

'Lollipops!' he screamed.

She returned seconds later, bearing a handful of brightly coloured lollipops.

This time, I would show him I could not be bought. 'No, I really can't accept any gift,' I said.

'Please. You TAKE lollipop!' he insisted.

I crumpled in an unprincipled heap. What was the point of going to the wall for the sake of a boiled sweet? I'd give them to the poor old producers in the office when I got back.

'Well, thank you very much,' I said.

I had now crossed the Rubicon, having accepted both a soft toy and a handful of lollipops. I began to understand how it was that MPs had been snared into accepting brown envelopes full of £50 notes. Sensing, perhaps, that he had me in his evil grasp, Al-Fayed continued his conspiracy theories. Despite everything he had done for Britain, he was being balked by an Establishment that danced to the tune of 'de fuggin Jews'. His worth was more than his heroic efforts to embellish the nation's most famous shop. He had made major contributions to public life, bought dings, suffered dings, adorned dings.

By now I was beginning to worry about Ali, who was sitting in Al-Fayed's anteroom. We both ought to get back to the office.

'Mr Al-Fayed, this is very interesting, but if you're not willing to talk to me on camera, I really have to be going.'

'Aha!' he said, hitting the bell again. The young woman in the short skirt appeared again.

'Gold card!' he ordered.

She left the room, and returned with a piece of paper.

'You got 'Arrods Gold Card?'

'I'm afraid I don't really shop at Harrods.'

'You take 'Arrods Gold Card!' he shrieked, outraged. 'You will get best of everyding!'

This was, at last, serious. Proper venality. With an overwhelming sense of relief I saw that the piece of paper was a form which required me to enter my bank details.

'I'm terribly sorry,' I lied. 'I need my bank card to fill this in, and I don't have it with me.' A few minutes later I made my escape. I gave the teddy bear to Ali for his new baby, the lollipops to the producers on the desk in the office, and threw the Gold Card form in the bin.

In an earlier age, Al-Fayed might have been called a blackguard – in the late twentieth century he was just an absurdity. But why shouldn't he have had his passport? If he had been a South African sprinter or a Latvian rower he'd have been given it straight away. But he didn't understand that the way to get on in Britain is to be smooth and ironical. As Alan Bennett put it once, irony is the English amniotic fluid, the silver sea, 'the waters at their priest-like task, washing away guilt and purpose and responsibility. Joking but not joking. Caring but not caring. Serious but not serious.' It is a terribly hard thing to learn.

It's the production disasters that everyone remembers fondly. Or not so fondly. Throughout 1989 we had had a pretty good run covering the end of communism. We did not, of course, report the liberation of Poland, Hungary, Czechoslovakia and most of the rest of Eastern Europe impartially. All of us who had been in those countries during the communist years were well used to playing games with the generally boneheaded secret policemen who followed us about. And who could scowl at genuinely happy people excited by the prospect of freedom when the Wall came down?

There was perhaps another element involved. People who work in television seem to think that it should take precedence over just about everything. You are expected to be out celebrating your wedding anniversary? Cancel it, and make yourself available for interview. But in the end of communism, television definitely changed lives. Doubtless, the communist systems which enslaved most of the citizens of Eastern Europe would have collapsed at some point. But the fact that the mass media had made it clear to those citizens precisely what they were missing – cars and domestic appliances, to say nothing of free speech – undoubtedly hastened it on its way. On the night that the East German border guards gave up the unequal struggle and thousands of delirious Germans poured through the abandoned checkpoints, *Newsnight* hired a studio in Berlin, where reporter Olenka Frenkiel walked in on a Peter Snow discussion carrying a chunk of concrete chipped from the Wall. As between tyranny and freedom there was no impartiality.

At midnight on 2 October 1990 the country divided by the Cold War was to be formally reunited. East Germany and West Germany would cease to exist, the Freedom Bell would toll, the new flag of a unified country would be raised, anthems would be sung, speeches made, and there would be much celebration. Some bright spark in the office thought that the best place from which to cover this momentous event would be in front of the Brandenburg Gate. They had somehow overlooked the fact that on the night in question there would be approximately one million Germans in the square. They would be very happy. Many of them would be very drunk. There would be a lot of fireworks.

That night's edition of *Newsnight* was memorably described by the then Managing Director of BBC Television, a jowly, frightening man called Paul Fox, as 'the worst outside broadcast I have ever seen'. For understandable reasons (why would you?), no one had thought to ask the individuals invited to discuss the future of a reunited Germany how tall they were. It turned out that the two main guests were a bald six-foot-seven Teuton and a German Jewish lady who might just about have been able to muster five feet. In heels. Standing on a stage in the middle of the square in front of the Brandenburg Gate, I found myself alternately having to point the microphone to the sky and then to the ground.

'So you're confident that the new Germany won't be like the old Germany?' – gazing up the nostrils of the great colossus.

'I think we should be a bit concerned,' comes a voice from the floor of the stage.

Each of them was almost inaudible, because when a million people are celebrating the end of decades of enforced separation they tend to shout and sing and dance. My colleague and pal Charles Wheeler, a great reporter and human being, did not help matters by interjecting, 'This thing is pure *Monty Python* – trying to have a serious political discussion in the midst of a firework display.'

Charles had been part of a secret Royal Marine raiding unit which had swept into Germany after D-Day, ahead of the main Allied advance. In the circumstances, my response – 'I'm just obeying orders, Charles' – was not well-judged. Somehow we reached the end of the show, and I said 'Goodnight from Berlin' with a profound sense of relief. Before heading off to the cheap hotel in the former East Berlin where the BBC had booked too few rooms, we gathered at the Portacabin we were using as an office. As a mark of possession, someone had scrawled 'BBC' on a piece of paper and stuck it to the door. The producer called London.

'Well, I thought that was rather good,' said a voice at the other end. 'You really felt you were there.' It was certainly true that you felt you were there, though this was the last time the word 'good' was used to describe the event. By the end of the following morning's Programme Review the verdict had been reached that it had been a shambles. Our phone conversation was cut short, anyway, because the hut had begun to rock backwards and forwards. Dozens of soldiers stationed at the British garrison in Berlin had seen the home-made notice and were trying to effect an entry, chanting, as the place swung to and fro, 'We want Kate Adie! We want Kate Adie!'

* * *

It took a little while for the collapse of communism to shake Yugoslavia to pieces. When that happened, it was horrible, though not without absurd interludes, one of which was provided by a man rejoicing in the name of Milan Panić, who turned up in our spartan subterranean Green Room one evening accompanied by men with briefcases, well-made-up 'spokeswomen' carrying clipboards, and much American tailoring. He had decided, he said, that he should be the next President of what was left of Yugoslavia. According to the biography handed out by his acolytes, he had fought with the Yugoslav partisans during World War II, before making uncountable millions from a chemicals company in America. The handouts did not mention his brushes with the American Securities and Exchange Commission.

In a blizzard of management-speak this Rufus T. Firefly explained that what his country needed was some Western management – downsizing, upsizing, sideways-sizing, and doubtless some hot-desking too. He sounded like a man with a business plan for a Chevrolet dealership in Delaware. He would run a flag up the pole and see who saluted. Unfortunately for him, when it came to elections in the rump state, not many did, and the bullet-headed nationalist Slobodan Milošević won the presidency, which enabled him later to become the first European head of state to be prosecuted for genocide and war crimes. Though he never graced the *Newsnight* studio, we were frequently treated to down-the-line rants from his ally Radovan Karadžić, a long-haired psychiatrist and part-time poet who led the Serbian enclave inside Bosnia, where he earned himself the nickname 'the Butcher of Bosnia'.

The Balkans are virtually incomprehensible to most people at the best of times. Before the collapse of the Berlin Wall, like most Western Europeans I was incapable of distinguishing between Slovenia and Serbia, Bosnia and Croatia, Macedonia and Montenegro. Landlocked Kosovo might have been anywhere, and the version of fourteenth-century history I had learned at school was more preoccupied with the Battle of Bannockburn than the fighting which had taken place there in 1389, and which Serbia seemed unable to get over. The last time I had visited any of those countries was hitch-hiking back from Greece after my youthful kibbutz interlude. Then they had all been part of Yugoslavia. My main recollections were of a stunningly beautiful coastline, waiting five hours for a lift on two consecutive days, and a kind peasant woman who gave me some berries to chew to calm my diarrhoea.

By the early 1990s the hotels and holiday villas were filled to bursting not with tourists but refugees who had been driven from their villages by armed thugs. If there is a sadder human being than a refugee grieving for home and loved ones, it is hard to imagine. But then, almost everything in that part of the Balkans seemed unutterably sad. The frequently disgusting events which unfolded in Bosnia, Serbia and Croatia also revealed the feebleness, cowardice and mendacity of international organisations like the European Union and the United Nations.

At the collapse of communism, Slovenia, the wealthiest part of Yugoslavia, slipped away to independence just as soon as it could, after a war that lasted all of ten days. When ethnic tensions in the rest of the former Yugoslavia erupted in demands for Serbs, Croats, Bosnian Muslims and Bosnian Serbs (to say nothing of other groups) to have their own states, the EU affected concern and promised to act. With its usual deference to the status quo, the organisation claimed to be committed to keeping the clearly defunct Yugoslavia together. This was like holding a ticking time bomb in your hands and swearing you will make sure its casing stays intact. In late 1991 Germany broke ranks and announced that it would recognise Croatia as an independent state, thus discrediting the EU in an instant. Britain and France blustered at the United Nations, but soon bent the knee – there was nothing they could do to stop Germany helping its World War II allies to get what they wanted.

Several of the great faultlines in Europe crossed the area – Christianity and Islam, Orthodoxy and Catholicism being the obvious ones. But however earnestly we tried to interest the viewing public in this appalling saga of diplomatic incompetence and indigenous brutality, there was a strong feeling of indifference – all the newly emerging entities seemed a very long way away. In 1995, with the Bosnian Serb militia on the rampage and a genocidal massacre of Muslims a real possibility, I managed to get the BBC to send me there, even though I had not, and never have, done a 'hostile environment' course. (In these courses retired soldiers take journalists from comfortable outer London suburbs into the English countryside to show them how to survive kidnap, or what to do if a colleague's intestines get blown out. Attending one of them is now compulsory if you're to visit a war zone, and having lost friends in such places, they seem to me to demonstrate an admirable duty of care: you cannot remove danger, but you can learn how you might cope with it.)

Our journey to Bosnia began in Croatia, where we picked up an armoured Land Rover to which we attached white tape spelling out the letters 'TV', which was supposed to deter snipers. The last representatives of the EU 'peace initiative' were wandering about one of the few remaining hotels still accepting guests, wearing white trousers and jackets and looking as if they had just walked off the set of a Persil advertisement. Their job seemed to have been reduced to merely keeping track of the killings.

Just before we crossed the border into Bosnia the next morning we were stopped at a roadblock while gunmen leafed through our passports. One of them stood back, playing with his rifle. The oddest thing was that he was wearing a British Army Glengarry cap – the war had sucked in volunteers and riff-raff from all over Europe. I made eye contact with him, and attempted a smile. He gave me one of the deadest-eyed stares I have ever experienced. There were more chilling sights inside Bosnia, where village after village resembled European settlements everywhere from Norway to Romania, provided only that you ignored the blackened shells of houses which had been burned out because they were occupied by families of the wrong religion or ethnicity. That evening, as the heavy old Land Rover strained its way into the mountains we looked down into the valley and saw the darkness broken by the eruption of fire after fire, as the militia continued their work. By now we were all very jumpy, and it was with enormous relief that we reached the fortified camp of a battalion of UN peacekeepers. We threw ourselves on the mercy of their Canadian commanding officer, who – in breach of his orders – allowed us to spend the night on his base. (If only all UN commanders had been willing to defy the unworldly orders they had been issued in New York, fewer people would have been murdered.)

From there, next morning it was a straight run along what the local peacekeepers called 'bomb alley' into Tuzla, an ethnically mixed town that served as the regional capital, where we joined the gaggle of foreign journalists drawn there to watch the next ghastly outrage. Outside the hotel where we all stayed, small boys operated a protection racket: your car would be safe (from them, no doubt) if you handed them a dollar or so to watch it overnight. In the bar of the hotel I discovered that the only business cards I had with me were the ones I had been given by *Esquire* magazine, for whom I was, at the time 'Fishing Editor'.

'You've come to right place,' said a young American photographer. 'There are some great-looking streams here.'

A couple of hours' drive away, at Srebrenica, Bosnian Serb soldiers were plotting the murder of thousands of mainly Muslim refugees. We spent a few days in Tuzla, where there were good enough facilities for us to be able to broadcast a 'Good evening from northern Bosnia' programme, a form of journalism which rather merits Dr Johnson's observation about dogs walking on their hind legs – the remarkable thing was only that it was done at all: this has been a common failing of television. While we scurried about town seeing if we could persuade people to talk to us, the Bosnian Serb army was planning precisely how they would murder over eight thousand men and boys. They moved in for their loathsome business after we had exhausted our budget and been recalled to London.

Although studio presentation often has as much to do with original journalism as an organ-grinder's monkey has to do with composition, it does still afford insights which are not easily come by.

'There's a recorded interview with Pavarotti at 4.30 in Claridge's,' said the editor one day. Not a brilliant time, I thought. It turned out to be when the great tenor got out of bed. Sure enough, at about a quarter to five a pair of dyed black eyebrows entered the room, followed by what seemed to be a multicoloured circus tent. Pavarotti had just finished his breakfast, which could probably have fed the entire orchestra and chorus of the Royal Opera House. He sat down and demanded to look through the camera that was going to be filming him. I pointed out that if he was looking through the viewfinder, he couldn't be in the picture. He then demanded that the cameraman set the shot and leave the room.

I can't recall whose idea it was to interview Sir John Gielgud on stage at the Old Vic about his life and times. A couple of years before Gielgud died in 2000, at the age of ninety-six, Dave the Driver was sent to collect him from his country house in Buckinghamshire. At the theatre, Dave took one arm and I the other as we manoeuvred the ageing actor up a set of steps. No sooner had he set foot on the stage than he said, 'I'm afraid I have to go to the lavatory.' Mercifully there is a loo in the Old Vic's star dressing room, where to my alarm he said, 'I wonder if you could assist me?' So I did, getting the very strong impression that I was not the first man to be so honoured. Business done, we returned to the stage and sat down. The interview turned out to need forty-two minutes of recording time. No story was ever finished, no joke ever had a punchline. Finally, I judged that we had enough to stitch together into a few minutes of conversation. I helped him off the stage and into the back of Dave the Driver's car, then returned to the *Newsnight* office. Many hours later, Dave turned up there.

''Ere, what did you give that John Gielgud to drink?' he demanded.

'He had one glass of water,' I said.

'Blimey! I had to stop for him four times on the way to his home.'

As in Whitehall, at the BBC the drivers are the people who really know what's going on – especially the one who was used by three separate executives to drive them to Acton for what the tabloid press call 'love trysts' with the same management figure.

'That Michael Howard – what did you do to him?' Dave once asked me. 'He spent the whole journey home saying, "Why didn't I say I couldn't remember?"' On other occasions, Ministers and party flak-catchers could be on the phone to their advisers, asking what line to take, which tended to be a useful source of intelligence. At the very least you could expect Dave to say, 'You've met him before, at a conference.' Possibly followed by, 'And it didn't go very well.'

No one should ever set foot in a live television studio without knowing what they want to say, and then making sure that they say it, regardless. It is surprising the successful people who don't. Vivienne Westwood once came in for an interview about the imminent death of *haute couture*, and did something I had never seen before.

'Does it really matter if *haute couture* dies?' I asked.

There was silence for what felt like ten seconds, which is an eternity in live television. Finally, Miss Westwood looked at the ceiling, looked at the floor, then said, 'Sorry. Do you mind if we start again?' I never discovered whether her silence was because the idea was so outrageous or because her mind had been elsewhere, but her personal assistant sent a nice note the next day to say how much she had enjoyed the conversation. She had, perhaps, been communing with the shade of Coco Chanel.

8

Dizzee Who?

Though there was widespread agreement that *Newsnight* was 'a good thing', we never really settled on a satisfactory form of words for what precisely it did. An honest slogan would have been something like 'Trying to find out what's happening', or 'You know what happened, but what did it mean?' The natural response when kicked in the shins by a total stranger – 'What was *that* for?' – would also have been adequate.

The programme worked like this. At 10 a.m. producers and reporters were required to attend a morning conference. When I joined, each was supposed to have three separate ideas, one of which might be for a longer-term film or investigation, while the other two were expected to be translatable into an item on that evening's programme. In the days of tyrant editors one sat in terror as the pointed finger made its way around the room: those who had duff ideas received a withering look, and were generally moved to some other programme as soon as possible. But once the BBC embraced a kinder, gentler way of doing things (I first noticed it when I tore a strip off an especially useless producer over a terrible brief, and the next day had a note from him thanking me very much for my 'feedback'), the meetings lost all their energy. The apex of pointlessness came when one morning someone I had never seen before glimpsed the pointing finger and exclaimed, 'Nigeria!'

'Nigeria's a country. It's not an idea,' I said. '*What* do you think we should be doing about Nigeria?'

'Oh I don't know,' she replied. 'But it's important, and we should do something.' That was when I decided life was too short to go to the morning meetings any more. There had always been a sense in which they were not what they seemed, for the 'editor of the day', or the producer in charge of that night's show, would have been in the building since 7 or 8 a.m., read all the newspapers and already formed an idea of the looming show that night during their frequent anxiety-induced trips to the lavatory. From the day of the Nigeria suggestion onwards, I would have a phone conversation with the editor of the day at about 8.30, and then head to the gym.

After the morning conference, most days followed a steady pattern, with stories assigned either then or after the short discussion involving the editor, editor of the day and presenter which followed it at eleven. There would then be an hour of indolence, coffee and conversation while someone went down to rifle through the filing cabinets in 'News Inf.' (News Information), collected slim buff folders of newspaper cuttings on the relevant subjects, and returned to the office. The arrival of desktop computers put paid to that interlude, and from then on producers hardly left their desks for the rest of the day. Lunch was a sandwich, and so was dinner.

The repeated pattern was the requirement to do more with less. When I arrived on *Newsnight*, the programme had separate domestic and foreign news desks, each with its own editor. That was a distinction erased in the nineties, though it was still the case that items in preparation for that evening's show had at least two producers, one of whom was designated as the 'lead'. By the millennium the two-producer item was a thing of the past, and within another decade you'd be glad to have someone on work experience.

In order to maintain distinctiveness, the programme had its own 'copy-taster', who watched what was happening on the news-wires and might occasionally say something enigmatic like 'They've burned down a Kentucky Fried Chicken shop in Bangalore,' in case it might be of interest. One of the copy-tasters was the delightful wife of the Oxford don who had supervised Bill Clinton during his Rhodes Scholarship. Another was a Serbian who had served with the British Army during World War II as, among other things, an interrogator. 'They *always* talked,' he said in a slow, slightly sinister Slavic accent. The copy-taster post vanished in one of the repeated culls which saw the number of staff cut to less than half its previous size. The production budget was reduced by a similar proportion. Of course, technology has light-ened the load a bit – when you can interview anyone through the lens in their computer, finding a studio in rural Manitoba is less of a problem. But there was no longer any safety in numbers – the producers who used to go and hide in the lavatories when the stress got too much would be noticed now.

But the laws of an editorial survival of the fittest have applied consistently. By mid-afternoon, the four or five possible stories which emerged from the morning meeting had been reduced to a likely three, either because no one could be found to say anything interesting about a couple of them, or because they had turned out not to be quite as presented in that day's newspapers. By five in the afternoon you wanted to have a rough idea who'd be sitting down in the studio in a few hours' time. By six, most of the interview briefs were under way, the tape reports in preparation and the stand-up rows with the dwindling band of graphics artists brewing up nicely. By seven the quiet of the office was broken only by the click of computer keys, the sound of people eating their second sandwich meal of the day, and an occasional shriek from someone who had had a mouse run over their feet to snatch the crumbs. By eight or nine, the driver had set off to fetch guests from distant locations – BBC programmes may seem in many ways to be as London-centric as ever, but the requirement to have voices from Sunderland or Wolverhampton has been very kind to the private hire trade.

The nice little man from the costume department who used to turn up offering to iron your shirt was made redundant years ago, but by ten the presenter was en route to the studio, via the make-up chair, which provided two minutes to sit and catch your breath while a human being from outside the journalistic maelstrom darkened your skin and powdered your face so you didn't wash out under the lights. I am not making a sexist observation when I say that the make-up process takes longer for female presenters. It just does. Some *grande dame* politicians – Barbara Castle was one – would turn up an hour early so they could experience the full respray and polish.

Like most live or as-for-live shows, *Newsnight* has a Green Room, or 'hospitality' suite. Once upon a time this was a panelled room with a groaning drinks cabinet. Then came the edict that spirits were only to be served when the former Prime Minister Edward Heath was in, because he refused to touch anything other than Glenmorangie. When Denis Healey heard about this exception, he managed to get it extended to himself. Since those days, the standard of catering has fallen off a cliff. The canapés went years ago, to be replaced first by curling sandwiches, and then by the odd packet of Pringles or Twiglets. This bleakness is not much offset by the fact that for the past few years the Green Room has been in the basement, furnished with ex-demonstration sofas in hideous colours, resting against walls which looked as if they were decorated during the H-Block 'dirty protest'. Problems with the drains in the newly-built extension to Broadcasting House have recently given the room a matching pong.

Guests who arrive before the programme begins must do the best they can to establish what is about to happen to them from the off-duty BBC staff earning pin money by working as 'hospy' men and women, their job to soft-soap the bewildered individuals who had been having a perfectly pleasant evening until someone arrived to drive them at breakneck speed to a building populated by young people seemingly on the edge of breakdowns. If the guests are lucky, the hospitality operative will have worked out that they are appearing approximately ten minutes after the programme starts, in a discussion about the decline of the seahorse population. If they are unfortunate, the person looking after them will have been told nothing by the young man about to have his breakdown, and will therefore assume that they have been invited in to discuss the Guatemalan debt crisis. This tends to spoil their evening.

I made a point of calling into the Green Room before the programme to put any nervous guests at ease, though I regretted it on the evening we had invited in a Coptic Bishop – in full clerical dress – to discuss the persecution of Christians in Egypt.

'Sorry about this horrible room, Bishop,' I said. 'Oh, look, someone's trying to brighten it up with this fruit bowl!' I leaned down to pick it up from the low table in front of his seat. It was his hat.

The most unattractive visitors to the Green Room were self-important figures like the late MP Greville Janner, who would arrive in good time before a discussion, accompanied by a gaggle of impressionable young people before whom he would show off. Most of the others, from the grandest to the least apparently important, bore out my conviction that, if you let them, most people will be nice.

The great danger in producing discussions which are expected to generate a lot of heat (always more attractive to less experienced producers than the production of light) is to let the guests spend too long talking to each other beforehand. That way, they often end up agreeing. When much heat was expected, guests would be kept in separate rooms before they went on air. Nuance and thoughtfulness are risky, whereas a good punch-up will at least get the audience talking (though the producer is really much more concerned with what the editor may say later than with what the unsuspecting viewer feels). The most unhelpful position to occupy, then, is to be reasonable. Common sense and amenability are a one-way ticket to obscurity. Television has a simple and stupid rule: noise matters. Yet perhaps the best discussion we ever had in the old *Newsnight* studio was about whether an Anglican any longer needed to believe in the virgin birth, between two bishops who had spent the evening having a jolly dinner together at the Athenaeum.

As the afternoon has worn on, the nature of that evening's programme has inevitably changed. Sometimes this is because something genuinely new and important has happened in the world. More commonly, the man or woman in charge of the show has just got bored – though changing plans almost always makes for a worse spectacle on air, it acts as form of calamine lotion, soothing restlessness. The final fly in the ointment is the common problem that things turn out to be slightly more complicated than they seemed at the morning meeting: there are not two diametrically opposed opinions on this subject, just a range of different emphases. When this happens it may fall to the unfortunate producer to make the most unpopular call of all, which is to tell the person who was booked at three o'clock and has already washed their hair, booked a babysitter, put on their smartest outfit and telephoned all their friends warning them to stay up late, that they are not wanted. Hannah MacInnes, an especially bold producer, developed a technique of ringing and saying, 'I've got wonderful news! You've got your evening back!', which wrongfooted anyone who might have been about to shout or cry. Everyone else dreaded the task. The only thing worse than making this call is receiving it.

There is, though, a worse way to hear the news. That is to be dropped from the show's running order when you are already being driven at breakneck speed to the studio. Worst of all, on several occasions guests have been discarded after they were actually on the premises. Since this can only decently be done face to face, the editor of the programme has to be torn away from their paperclip-chewing and sent down to reception to explain that Things Have Changed, and while it's awfully nice of the learned professor to have cancelled his wife's birthday trip to the theatre, he is in fact too dull to hold forth on television that night. There have been guests – including a distinguished member of the House of Lords noted for his apparently unflappable lucidity – who exploded at this point, crashing through doors demanding to know who the fucking hell these producers think they are. Others, including some hugely renowned figures, have put a brave front on this appalling rudeness by saying, 'Oh that's all right. I'll just sit here in reception in case you change your minds again.'

This sort of response seems horribly demeaning, but shows an intuitive awareness of a vital maxim: that television detests an empty chair just as nature abhors a vacuum. Be you never so dull, there may well come a day when you are the perfect guest, if for no other reason than that you are available. For many years I maintained a ban on the Conservative MP for Lichfield, Michael Fabricant, after he appeared on the programme discussing some policy or other and the following day the sole comment in the log of viewer responses was the observation that 'Mr Fabricius had a most inappropriate wig for a serious news programme.' Fabricant, a former disc jockey cruelly described by one political sketch-writer as having once been 'famous in several parts of Hove', does indeed have a collection of the most extraordinary blond hair-pieces. He also has a full set of standard-issue Conservative Party lines to take on everything from the European currency markets to manure subsidies. So one day the ban fell into desuetude when it had just turned 10.15 p.m. and there was an empty chair in the studio.*

At the opposite pole to those who cannot get into the amusingly named 'hospitality suite' are those you can't get out of it. Quite why anyone would want to spend hours of their life in such a miserable place is a mystery. But Kenneth Clarke, the one-time Conservative Chancellor of the Exchequer, was certainly ready to give it a go. I used to have to take the most junior researcher to one side and say, 'You can't leave until he does,' which often meant they were both still at it until almost one in the morning, when Clarke might head off to Ronnie Scott's. Norman Lamont, another Tory Chancellor who'd have looked quite at home at the counter of the Epsom branch of Betfred, was another who was willing to sully his liver with a glass or few of Burkina Faso's finest Riesling. Sometimes the producers who had been entertaining him, and had then moved on to entertaining each other, were roused from the Green Room by the dawn chorus of vacuum cleaners.

When I joined *Newsnight* in 1989 it was housed in two tin huts on the roof of Television Centre in White City – in high winds they rattled alarmingly and felt as if they were about to take off. Then the programme was moved into a purpose-built 'Journalism Centre', sharing offices with a quiet, tweedy bunch of radio producers who made a programme which went out on Radio Four at much the same time as ours, but with a rather more sedate tone – under the then fashionable nonsense of 'bimedialism' we were all

---

* If you're willing to risk it, the empty chair can also be a useful weapon. There was an entire week, during one of Peter Mandelson's periodic embarrassments which eventually led to him losing his government position, in which we requested an interview, to be rejected on each consecutive day. On the Monday we didn't mention it on air; on Tuesday we said we'd have liked to talk to him; on Wednesday we said that he had again declined the opportunity to explain himself; and on Thursday we cut to a shot of the empty chair which might have been graced by the ministerial bottom. He appeared on the Friday night.

supposed to be interchangeable, though neither television nor radio producers had the slightest interest in acquiring each other's skills. Finally, after spending over thirty years in West London, in 2012 the programme was moved to the BBC's hubristic new extension to Broadcasting House in the centre of town.

With each change of premises the operation was being shifted further into the bosom of the organisation, and a bit of sparkiness was extinguished. As time passed, the freedom granted to individual editors was more and more reduced. It was the inevitable consequence of increased ambition and fewer resources. The creation of a twenty-four-hour news channel reacting to the slightest sneeze not only removed many good reporters from journalism and turned them into studio automatons, it also required a centralisation which did nothing at all for the creative diversity on which programmes like *Newsnight* thrived. The audience is now much smaller than it was. But then, so are many television audiences: the show was devised long before the invention of many of the devices on which it is now consumed. *Newsnight* still employs plenty of clever, talented, witty people who deserve better. Given their freedom, they could flourish.

Whenever I used to interview a representative of that benighted trade union, the Prison Officers' Association, they would invariably say, 'Morale is at rock-bottom.' The BBC is a bit like that: everyone entering the building seems to have walked into Eeyore's bit of the forest, and a low moan can be heard almost anywhere. *Newsnight* is not the only programme to feel a bit unloved. Mercifully, the moaning seems to be in inverse relationship to the creativity.

During the course of my time there, editors came and went. I served under nine. Some – like Tim Gardam, who went on to run Channel 4 and was later reincarnated as a bigwig in academia; Peter Horrocks, who became Vice Chancellor of the Open University; or George Entwistle, who became the corporation's

Director General and was then defenestrated – were terribly clever. Others, like Peter Barron, who left the BBC to work for Google when the corporation decided he was too much of a free spirit, were among the most creative people in the country. One editor was a sinister figure who encouraged staff to stay behind after work to write up reports on colleagues, as if he were an officer of the East German Stasi. One drove some of the staff to tears (literally). Others drove themselves to tears.

Working in an ageing medium, all of them were at the mercy of technological fashion. One evening we would be appealing for viewers to send in video clips, as if we were becoming a version of *You've Been Framed*, the next we were turning the weekly highlights into a video blog for those who couldn't be bothered to stay up late. There was even an audio blog for a while, for people who preferred their television without the inconvenience of pictures. Senior managers were rather like dads at weddings taking to the dance floor. All the editors had the ability to appear strikingly confident: they had to be able to do so if they were to survive the strange combination of freedom and straitjacket with which they lived. They could put more or less what they liked on air, yet they could not ignore what the collective unconscious had decreed was 'news'. I listened to no fewer than three newly arrived editors say that their first ambition was to fire a spectacularly miserable reporter, only for each to discover that they couldn't do so – and nor were they able to do much about escaping the Buggins' turn routine in order to promote talent. More generally, I formed the distinct impression that the BBC management felt they could pay programme producers at a lower rate than they might earn elsewhere because there was no shortage of talented people desperate to work there. Editors tended to last about three years, until they burned out, their partners wouldn't put up with the disruption any more, or they had a divorce. Daily production was the responsibility of the 'editor of the day', a grand title for someone who generally spent the whole period in a state of existential terror, until they realised that the essential *Newsnight* running order could usually be boiled down to three pieces:

Item One: Isn't this Government Rubbish? (The latest political spat)
Item Two: Will it Kill Us? (Some public safety/food/science story)
Item Three: But is it Art? (An unsophisticated person's approach to culture)

Once you understood the template, you were fine. The great difference between a newspaper and a television programme is that while as a print editor you can endlessly change your mind and fire up a new story at the drop of a hat, spiking another you have spent ages working on, a television programme has to be built, which takes time: stories are not of equal weight or style, and the wise producer recognises that the audience needs to be carried from one to another. It is asking a lot of people to start watching a show at 10.30 and stay with it until after 11.15.

But why did it matter how many people were watching *Newsnight*? After all, it wasn't as if the show had to survive by selling advertising spots. In one way or another, that question of audiences lies at the heart of the BBC's identity crisis. The basic purpose of a commercial broadcaster is to make money. It does that by supplying a product which people want to watch and will pay for, either directly (like Netflix) or through advertising (like ITV). The BBC is immune from such commercial pressures. How then does it decide what to put on its screens? Periodically, governments and the corporation agree targets, which include vacuous forms of words like 'sustaining citizenship and civil society', or 'delivering to the public the benefit of emerging communications technologies and services', which sound like mission statements concocted by expensive and not-very-good management consultants. In the end, the BBC cleaves to the motivation encapsulated in the three verbs chosen by its first Director General, Lord Reith, which have endured for generations: it exists to 'inform, educate and entertain'. It is precisely because it is immune from commercial pressures that private-enterprise media businesses hold the corporation to higher standards than those to which they hold their other rivals (or, it often seems, themselves). Since people have no choice about whether or not to pay the tax which funds the BBC, this is right and proper. But it raises the intriguing question of how these higher standards can be met.

The confusion about the BBC's purpose was made abundantly clear in an absurd ritual which news programmes were made to go through every six months for much of the 1990s. On balmy weekend afternoons, each programme's staff was tested to ensure that they understood how to break the news to the nation that a prominent member of the royal family had died. The dubious honour of unexpected death was usually given to the Queen Mother, who was then in her nineties. There is an argument to be made that the death of a little old lady is hardly news at all: most of us will not make it, as she eventually did, to an age of over a hundred.

If, because of the person involved, a death really is news, you might think that the mature thing to do would be to tell the nation about it in as straightforward a way as possible. Not at the BBC. The scenario always began in the same way. *Newsnight* was notionally on the air and in the midst of a riveting discussion on something like the Common Agricultural Policy. A voice would come in over the presenter's earpiece saying, 'We're getting reports of a fatal car accident near Windsor.' This was a test, for on hearing this news you were to continue talking about sugarbeet or turnips while the producers purged their minds of everything they had so assiduously imbibed about European root-vegetable policy and hammered the telephones to try to discover what had happened on the M4. Only when they had established the facts, and had then been authorised by a senior figure in the organisation, could the presenter acknowledge what had happened.

This did not, however, involve anything as simple as saying, 'We're just receiving news of a traffic accident on the M4 near Windsor.' Instead, on confirmation of the accuracy of the news the programme was to fade to black, and a caption would appear on screen with words to the effect, 'Stand by for an important announcement.' At this point the presenter was to leave the studio, run down the corridor, take the lift to the sixth floor, sprint down another corridor, take from their pocket the key they had been instructed to carry on their person at all times, and then open a wardrobe. Inside was a rail from which hung a row of identical grey suits, white shirts and black ties (or, as an official memo put it, 'In the case of female presenters, black shawls').

Hoping you had not grabbed Nicholas Witchell's suit by mistake, you were to hop down the corridor inserting your legs into the trousers, take the lift back to the ground floor and return to the studio, where the caption would be faded down and you were to articulate two sentences from which no deviation was allowed: 'It is with deep regret that the BBC announces the death of Her Majesty, Queen Elizabeth, the Queen Mother. She was …' This announcement was to be followed by several minutes of choco-late-box pictures showing images of the old girl at various stages of her life. The presenter would then reappear on screen, and repeat exactly the same form of words, for the benefit of anyone who had missed them the first time around. The chocolate-box pictures would be reshown. Some time after that, reporters would deliver live reports from the nearby multi-storey carpark, pretend-ing they were standing outside Clarence House, while producers sat in the studio impersonating elderly former courtiers and the Archbishop of Canterbury. There were a number of flaws with this approach, not the least of them being that while BBC presenters were running up and down corridors and introducing videos over-laid with saccharine music, all the other channels would be treat-ing people as grown-ups, and telling them what had happened.

Inevitably, the elaborate rehearsals did not survive contact with reality. When Diana, Princess of Wales was killed in a Paris under-pass in 1997, the news had to be passed on in as straightforward a way as possible – and indeed, when the Queen Mother succumbed to natural causes five years after that, the BBC newsreader on duty, Peter Sissons, announced the news inside the burgundy tie he happened to be wearing at the time.

The wardrobe which held the rack of identical shirts, ties and jackets survived for a while, and did make one contribution to broadcasting, when *Newsnight* staged a discussion about the planned enlargement of the European Union to take in a raft of formerly communist countries. We planned to devote the entire programme to a discussion of what the effects of this expansion would be. The future Labour Foreign Secretary, Robin Cook, agreed to take part, along with the Latvian Prime Minister, the Lithuanian Foreign Minister and numerous other Eastern European statesmen and women. Cook was a fan of the European Union, but could be very prickly. He insisted on being treated differently from the mere Continentals, and therefore would not be joining them beforehand in the Green Room. So he was invited to have a coffee in the editor's office instead.

Things got off to a slightly testy start when the representatives of the would-be new member states were shown into the studio. The producer had gone to a lot of trouble, and enormous flags hung from the ceiling, above a semi-circle of chairs.

'Why do you want me to sit beneath the flag of Estonia?' asked the Lithuanian.

'And why am I sitting beneath the Czech flag?' asked the Latvian.

Few of us having any idea what their respective national flags looked like, I mumbled, 'Just symbolic.' At this moment, five minutes before the programme went on air, Robin Cook entered the studio, carrying a Styrofoam cup of coffee. I showed him to his seat just as the sound engineer stood up, having been bending over to attach a microphone to the Hungarian Ambassador's tie. The engineer stepped back, straight into Cook's coffee, which upended itself all over his shirt and tie. To describe him as angry fails to do justice to his feelings.

'I refuse to appear like this,' he said, dripping.

'I'll find you some other clothes,' I said. The plainclothes police-man acting as his bodyguard began taking off his tie.

'I am not wearing *that*,' said Cook, looking at what seemed to be some sort of club tie, but speaking as if he had been offered a tutu. The policeman looked a little crestfallen.

At this point I recalled the existence of the wardrobe, pulled from my pocket the key we were instructed to carry at all times, and knew that the day was saved, even if the Shadow Foreign Secretary did look as if he was attending a funeral.

People often assume that those who report on politics have known the politicians they interview for years. It isn't true. If I had known politicians socially I should perhaps have been better at small talk. Around the time Theresa May became Chairman of the Conservative Party she came in for an interview. She is notoriously bad at gossip, so I struggled to find something to chat about in the ten minutes before the programme went live. Had she been surprised, I asked, by the amount of attention the newspapers had paid to her shoes? This was a stupid subject to raise, since I know even less about shoes than about quantum physics.

'Yes, I have been,' she said.

The only thing I could recall about her shoes was that they seemed to be in a leopardskin pattern. I had been reading the previous day about divisions in feminism. During one spat, Germaine Greer had attacked the journalist Suzanne Moore for her hair, cleavage and 'fuck-me shoes'. I assumed this was a recognised category of footwear.

'Are they what they call "fuck-me shoes"?' I asked Mrs May.

Bateman would have struggled to do justice to the expression on her face.

Just as I had kept away from student politicians in my university days, so I made no attempt to enlist politicians as friends during my working life. It was not that there was anything innately dislikeable or dishonourable about them, just that I have always found my friends in shared interests. But there comes a point when you start getting invited to drinks parties at the Foreign Office or receiving Christmas cards from the Prime Minister, the leader of the opposition, the Chancellor of the Exchequer and so on. Since both the invitation list and the Christmas-card list have undoubtedly been drawn up by some dogsbody, these amicable gestures would be meaningful only in a parallel universe. It may be amusing to stick on your mantelpiece a photograph of the party leader and his or her unfortunate spouse posing as the Holy Family, but the comedy soon tires.

But work will undoubtedly throw you together with politicians. I had met Tony Blair only once before he became leader of the Labour Party, when we had both been invited to speak at a conference organised by the Prince's Trust to encourage young entrepreneurs. He was dressed in his usual corporate lawyer's subfusc, and as we sat in awkward silence backstage, waiting to do our stuff, I looked at his feet and said, 'Those are very well-polished shoes.' It wasn't much of a gambit, but it immediately drew the toothy grin we all later came to know so well, and the words, 'Yes, yes, I really can't go out if my shoes aren't properly polished.' Up to that point I had been thinking, 'We're really pretty similar – middle-class minor public schoolboys with liberal prejudices.' The Iraq War deception and an unappealing fascination with the very rich were what really did for his reputation, but – as the jeans at Camp David demonstrated – he was always a man with an unusual preoccupation with his image.

But from a reporter's point of view, the great thing about Tony Blair was that he did believe in accountability and communication. (We should give some of the credit for that to his PR man, Alastair Campbell. So what if he tried to browbeat reporters and editors? That was his job, or part of it. More fool his victims when they succumbed.) Unlike some of his successors in Downing Street. Blair was willing to put himself up for interview, and seemed positively to enjoy the impertinent or unexpected question. Before the 1997 election which brought him to power he had set out to woo Britain's most powerful newspaper baron, Rupert Murdoch, whose *Sun* newspaper had been the Tory attack dog in the previous election. It was generally reckoned that its vicious attacks on the then Labour leader, Neil Kinnock – including an election-day front page in which his head was superimposed on an image of a lightbulb, with the caption 'If Kinnock wins today will the last person to leave Britain please turn out the lights', had done Labour tremendous damage. After Blair won the party leadership in 1994 he literally flew halfway around the world to dance attendance on Murdoch when he gathered his lieutenants together at a luxury resort in the Whitsunday Islands, off the coast of Australia. It paid off, and in 1997 the *Sun* came out for Blair, telling its ten million readers the country needed his 'vision, purpose and courage'. Blair returned the compliment by writing an article for the paper, begging for its readers' support.

To most people the re-election of John Major's calamity-prone party was almost inconceivable, and Labour's eighteen wilderness years looked to be at an end. But what to ask Blair in the one interview we had with him before the country voted? By now I was a firm believer in the importance of beginning any interview with a question that would deflect the interviewee from their prepared blather. You needed to ask something which you imagined they not only wouldn't be expecting, but wouldn't really want to deal with. Ideally, you wanted not to be able to guess how they'd answer. Travelling to Gloucester, where the encounter was to take place, it suddenly dawned. What did he think about his *Sun* article appearing opposite the breasts of a naked Page Three model? And what did his wife Cherie think about it? The question threw him, but only for a moment. The smile flashed, he drew breath for a second, and then he was off.

There followed numerous other interviews with Blair over the years of his premiership, including several in Downing Street at various junctures on his journey away from Received Pronunciation to Estuary English (did he have a voice coach to learn the glottal stop, or was he home-educated?). Just before one of these interviews it had become public that the Labour Party had accepted a £100,000 donation from the newspaper proprietor and pornographer Richard Desmond. I had guessed that Blair would be uncomfortable talking about his religious beliefs (it is one of the big differences between political life in the United States and Britain), and indeed he was. How, I asked, was taking money from a pornographer consistent with his Christian principles? That satisfying expression of alarm flashed across his eyes, and then he tried to duck the issue. Did I mean the owner of that highly respectable organ, the *Daily Express*? Not being familiar with Mr Desmond's empire, I had asked a colleague to find the names of some of his magazines before I left for Downing Street. 'Yes. He also publishes *Horny Housewives*, *Megaboobs*, *Posh Wives* and *Skinny and Wriggly*. Do you know what these magazines are like?'

The nervous smile creased his face again. 'No, I don't. But if someone is fit and proper to run a major newspaper group, then there's no reason we shouldn't accept donations from them.' With one bound he was free – that was just how modern Britain was. I should have asked a further question on the subject, because his answer might have told us a lot about Tony Blair, but I feared that banging on about pornography risked just sounding priggish. (Why? The general coarsening of everyday life through the proliferation of betting shops, 'gentlemen's clubs' and binge-drinking is surely the concern of politicians.)

On the journey back to the office, it suddenly occurred to me that perhaps *Skinny and Wriggly* was a magazine for worm breeders. My request to check it out must have been one of the oddest assignments ever to be given to a desk producer. I sighed with relief when she told me it was devoted to 'sexy slender lovelies'.

On several occasions Alastair Campbell sat in on my interviews with Tony Blair – once with Blair's son, the two of them scoring the encounter as if it were a football match. New Labour understood that interviews were as much about performance and confidence as they were about facts and policy. Of all the British politicians I have interviewed, Blair was the most capable of thinking on his feet. But he could do facts, too. He had the barrister's ability to master a brief and then to extemporise: when Campbell interrupted an interview to correct a figure his boss had just given for Afghan heroin production, Blair muttered, 'Well, that was what it said in the brief.' I checked later. Blair was the one who had been right. He had begun that day having breakfast with the Canadian Foreign Minister, then chaired a Cabinet meeting, and after our interview was lunching with the Polish Prime Minister. He was now doing three half-hour interviews on foreign policy, domestic policy and political objectives back-to-back. His command of detail in such circumstances was remarkable.

Eventually, this ability to absorb information and then to seem to be speaking from the heart (George Burns's celebrated advice that 'Once you can fake sincerity, you've got it made') made Blair think he could walk on water. Notoriously, his last years in Downing Street were overshadowed by his calamitous relationship with George W. Bush and the invasion of Iraq, which cost hundreds of thousands of lives, including those of nearly two hundred of his fellow citizens. Time will doubtless dull the findings of the investigation into Blair's decision to take the country to war, but it will never negate the judgement that he acted on flawed intelligence and inadequate legal advice, and failed to plan for the consequences of destroying the regime of Saddam Hussein. Many lives were snuffed out because, having given Bush a promise that he would be with him 'whatever', Blair preferred to use force rather than to exhaust all the peaceful ways of trying to get the dictator to disarm. It's no good running for high office if you allow the public to see your doubts. But once you can't recognise them yourself, you can do some very foolish things indeed.

Where did that cavalier disregard come from? Tony Blair always seemed more of a religious figure than a politician – he once talked about bearing 'the scars on my back' from attempts to reform the public sector. It was as if he believed in the mortification of the flesh. There was something of the masochist about him: before the Iraq War he had been willing to debate the issue with a room full of largely hostile people we had assembled in Gateshead. Having no evidence otherwise, I had to take at face value his assurance in that discussion that he did not pray with Bush. In the context of his attitude and his subsequent behaviour it was a justified enquiry. Like all of us, Tony Blair had many failings and made some serious misjudgements. But you had to admire his willingness to be held accountable for his beliefs.

The man with whom Blair struck his deal to lead the Labour Party after the death of John Smith in 1994 was a different kettle of fish. As Chancellor of the Exchequer he too believed his own propaganda, notably the nonsense about 'ending boom and bust' and how the Private Finance Initiative was somehow good for the taxpayer: say anything often enough, and it can enter your soul.

In the mid-nineties, when I first interviewed him, Gordon Brown was Shadow Chancellor of the Exchequer. There was no doubting his passion for social justice, or his intelligence – even though he made a point of telling me off-camera about the time he had been watching *University Challenge* as a student and been astonished when a question beginning with the words 'A shortage of Osage orange wood on the prairies …' was interrupted by a student from Oxford shouting 'Barbed wire!' before the rest of the sentence was out. Brown had concluded that he wasn't quick enough to compete himself.

At one of the party conferences before the election which brought Labour to power in 1997, we tried to get a sit-down interview with him about the party's alternative economic strategy, and were refused. Then someone recalled that Brown had written a biography of James Maxton, the brooding 1920s 'Red Clydesider' MP. Perhaps, we asked Ed Balls, his economic adviser, Brown might like to give an interview which dealt with both the state of the economy and the life and times of Maxton? Yes, he would. Tomorrow morning in the conference hotel?

We began, of course, by talking about the current state of the economy, not merely because it was the most topical subject, but also because it was the one Brown did not want to deal with, for some reason. After a few minutes an aide who had been sitting out of shot stood up and interrupted with, 'Right, that's it! Time's up.'

'But we haven't finished yet,' I said.

'Doesn't matter. You've had your time.'

Brown gave me a withering stare and said, 'You didn't even mention James Maxton.'

'I was just about to get to him,' I protested.

'This is just typical of the way you people behave,' the Shadow Chancellor spat out, with what appeared genuine venom.

It was only years later that the talk of Brown's 'psychological flaws' began, after his uncontrollable temper, conspiracy theories and obsession with micro-management of the media became common knowledge. It turned out later that Brown and Balls had spent hours mugging up on James Maxton and the Red Clydesiders, under the impression – said Balls – that they would form the greater part of the interview. If that was genuinely what his memory told him, he had been either wilfully blind or astonishingly naïve: not to have dealt with what was happening in the economy would have been derelict.

On other occasions Brown, who had once been a television reporter himself, could be quite astonishingly charming. Just about the first serious economic decision that the incoming Labour government took in 1997 was to allow the Bank of England to set interest rates, free of political interference. This was bold and wise and completely unexpected, and I was sent to number 11 Downing Street to interview the new Chancellor of the Exchequer about it. I found him in a cheerful mood, and before we sat down to do the interview he took me on a tour of the building.

'This is my study,' he said, sweeping his arm around a little room dominated by a large table, 'where I'll write the Budget … And that door there goes into the Chief Whip's Office, I think.' He tried the handle, and when the door opened, a doorman greeted him with, 'Welcome to number 12 Downing Street, Chancellor.' (There is an internal corridor running from number 12, through number 11, to 10 Downing Street. It was characteristic of Blair's tenancy that much of number 12 was soon colonised by Alastair Campbell and his team of media mavens.)

After Labour's election in 1997 Gordon Brown seemed like a delighted young child given the run of a toyshop. But the longer he remained in Downing Street – either as Chancellor, or later as Prime Minister – the less he seemed to enjoy it, and certainly the less willing he was to spend time with the media. During the three years he was Prime Minister, he avoided interviews with us. He was quite entitled to do so, though Downing Street contacts told tales of a horrible working environment in which people were shouted at and things were occasionally thrown. Brown seemed tortured by having accomplished what he had set out to achieve.

The contrast with his friend and colleague Tony Blair could hardly have been plainer. Blair loved risk, and was eventually undone by it. Brown did not, and was undone by that. Of course a Prime Minister has a democratic legitimacy that journalists do not have, and he or she is perfectly entitled to choose who they talk to, and when. But the danger in ducking dealings with the media is that the longer you do so, the bigger a deal it becomes. Stories begin to appear in the press suggesting nervousness, and people expect their Prime Ministers to be made of sterner stuff. When the 2010 general election came around, Brown could put us off no longer. In person, he always strikes you as a man not really at home in his own skin (but then, people used to say that about me), and the short time we had together before the exchange, which was shot in an empty office block in Paddington, was awkward.

Things got more tricky once the interview was under way. 'Why don't people like you?' I asked, at which Brown struggled to force his expression into a smile when he clearly – and understandably – wanted to punch my teeth out. He could only mutter, 'You're such a nice guy, Jeremy.' This, I think, was the unkindest question I ever asked, for it has no satisfactory answer: deny it and you look smug, try to explain it away and you look weak. 'It's not my job to be liked. It's my job to be able to make this country better,' is perhaps the only form of words that might have worked.

You wouldn't ask such a question in a normal social relationship. But however much they may appear to be conversations, interviews are not part of a normal social relationship. Did I feel shitty asking it? Yes. Do I wish I hadn't asked it? Yes. A cantankerous, irritating media obviously makes for a better democracy than a bunch of lickspittles. All governments assume that they know best, and arrogance is the default position for most politicians. (How often do you hear one of them say, 'Gosh, I might be wrong'?)

But there is an arrogance to the way the media behave, too. There had been occasional 'Who do they think they are?' outbursts from politicians before.

But as time went by I became increasingly troubled. To psych yourself up for a big interview you must believe that your questions are worth asking, and that they're entitled to an answer. Yet the opening tussle in an interview to establish the terms of engagement had started to seem a bit fatuous. It reached a very silly state when David Cameron ran for the Tory leadership in 2005, in a week when the party was agonising over young British people's drinking habits. I opened by asking him, 'Do you know what a Pink Pussy is?' An 'Umm …' came forth, which I silenced with, 'Do you know what a Slippery Nipple is?' Cameron then twigged that they were both cocktails served at £8 a jug in bars belonging to a company of which he had been a director. I could – and did – defend the questions later, though Cameron harboured a grudge about them for years. And really, what was gained?

Many of my most enjoyable interviews weren't with politicians at all. The obvious questions are always best (though they are often also the easiest to forget to ask). Wasn't Richard Dawkins' passionate belief in science akin to religious conviction? How did Daniel Barenboim remember all of Beethoven's piano sonatas? Didn't Major Tim Peake fear that spending six months floating around in a metal tube in space might be a little bit, er, boring? These were the enquiries which drew the intriguing responses, not yet another recitation of political intentions.

Much though editors, producers, reporters and – most especially – managers like to maintain that the editorial principles of the electronic media are Olympian and unchanging, the fact is that fine thoughts are less important than technological feasibility: if you cannot see and hear someone say something, it might just as well not have been said. So there is a consistent trend in television that what has been shown to be technically possible soon becomes editorially imperative. The Vietnam War was reported by correspondents whose despatches were frequently recorded on film and then 'pigeoned' out of the country in the luggage of a passenger on an aeroplane. The film might be processed and edited in Hong Kong, before being sent to London. By the time the report was broadcast in Britain, the words and pictures were often at least twenty-four hours old. Today, if the story is thought important enough, the reporter appears live on the *Ten O'Clock News* from the scene of the action. It makes for greater immediacy. Whether it makes for better understanding is another question.

The easiest country from which to report is the United States, since just about every town seems to have a television station, and no one questions the (self) importance of the media. Reporting from America was considered one of the most desirable assignments, and was rarely given to the programme presenter. But even if you were unlucky enough to find that, understandably, the editor felt that a presenter ought actually to be available to present the show, rather than being off on the road somewhere, you were at least guaranteed a trip to Washington every four years, when the United States chose a new President. Embarrassingly large numbers of BBC people made the trip, though there was generally a good reason for most of them to be there, given the corporation's huge number of outlets, from programmes in Farsi to pop radio channels. Entire floors of hotels were hired, though the senior managers who had decided that their presence was essential, even though unconnected with anything being broadcast, generally stayed somewhere rather smarter.

Apart from George W. Bush's protracted attempt in 2000 to win the presidency through the law courts, these were generally pretty short visits, with much of the programme being delivered from the roof of an office building overlooking the White House. Although every presenter liked to give the impression that they had exclusive access to this plum position, you were generally standing along-side Norwegians, Japanese, Indonesians, Swiss and reporters from many more countries, all of them explaining the workings of democracy through clouds of hairspray and earnestness.

The first day of coverage of presidential elections was generally pretty straightforward. When Barack Obama became the first African-American to win the White House in 2008, our producer, Shaminder Nahal, decided it would be intriguing to ask on the second day how long it might be before Britain had a black Prime Minister. Valerie Amos, a one-time Chief Executive of the Equal Opportunities Commission who had been sent to the House of Lords by Tony Blair, agreed to discuss the subject down the line from London. The other guest was the rapper Dizzee Rascal. Grime being a style of music unknown to most *Newsnight* viewers (and presenters), Rascal was an unusual, amusing booking. Since the programme's rather buttoned-up style generally involved calling people Mr or Mrs, or Lord or Lady this or that, his presence raised an entertaining question of etiquette. To call guests by their first names suggests to viewers a relationship from which they are excluded. For all her time in Equal Opportunities, Valerie Amos would expect to be called 'Baroness', or at least 'Lady Amos'. Would it not be patronising to call Dizzee Rascal by his first name? But it seemed odd to call him 'Mr Rascal'.

Midway through the discussion, Amos raised the question of Britishness being something 'we don't talk about in the UK'. This led to the 'Mr Rascal, do you consider yourself British?' question, to which he answered, 'Of course I'm British, man!' Unfortunately, as it was a recorded interview, someone in London was able to edit the discussion and then release clips to the media as 'an interview about Obama's election with Dizzee Rascal'. Out of context, the question about whether he considered himself British looked tantamount to racism. I was very embarrassed. But several months later Mr Rascal's agent called. His client was appearing at

Glastonbury. Would I mind if he went on stage to the *Newsnight* theme tune and then introduced himself as 'Mr Rascal here.' I've bumped into him a couple of times since, so occasionally I get the chance to greet him again with 'Good evening, Mr Rascal.'

Something quite unexpected – but, when you think about it, quite predictable – happens when you present yourself, uninvited, in people's sitting rooms. Viewers form an opinion about you, and sometimes they let you know what it is, however mad. 'I shall get straight to the point, Jeremy,' a letter from a man in Edgware began. 'I am having a party at my house on December 5th and you have simply GOT to be there.' He had promised his neighbours that the party would be over by 10 p.m., 'but if you get too drunk and lose track of time, you can stay over in the spare room'. Unfortunately I already had an engagement that evening.

God knows what would have happened had I turned up on his doorstep. It is a false familiarity. Human beings are unsophisticated creatures, and can only really cope with one idea of a person at a time: nuance comes from proper acquaintance, not the bogus electronic intimacy of television. I first became aware of this monocular impression when I was buying some apples from a market stall before I had even begun working on *Newsnight*. 'I know who you are, don't I, guv?' said the man on the stall. I began to stumble through where I lived, to be interrupted with, 'Don't tell me!' I stood in embarrassed silence, waiting for him to answer his own question. 'Yeah. You're the bloke off the telly.' There was a pause while he checked that his synapses were firing properly. 'Yeah, you're the 'orrible one.' There were plenty of similar observations, by post or email, usually objecting to robust interviews. 'I suggest you look in the mirror and ask if you're the fairest of them all,' wrote a woman from Oxford. 'I suggest most definitely not.'

Appear in any capacity on television, and pretty soon you start getting letters from local charities asking you to give something to auctions they're running. It's exhilarating to realise quite what a vast number of people there are doing good around the country – I found that books I had written and signed, or ties in which I had 'presented' a programme, were suitable for auctions, and I needed two or three recipes for all the fund-raising recipe books being compiled. People send you birthday, Christmas and Valentine's Day cards, and anyone feels free to tell you their opinion of you:

Sir,
I think you are an ignorant lout

was the entire text of a letter from a Dr Ward of Newry, County Down.

Then come the invitations to appear on daytime television or radio shows. After that are the requests from national charities to become a patron or to speak at a fund-raiser. Around the same time you begin to notice your name in the newspapers, attached to inconsequential bits of gossip, and quite often to entirely made-up stories. It is at about this point that you begin to develop a certain caution at social gatherings. You are having a private conversation when you suddenly realise there is an extra ear involved, often belonging to someone from a gossip column. For a couple of years I was hated by bird-lovers because I was once seated across the table from an Icelandic woman at lunch and confessed my ambition to eat the Icelandic delicacy, smoked puffin. 'You must go meet my father,' she said. 'He is puffin strangler. He will take you.' My eagerness to experience a field sport I had never dreamed existed was all over the following day's papers. The death threats from puffin-fanciers had just abated when, discussing the plague of cats in West London, I suggested at another party that we ought to form a pack of cat-hounds, and meet for stirrup cups on Shepherd's Bush Green in bright-blue jackets for the occasional morning of moggy-mauling. It was over a year before the hate mail from cat-lovers died down. Rule one: newsdesks don't like humour.

Rule two: just ignore what they say about you, good or bad. I was once sufficiently irritated by some garbage in the *News of the World* to consult lawyers. But, having paid a bill of almost £6,000 for two meetings and a QC's opinion and been told, 'We reckon there's a 90 per cent chance of victory' if I was prepared to wait a year and a half for the case to come to court, then to face a 10 per cent chance of losing and certainly to see the whole thing ventilated again, I decided that on the whole, it was better just to let it lie.

If you have a gappy memory you can fail to recognise the danger signs of a looming tabloid attack. At the launch party for a friend's book a woman in a strange green trouser suit asked how my insomnia was, and I listed the remedies I had tried – hypnosis, sedatives, breathing techniques and much more, none of which worked – only to see the next day that I had 'poured my heart out' to the *Daily Mail*. I should have realised that I didn't know anyone likely to turn up to such an event dressed like a badly tied party balloon.

Then there are the invitations to play yourself on television and to appear on chat shows, talent contests and reality shows. I declined to go on *Desert Island Discs*, *Celebrity Big Brother*, *Have I Got News for You* and *Strictly Come Dancing*. I had no ideological objection to any of them. At the time, I just couldn't see the point. I did accept an invitation to play myself in a Bridget Jones movie, because I had never been on a film set. It turned out to be in an office block just off the North Circular, and while everyone was exceptionally friendly, the morning seemed to last forever. There is no rhyme or reason to these invitations. They have nothing to do with whatever talent you may or may not possess. They're just the consequence of having a recognisable face, which is, in the end, most of what being a 'celebrity' is.

The relationship between the viewer and the media 'personality' is entirely vacuous, the antithesis of real life, which is perhaps why people sometimes do not recognise the boundaries of polite conversation. Out of the blue one day I received an email from a woman in outer Manchester which read, 'Dear Mr Paxman, I really think you should stop dying your hair.' My hair at the time was quickly turning grey.

'I DON'T dye my hair,' I replied. 'If I did, do you honestly imagine I'd choose to colour it grey?'

To which she replied, 'Of course you dye your hair. My father is your age, and he dyes his hair.' Her logic reminded me of the famous false syllogism:

All cats have four legs.
All dogs have four legs.
Therefore my dog is a cat.

There was nothing more to be said. But the impression that I might choose to tint my hair grey is not uncommon. 'For God's sake, what's with the hair? It looks RIDICULOUS. Leave that sort of thing to those as false and weird as Tony Blair,' wrote Bob March from WC1.

A rather frank man in Maida Vale began his letter by saying, 'I suffer from a potato allergy and usually when I wake up, I send someone a stinking letter about Europe ...' before going on to outline just where I had gone wrong on Brussels. 'Last night I dreamed we were in bed together,' another letter began. 'You began by kissing me passionately and then you sucked my nipples. You ran your tongue down my stomach,' it continued, going on in total for seven pages, in ever more graphic detail, until it reached its climax in a series of out-of-context biblical quotations, each only a few words long but instantly recognisable as the work of a Jehovah's Witness. Though she was taking an unusual route to finding it, the anonymous author wanted to save my soul.

One of the oddest pieces of mail was a big cardboard box which arrived in October 2000. I had been away filming for a few days, and arrived back in the office to be met by David Sells – by a long margin the oldest reporter on *Newsnight* (he had covered the 1956 Suez Crisis) – who asked me to remove the great parcel by his desk which had been sent to me. He kept tripping over it. I borrowed a pair of scissors from the unit manager and cut through the many layers of brown sticky tape covering the box. Inside, there was an overwhelming smell of old-fashioned lubricating oil. Digging into the packaging I reached a wooden box, which I lifted out. As I opened its hinged top I joked to a colleague, 'Maybe it's a bomb.' 'Don't be silly,' said the office manager. 'All your mail is X-rayed.'

The security X-ray machine had failed to register anything at all suspicious about a collection of bits of metal, wires and cylinders inside a tightly-bound parcel. It might have been a typewriter that the wooden box contained, but because I had seen one before, I recognised it as a Nazi Enigma code machine. There then followed half an hour of the sort of silliness of which only a well-meaning organisation like the BBC is capable. 'We won't be reporting this,' said a senior figure. 'Why on earth not?' I asked. 'There's a news blackout,' he replied.

What he knew, and I did not, was that the machine had been stolen six months previously from the museum at Bletchley Park, the secret wartime 'Station X' code-breaking establishment. A fortnight earlier there had been a ransom demand for its safe return – there were only two surviving such machines in the world. I called the boss of the museum and told her that, for reasons I did not understand, someone had sent me her missing exhibit. She said she was delighted, though her excitement seemed strangely muted. That night we reported what had happened, of course, and a couple of policemen turned up to take the thing away, and a couple more to turn my account of events into the requisite 'I was proceeding in a northerly direction' police-statement idiom. A year later a Nottinghamshire antiques dealer who said he had been acting for a mysterious figure in India known as 'the Master' was sentenced to ten months in prison for handling stolen goods. Why the device had been sent to me I can only surmise. Whoever put it in the post must have been confident that its arrival was bound to become public, thus scotching any talk of its having been destroyed.

Nothing is off-limits to the public. I had grown a beard, for example, during several summer holidays, but had always shaved it off at the beginning of September. But in 2013, when I returned to work I suddenly thought, 'Why?' The BBC is – or was then (this was before the hipster beard became omnipresent) – pogonophobic, restricting facial hair to Uncle Albert on *Only Fools and Horses*, Demis Roussos and various fundamentalist bigots. The first night I presented *Newsnight* with a beard, it trended on Twitter and appeared in all the newspapers. Whether this indicates the innate triviality of the medium, the innate triviality of the audience, or the innate triviality of the commentators who accuse television of triviality, is a matter of taste.

Underpants, though, are a much more serious matter. I was getting dressed in the gym one morning in January 2008 when, as I put my leg through my Y-fronts, the elastic came away from the cotton. 'Any of you blokes had any trouble with pants?' I asked of the other changers. There was a general feeling that there had been something of a falling off in Marks & Spencer underwear in particular. My father used frequently to insist that Marks & Spencer had done more for ordinary people than Karl Marx and Herbert Spencer ever achieved. I was therefore in no doubt of the potential importance of a perceived pants failure, and emailed Stuart Rose, the chief executive, that afternoon, not to complain but to warn him of what might be a looming crisis. He replied immediately, saying, 'Come to lunch. Not just any lunch, an M&S

lunch. Bring your pants.' Nimble PR, I thought, and showed the email to the producer of that evening's programme as an example of how to manage customer relations. This was a silly mistake, for the producer in question had a voice like a foghorn and all the discretion of a neon advertising hoarding at Piccadilly Circus. As I ought to have predicted, he duly regaled other producers with the story.

A couple of days later came the inevitable call from the *Mail on Sunday*. 'I gather you've complained to Marks & Spencer that their pants don't give you adequate support.' It wasn't quite true, but it was true enough. I could see that it made an entertaining piece, and it got the whole of page three that Sunday. In the aftermath, the pants story went global – I was even emailed about it from Dunedin in New Zealand, twelve thousand miles away. Members of Deep Purple and ABBA called to ask if they could join the Campaign for Better Pants. People stopped me in the street to say 'Good on yer, mate!' In St James's Square a couple in their sixties accosted me: 'You are the man has problem wiz his pants, I zink. We read about you in ze newspaper in Switzerland.'

For weeks I was inundated with brown paper parcels from manufacturers and underwear enthusiasts. Each time I returned to the office the pile of boxer shorts, Y-fronts, briefs, thermal pants and even woollen versions of what used to be called 'coms' had grown a little higher. A New Zealand company called Ball Control sent some of their products, proclaiming that they had been treated with an 'antimicrobial agent', 'to ensure your gear stays fresh'. Friends from Canada, Australia and South Africa were in touch with sensational tales of Commonwealth underwear – the only continent untouched by the story seemed to be Antarctica. But most bizarre of all were the letters from total strangers, who frequently sent in their own underwear. Reader, there are some very strange things being worn under the trousers you pass in the street.

The story went through the usual predictable phases, from the initial (quite funny) piece in the *Mail on Sunday* to pickups by other newspapers and broadcasters, then to the wisdom dispensed by commentators and profilers, a characteristic of which is that no one ever bothers to call you for an answer to their question (What possessed him to make such a fuss about pants?), because they prefer to lay out their own theory (e.g. He's gone mad). Stuart Rose gave an interview to *The Times*, asserting that the real problem wasn't his pants, but the fact that as men get older, their balls hang lower. The Controller of BBC 2 suggested that I launch my own brand of underwear, and at a charity auction Rory Bremner flogged a 'similar' pair of Y-fronts for £1,400. My brother Giles, at the time the British Ambassador in Mexico, found that the first thing the Environment Minister there asked him when they met was whether he had any intelligence on The Great Pants Issue.

After several weeks the story – and the avalanche of underwear – abated a little, and I judged it safe enough to contact Stuart Rose again and see if the offer of lunch was still, as it were, on the table. It was. Rose had assembled the Head of Pants, the Head of Socks and the Head of PR in the company's new headquarters in Paddington. There was a Monet print on one wall and a Lowry on another. Before we could eat there was a demonstration of a Heath Robinson contraption which tested the elasticity and support strength of socks – it looked rather like a prosthetic leg with various winches attached. After ten minutes, Rose said, 'This is a bit boring, isn't it? Let's go to the table.' We sat down to sea bream, salad and a glass of white wine.

I had hardly lifted the first forkful before there was a knock at the door, and through it came a bronzed, muscled and well-endowed young man. The odd thing about this young man was that he was wearing nothing but a pair of underpants.

'Ah, Remko, come in. What are you wearing there?' asked Rose nonchalantly.

The young man explained that they were cotton Y-fronts.

'Let Mr Paxman have a closer look,' Rose said, and I laid down the mouthful of fish I had been anticipating as the model came to stand with his groin at my right shoulder.

'Have a feel of the cotton,' said Rose. Never having handled another man's pants – especially when he was inside them – I declined the invitation. The young man left the room, and I picked up the forkful of fish.

Two mouthfuls later there was another knock at the door. This time the model was wearing the skimpiest of red briefs. There followed much discussion between him and Stuart Rose about technical aspects of the pair of pants in question, in which the key word was 'access'.

Three minutes later he was back again, this time wearing a pair of boxer shorts. 'Do let Mr Paxman have a good close look,' said Rose.

And so it went on until we got to pudding. It was the oddest meal I have ever attended, and – as Rose had predicted – 'not just any lunch'. The effect of 'Pantsgate' had been measured in lost sales to M&S, and they had got revenge of sorts. Rose explained the real challenge the company faced: that particular young man may have had the precise specifications for their underwear, but most men – fat or thin, tall or short – expect to find pants that fit them. It was, so to speak, a tall order.

It took me another few weeks before I realised the true cause of the problem with which I had embarrassed the boss of M&S. Once your pants have been through the wash a few times, you have no idea how old they are. As I have since discovered – because I had to buy my underwear elsewhere for a while – it doesn't matter what brand they are, eventually all pants just start to fall apart. Who knows how much of the nation is wearing elderly underwear? It should all be sold with a 'best before' date.

* * *

Another of the dangerous consequences of appearing on television is that, unless you are very careful, you enter that hall of mirrors which distorts the perceptions of so many people in public life. You might easily start to take yourself seriously. What was I to make, for example, of an invitation to lunch with the Princess of Wales in her private apartments in Kensington Palace, where she greeted me with, 'Jeremy! So nice of you to come. Just the two of us. Can you cope?' – as if I were in the habit of dropping in to dine with royalty. The experience was never repeated, though a few years later Prince Charles invited me to stay with him for a couple of days at Sandringham. Again, we turned out not to have much in common, though seeing some of my fellow guests simpering to their host was rather revealing. The Crown Prince of Belgium (now the King of the Belgians) invited me to tea at the London Embassy to discuss an issue that was bothering him. He was impressed by the way Britain had handled immigration and race relations.

'We have a lot of Moroccans in Belgium,' he said. 'Do you think we should give them the vote?'

I told him I thought it might be a start.

I have no excuse beyond curiosity for accepting an invitation to lunch from the former Prime Minister, Sir Edward Heath. It was to take place one November Sunday at the beautiful house he had bought in the shadow of Salisbury's sublime cathedral. There were about a dozen of us, including the Conservative Chief Whip in the Commons and his wife, plus a couple of businessmen who I imagined to be party donors. All the men wore dark suits, white shirts and ties. Heath entered the room where we were being offered drinks wearing moulded grey shoes, duck-egg-blue trousers and a hooped red, white and blue jumper carrying the logo 'Superbowl Souvenir'. He worked the room, saying hello to everyone, but was clearly already bored. As a waitress filled my glass I heard him say to her, 'How long?'

She replied, 'About ten minutes I think, Sir Edward.'

'Well,' he grumbled, 'hurry it up.'

Lunch was a pretty standard roast beef and Yorkshire pudding. With some relief I found myself at the opposite end of a long table from my host, seated next to a very nice woman who was acting as his hostess for the day. 'I'm sorry about the colour scheme,' she said. 'I tried to make some suggestions, but he was determined to make it look as if the place had been decorated by someone from the Foreign Office.' Coffee was to be served in the drawing room, where every surface was covered in silver-framed photographs of the former Prime Minister with world leaders, or studio photos of the potentates themselves. I noticed that whenever he sat down to play the piano Heath seemed fated to gaze at a photo of Sultan Qaboos of Oman.

As we walked into the room, he accosted me. 'Do you know what our trade balance is with China?'

I made the mistake of pausing for a moment. 'Umm ...'

'No, of course you don't!' he snapped, turned on his heel and went off to find someone else to talk to. He was right. I hadn't a clue. I went for a walk around the cathedral.

If Heath had been genuinely curious to find out about trade with China, he might have invited any one of dozens of authorities on the subject, just as the future King of the Belgians might have had tea with someone who really understood immigration and citizenship policy. But – on those occasions at least – they did not. It would be easy to get your head turned by having Important People ask your opinion, even on subjects about which you know virtually nothing. Though I had justified accepting these invitations on the grounds that to do so would satisfy my curiosity, perhaps my head really had been turned. How congenial seems the embrace of the Establishment!

Having never felt I truly belonged anywhere, I had been very lucky to find an occupation, an employer and an outlet which opened doors, while not requiring too many concessions on my part. But rubbing shoulders eventually removes all spikiness. Britain's mainstream media devote most of their energy to reporting upon mainstream issues as seen by mainstream institutions – like reports by committees of MPs on how the government has handled the country's housing shortage. They do not see how immensely remote MPs and the government are from the lives of great numbers of people, and that affordable housing is unfindable in many areas of the country. Those who report upon politics and those who practise politics inhabit the same social world. It is not the world lived in by most voters.

Soon after he finished his second term as US President, I went to New York to interview Bill Clinton. Men and women running for the White House don't much bother to undergo interviews with the foreign press, for the simple reason that we don't appear to be able to deliver any votes.* But soon after he left office, like all of his recent predecessors, Clinton set about trying to secure his place in history. Edward Heath's attempts to see that his house in Salisbury's Cathedral Close became a shrine to himself seemed very homespun by comparison. Bill Clinton had decided that the foundation bearing his name would tackle a great range of worldwide problems, from fighting preventable diseases to empowering girls and women – you certainly could not accuse it of lack of ambition.

Whatever it is that Clinton has got (and it is certainly more than the aroma of power) would be worth a fortune to anyone who could bottle it. I have seen many powerful men and women close up – Indira Gandhi (brave and not to be crossed), Benazir Bhutto (also brave, but she somehow considered her country a family

---

* Once a President is in office, if a group of foreign correspondents in Washington get together and are persistent enough, there is a chance that they may be granted a collective interview. These tend to get precisely nowhere, because the focus is all over the place.

business), Hillary Clinton (a toughie, but vulnerable to a bit of flirting), Valéry Giscard d'Estaing (all sophisticated, supercilious charm), Mikhail Gorbachev (resolute but sensible), to say nothing of a host of European Prime Ministers and Presidents. Power gives people a kind of patina. But Clinton had something special. Of course he commanded the crowded room in Harlem where we were meeting. But there was something more, a sort of animal magnetism. Over half of the people in the room were young women, and I have yet to meet a woman who has been in a room with Clinton in his prime and would not have gone to bed with him if he asked. But it was more than sexual magnetism. They *believed*, with that radiant joy you see in evangelical churches on the faces of people who think they've been 'saved'.

Clinton was also quite remarkably fluent. At the end of our interview, as we were sitting making small talk (he rather liked the tie I was wearing, and wanted to know if it came from Thomas Pink), one of his aides asked if they could please borrow our camera. I said it was up to the cameraman, who agreed that he would film whatever it was they wanted to record. The aide had scripts for two video contributions to be played at conventions to which Clinton had been invited, but which he wasn't attending. The former President took out his glasses, looked at the first script, put it in his pocket and then declaimed from memory how sorry he was that he wasn't able to be present at the Biloxi orthodontists' convention. The speech took little more than thirty seconds, and it sounded as if every word had just come into his mind as he thought about what a fine job was being done by the dentists of Mississippi. The second script was much longer – a couple of sides of paper addressed to another convention he sadly wasn't able to attend. Clinton took out his glasses again, scanned the paper and said, 'You seriously expect me to remember all of this?' Then he folded the paper, put it in his pocket and recited the speech to camera – without hesitating, deviating or repeating himself – for what seemed to be a full two minutes. The longest piece-to-camera I have ever perpetrated described the Charge of the Light Brigade, and lasted three minutes. It took me half a dozen attempts to get it right.

9

What is *Torschlusspanik*?*

I was sitting minding my own business in one of the tin sheds on the roof of a BBC building in White City when the phone rang one day in 1994. A voice introduced itself as belonging to an ITV producer. The producer had an idea.

'We've still got the rights to *University Challenge*,' he said. (The show had once been a stalwart of the channel, but had died a lingering death, spending several years being shunted around the schedules. It had not been broadcast for the best part of a decade.) 'We reckon we can sell it to the BBC. Would you be interested in presenting it?'

I knew the show, of course. I even had dim memories that after dinner one night at Cambridge there had been a quiz to choose a team to compete on behalf of the college. If I had managed to tackle any of the questions, the answers had certainly been wrong, and the college was represented by a team of four memorably described by my friend Andrew Nickolds as 'geographers now doing well in Saskatchewan'. (They weren't, and aren't, but the description caught something of the college.) In those days *University Challenge* was a sort of national institution, on which clever young people with home-made jumpers and odd haircuts showed off how much they

---

* Gate-shutting panic – a sense of alarm at the passing of life's opportunities.

knew. The question master, Bamber Gascoigne, had presented the show since 1962, when I was twelve years old. He was a tall, thin, bespectacled toff, possessed of a languid Etonian charm. It was a mark of how little ITV valued the show that the entire set appeared to be built out of nasty beige carpet.

'Might you be interested?' the producer repeated. I was both flattered and fearful. You do not get offered pieces of the nation's cultural furniture very often, yet part of me sensed that I would only suffer by comparison with Bamber Gascoigne, who seemed to eat dictionaries for breakfast cereal. After thinking it over, I called the producer back. 'It's terribly nice of you to ask me,' I said, 'but it's Bamber Gascoigne's show, and I think you should ask him.'

'Times have changed,' he replied. 'The zeitgeist is different.'

'Well,' I said, 'that's your call. But you really ought to offer it to Bamber, so I think I'm out.'

A week or so later I was in the glorious old Reading Room at the British Museum. With its great dome and leather-topped desks radiating out like the spokes of a wheel, it was the sort of place where you could doze away the whole afternoon and still be convinced you were becoming wiser. Though fully half of the people working there were clearly insane, it felt as if any writer of note in the last 150 years, from Marx and Gandhi to Shaw and Orwell, had worked there: you could sense their ghosts. I looked up from my snooze and saw Bamber Gascoigne standing by the inquiry desk. I walked over.

'We've never met,' I said, 'but I think you ought to know that Granada believe they can make *University Challenge* and sell the shows to the BBC. They're looking for a presenter, and if you're interested, you should get in there.'

'Oh yes,' he said. 'They rang me about that about six months ago, but I don't like the sound of it. Too much like hard work.'

So much for the changing zeitgeist. I called the producer back.

* * *

Mercifully, they had not found anyone else in the intervening period, and a few weeks later I travelled to the 1960s office block which was the headquarters of Granada Television in Manchester. (Most of what used to be Granada productions now come from a rented building in the wilderness of Salford docks.) There I met the man who had invented the format (as a way of keeping troops entertained during World War II), a charming old Canadian, Don Reid, who was thrilled to see his invention taking to television again – its American counterpart, *College Bowl*, had been off-air for years. He gave us one invaluable piece of advice, which was at all costs to keep the five-point penalty for incorrect interruptions to starter questions. The producers had been planning to remove it as an unnecessary complication, but he was right – it brings an additional sense of jeopardy to the contest.

The first series was duly filmed, and was won by a team from Trinity College, Cambridge, captained by a man called Kwasi Kwarteng who seemed to know everything there was to be knowed. Not a single member of the production team noticed that on several occasions his conferring with fellow team members had been punctuated by a whispered, 'Oh fuck, I've forgotten.' Viewers, unfortunately, were less cloth-eared. At the time I too had not noticed, and had just thought, 'What a great advertisement to young black people,' imagining he had fought his way up from an inner-city housing estate. After recording the final, I asked him where he had gone to school. Without batting an eyelid he replied, 'Colet Court and Eton.' His origins turned out to lie in West African royalty.

The other day I read a comment by Kwasi – now an MP sitting for a safe Conservative seat in Surrey – about my style on the show: 'One often got the impression that he didn't know what he was talking about, but he always said the answer with great authority.' The authority is for others to judge. But as far as content went, he was spot on. I do my best to get my head around the questions, but a Grade E Physics O Level is no solid foundation for asking questions about science at this level. The vital ability when bluffing is the capacity to understand what is an acceptable near-miss. It's easy enough if someone says 'Sixty-six per cent' when what you were expecting was 'Two-thirds.' It is much more tricky when dealing with scientific properties.

Since much of the production team was similarly badly equipped, briefing sessions were arranged with two scientists, Neville Cohen, a Liverpudlian physics lecturer, and Stan Shaw, a biologist from Manchester, before each recording block. Neville was a wiry, bearded man who spent his weekends wearing garish waterproof clothing and scrambling about on the moors. Had there been any meat other than gristle on him, Stan could have eaten three of Neville, for Stan was round and jolly and slow to anger. The sessions with the two of them went on for hours. 'Oh no, Neville,' Stan might say. 'I think you'll find that there's a confusion here between the general two-dimensional convection-diffusion equation and the Fokker-Planck equation.' The hours spent trying to grasp concepts like this, locked in an airless room with only a wilting ham sandwich for company, were some of the longest in human history.

The first show we recorded was a disaster. In recognition of the supposed new zeitgeist it pitted the University of North London against New College, Oxford. The New College team consisted of four terrifyingly clever young men, two of whom were, I think, Rhodes Scholars. There had been some difficulty with the North London team, since – in a sign of how little the zeitgeist there had changed since the sixties – the place was in the throes of a student occupation when the invitation to appear on the programme arrived. The business of choosing a team is the responsibility of the student body, and the only duty of the academic authorities is to certify that they are all genuine students: it had taken ages to make contact with the besieged administrators. The four from North

London were all women, including a feminist stand-up comedian who had changed her name to 'Viv Acious'. I looked at them and predicted trouble – they'd probably claim the questions were phallocentric. The young men from New College settled into their seats with a comfortable look of intellectual ascendancy (well-merited, as it turned out, since they went on to emerge runners-up in the entire series). One of them was even wearing a blazer.

To my delight, the first starter question was won by North London. I picked up the first card off the pile of three-part bonus questions. Even better – it was an easy one. 'How many permanent members are there on the UN Security Council?' The North Londoners conferred eagerly, but the captain was so anxious to hear all points of view that they seemed to have no way of reaching a decision. Over the microphones you could hear the number of countries being talked up. They were always having elections to the Security Council, weren't they? Their agreed final total was enormous.

'I'm terribly sorry,' I said. 'The correct answer is five. I expect you were thinking of the *total* membership of the Security Council, which as far as I recall is fifteen.'

I looked down at the card. The second bonus question read: 'What is the *total* membership of the Security Council?'

'I'm terribly sorry, I've made a mess of this,' I spluttered. 'There's no way to salvage it. We'll stop the recording, and I'm going to give you an alternative bonus set.' I reached down to pick the next card off the pile.

'You can't do that!' barked one of the New College team. 'They've already had one bonus question, so they should only have two more.'

'Look,' I said, 'this is the very first show we've recorded. We're obviously going to have to edit out the first bonus question. If I only offer them two bonus questions instead of three, the audience won't have a clue what's happening. Please, will you just accept it?'

'I'm afraid not,' said the New College captain. 'It's not fair.'

I looked at the four young men whose education had set their careers on cruise control for life.

'Look, there are ten points on the board, and the best part of half an hour to play. I'd appreciate it if you just accepted this, and let's get on with the game. It's all my fault, and I'm sorry. But that's all we can do.'

'Well, we're not accepting it.'

Impasse. At this point the producer's voice came in my hidden earpiece. 'Remind them of Rule Nine.'

Rule Nine was the rule that said the rules were whatever we said they were. I remembered, too, that we had a reserve team whose scores on the test paper had not been quite good enough for them to get onto the televised section of the competition, but who lived in hope of a student union minibus being wiped out on the motorway to Manchester. At this moment they were corralled in the horrible little 'hospitality suite', being force-fed Cheesy Wotsits and cans of Boddingtons.

'OK, well, if you won't accept it,' I said, 'we'll just have to get the reserve team in, and they can play instead of you.'

At this point the Oxford team's principled objections evaporated. They went on to steamroller the students of North London, who left the contest with the finest display of good manners and charm, with much thanking of everyone involved. In contrast, I overheard one of the New College team saying to another, 'There's nothing we can do now – everyone hates us.' He was right. But that is the only team I have ever had mixed feelings about on the show.

Periodically some ignoramus asserts that the programme is biased in favour of Oxbridge colleges, or against them, or is anti-Welsh, or something. In fact the only bias is in favour of entertaining television (which – dark secret – is the reason that when we get an occasional long run of unanswered starter questions it gets edited out. No one wants to watch people not knowing things, and viewers are taxpayers and like to think the higher education budget has been well spent). Sometimes you get the sense that the invitation to enter a team never got beyond the office of the student union, since the team seems to be made up of its President, Treasurer, Secretary, and perhaps an associated boyfriend or girlfriend. There are one or two dull institutions which take the thing far too seriously, and coach potential players. But most of the teams have been chosen in competitions of one sort or another, and represent a remarkable range of human types, from the impetuous to the considered, the troublesome to the easygoing. Extroverts tend to be over-represented, but then it *is* a sort of performance. The best teams of the lot are those that want to answer very difficult questions, yet understand the whole thing is only a TV quiz after all. There's not even any money at stake, just a trophy which usually ends up behind the student union bar or propping open a common-room door somewhere.

I love it precisely because the stakes are so small – there's not only no money, but no razzmatazz, no sequins. It is old-fashioned family viewing, watched by young and old, and sparking a thousand competitions in houses across the land every night it is aired. I've no idea whether it's cool or terribly uncool, and I don't care. Most of all, I'm glad Bamber Gascoigne turned the job down, because I like students, enjoy their enthusiasm, and am often astonished by their knowledge. And sometimes by their ignorance. The most entertaining teams are the ones which simultaneously care and don't care. Occasionally, though, we do get someone who becomes overwrought. Once, three quarters of the way through a recording in which four women from one of the Cambridge colleges were failing to demonstrate that they knew anything much (sometimes it just goes that way – you get a couple of tricky questions, buzz in with a wrong answer, and before you know where you are, you're a hundred points behind), one of the team put her hand up. Could we have a break, please, so she could go to the lavatory? I stopped proceedings.

Ten minutes later, she had failed to reappear. We sent the team captain to the ladies, and she too was gone for longer than expected. She finally returned, saying, 'I'm afraid she won't come out.' Since they were so far behind that the outcome wasn't in doubt, I asked if they'd mind playing the remaining few minutes with a three-person team. They were quite happy to do so, but the television audience viewing the eventual broadcast would never have been able to understand why, in the show's signature split-screen shot of the two teams, one of them suddenly only had three members. We were saved by a clever picture editor, who pasted in shots from earlier in the show. If you looked very closely at the team at the top of the screen, the contestant on the right didn't move a millimetre.

If only she'd realised that there is no shame in not knowing answers to very difficult questions. For any contestant who is accused of ignorance for failing to have pressed their buzzer, the perfect rebuttal is to point out that they were there, and their accuser wasn't. The tedious complaint from self-proclaimed 'experts' in middlebrow newspapers (though 'expert television watcher' is surely something of an oxymoron) is that the questions have got easier. This is invariably and thoughtlessly described as meaning that the programme has 'dumbed down'. It is demonstrably false: in fact we have deliberately made the questions harder. In the very first series of the black-and-white *University Challenge* in 1962, one question asked students for the equation in Einstein's Theory of Special Relativity that expressed mass–energy equivalence. We would never ask anything that simple now. (Interestingly, as the questions have got harder, the average audience size has grown; proof that you do not need to treat viewers as idiots.) All knowledge exists in a cultural context, and just as early-twenty-first-century students are more knowledgeable about science than their predecessors, they are also much more ignorant about the Bible and Greek mythology.

The obvious way to disprove accusations that the questions have become easier would be to match winning teams from previous eras against their contemporary equivalents. But that could not really be a fair contest, since mere longevity suggests that older people know more – knowledge should stick to them like flies to flypaper. On the other hand, their reactions are slower. And each time we have invited previous winners to come back to take on the current winners, they have tended to be soundly thrashed.

'Did you enjoy it?' I asked Sir Nicholas Montagu, then the Chairman of the Inland Revenue, after he had led his reunited team from New College, Oxford in a match against younger contestants.

'Terrific fun!' he said. 'But my, times have changed. When I was an undergraduate [in the early sixties], we were sent a first-class rail warrant and accommodated at the Midland Hotel in the centre of Manchester. This time, we were given Supersaver train tickets. And they wanted us to stay in something' – his voice rose in wonderment – 'called a *Travelodge*.'

If only he know how lucky he'd been. The fatted-cow days of television are long gone, and *University Challenge* is probably the cheapest show on prime-time television. The fabled catering provided in the Green Room is reduced to a few packets of crisps and whatever beer Costco happens to have on special offer when the runner is sent down there that week. The students are indeed put up in cheap hotels, although that is a great improvement on the arrangement a few years ago, when they were expected to stay in digs in Salford and strongly advised, 'Don't leave the building after dark.'

And still they come. Each year throws up another phenomenon or two, social media ensuring that their obscure research topic, assertive knowledgeability, quivering on the buzzer or bizarre dress sense at the recording session (which happened months previously) trends on Twitter and enters the newspapers. One evening just before the general election of 2015 I met Dame Judi Dench at the theatre. 'And how is dear Loveday?' was her opening gambit, referring to the Cambridge law student who was that year's intellectual *enfant terrible*, famous for cable-knit jumpers and for correctly answering no fewer than ten starter questions. He was, said the author of the *University Challenge* Cuties blog, 'the definition of a UC cutie'. There's at least one of these cuties every year, though it tends to be the females, like Sarah Fitzpatrick (who went on to become a great panjandrum in Whitehall) or the classicist Gail Trimble (dubbed by the press 'the human Google' for the breadth of her knowledge from Kipling to Kazakh banknotes) who get asked by a tabloid paper whether they'd like to pose wearing nothing but an academic gown and mortarboard.

Unsurprisingly, the certainty of coming to public notice attracts attention-seekers, although mercifully, most of them get seen through straight away. What matters – all that matters – is whether they can answer the questions. Inevitably, though, there are a few each year – blokes in cravats, or girls with too much cleavage on show – who flare up like cheap indoor fireworks in the early rounds, and then quickly fizzle out. On one occasion I was accosted in the Green Room by a female student from Cambridge with the question, 'How can I get your job?'

'Which bit of it do you want?' I asked. 'I'm a journalist. I do this for fun.'

'I don't care,' was her breathtaking reply. 'I just want to be on television.'

She went on to complain that a school contemporary of hers was now 'showing off the prizes' on a Saturday-night game show. 'I look at her and I think, "That could have been me!" Life's *so* unfair!'

It is sometimes hard to convey the frenetic urgency of the news business.

This photograph is credited to the production team of *Who Do You Think You Are?*, in the archives which disclosed in 2006 that my ancestors were a long line of illiterate Suffolk peasants. On the other hand, it might have been an attempt to understand BBC regulations on representation of the Liberal Democrats.

Zambezi, 1989. I have no idea what this fish is, though it may be the one said for about five hours to be the world-record three spot bream caught on a fly.

Discussing world affairs with one of China's most high-profile ambassadors. Chengdu, 2014.

Messing about in a boat, Glen Affric, 1993. The picture is too low-res to show the clouds of midges.

Deer-stalking in Glen Affric, 1995.

July 25 2002

Jeremy Paxman

B.B.C., London

Sir,

    I think you are an ignorant lout.

        Your, etc

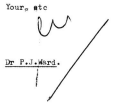

        Dr P.J.Ward.

Dr. P. J. WARD, MBE., JP., DL., LRCPI., LM., LRCSI., MRCGP., AFOM., DPH.

It is always a pleasure to hear from viewers.

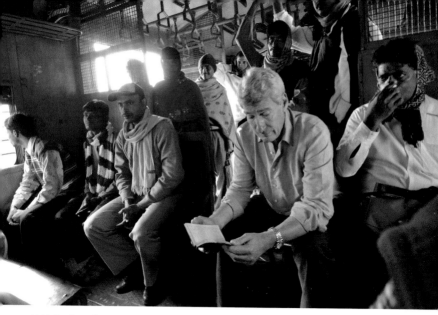

2008. Reading a letter on a Kolkata commuter train – even a fellow passenger seems outraged.

2011. Waiting to be told to do some damn stupid thing by a director, Chennai (Madras).

2009. Being beaten at dominoes in Cairo.

2011. Among the Ethiopian and Coptic churches defying
Christian unity on the roof of the Holy Sepulchre, Jerusalem.

2016. Outside the European Commission's lair.

2010. A non-Test-match day at Sabina Park, Kingston, Jamaica.

2015. Admiring Rembrandt's *The Conspiracy of the Batavians* from the correct position.

2015. Interviewing the French provincial lawyer pretending to be Napoleon
at the re-enactment of Waterloo. He tried to claim he'd won.

'Hang on. You're at one of the best universities in the world, spending three years having to do nothing but study a subject you enjoy. And you're jealous of a bimbo in a spangly dress?'

Something very odd is going on. My suspicion is that the rise of celebrity culture is to do with the decline of religion. Once our basic needs of food and shelter have been met, the one thing we all seek is significance. Many of us will find it in the love of a fellow human being, in our parents or our children. For centuries, millions of people found reassurance through a belief in God: whatever happened in life, you mattered to Him. But as religious congregations dwindle, exposure on television in homes across the land – the product of nothing more than a producer's patronage – offers instant acclamation and significance. It is not necessary to do anything very well; the mere fact that you are seen by others – even if you are only being a bit of Saturday-teatime arm candy – seems an affirmation: you have not lived in vain. Appearing on a quiz show, where merely pressing a buzzer will guarantee a camera's crash-zoom and the screen filling with your face, must promise satisfactions beyond the merely intellectual to some.

In one of my earliest instances of journalistic incompetence, when editing the student newspaper at Cambridge I failed to print a story that the Jewish Society was serving bacon sandwiches at its meetings. Years later, Peter Weil, the friend who had unearthed the story (which he never forgave me for not printing) became a researcher on Bamber Gascoigne's *University Challenge*, and would regularly walk into the office to find the producer happily drunk and asleep on the floor. (Later in his career Peter became the first producer to have his expenses returned to him with a scrawled note from the editor reading 'Eat less!' When Granada finally parted company with him, his leaving present was a one-way rail ticket from Manchester to London.) Though our current, longstanding producer, Peter Gwyn, is no teetotaller, twenty-first-century working life is duller. But the *Challenge* office and studio are happy places.

It is increasingly common to find television studios crewed by robotic, remote-controlled cameras. Newsrooms have been like that for years – those earnest figures who seem to be looking you straight in the eye are just talking to a piece of glass, often without even a human being behind it. *University Challenge* cannot be made like that, simply because too much of it is unpredictable: any one of eight contestants might buzz in with the answer to a question, which requires split-second camera moves and button-punching by the vision-mixer. We are lucky to have a devoted studio crew – some of whom are now well past retirement age. It often seems that the dates of the planned next recording blocks are the first thing they put in their diaries.

The closest we ever get to a scandal on *University Challenge* are embarrassments like the one a few years ago when it turned out that a student on a brilliant team from Corpus Christi College, Oxford, had been unable to get funding for the PhD he was planning, and therefore found himself a job before the recording of the final. Yet he still introduced himself as a student. Had he mentioned his problem to one of the production team, we would doubtless have tried to find a form of words to enable a way around it. But he didn't, and if you allow people to pass themselves off as students, you open the door for teams to play all sorts of ringers. His team had to be stripped of the title, and see the trophy given to the runners-up. Because there had been a minor flurry in the news-papers, senior figures at the BBC went into one their periodic fits of the vapours, and ruled that henceforth the whole competition would have to be recorded within a single academic year. Since holding auditions in the Christmas term would make it almost impossible for freshers to take part, and in the summer term everyone is preoccupied with exams, this means that the entire series, including the final, is now recorded within a few weeks in the spring. As transmission doesn't generally begin until the summer, one lives in constant fear of some awful tragedy striking a team in the interval between recording and broadcast. There is a precedent in *Songs of Praise*, which often had a similarly long gap between the time elderly church congregations were filmed singing hymns and the images being transmitted. It became known as 'The Resurrection Show'.

Wanting to show off your knowledge (or ignorance) on national television is not a normal activity, so the teams are not cross sections of humanity. Yet the competitors are at least much closer to some mother's son or daughter than many of the dusty apparitions who haunt the black chair in *Mastermind*, which is one of the very few places where you might find questions approaching the same level of difficulty. 'Good guess', I once said to a Cambridge student when he answered a question with 'W.H. Auden.' 'It wasn't a guess', he muttered under his breath. The most enjoyable questions, I find, are the ones that require students to work something out on the spot, like 'If the numbers one to ten are written out as words and the order of the letters is reversed, alphabetically, which one comes first? The words were no sooner out of my mouth than a student buzzed in 'Three.' Anyone can attempt the question at home. It's the speed of processing that's impressive.

A few years ago a producer working on *University Challenge* called it 'the little black dress of quiz shows', suggesting that it should be able to go on from year to year, regardless of fashion. Perhaps it can – the audience figures are evidence of its popularity. There is certainly something unalterably wholesome about the show itself. But the chances are that one day someone will come along wanting something grittier, fluffier or differently paced. Then I shall be toast.

* * *

The invitation to chair *University Challenge* was a direct consequence of my appearing on *Newsnight*. It was not the only one. A man from Radio Four asked me if I'd be interested in presenting a show on Monday mornings. *Start the Week* was one of a trio of programmes – the others being *Midweek* and the now defunct *Stop the Week* – known respectively in the trade as 'Pluggers', 'Nutters' and 'Wankers'. *Start the Week* had acquired its unhappy moniker because it was the programme of choice for publishers wishing to introduce the middle class to a new book. I rather enjoyed listening to it, even though it induced a guilty feeling that 'I really ought to read that' (or watch that film or listen to that lecture, both of which also featured). If I presented the show, I need never have that sense again.

This was a very silly thing to think, because it came at the price of reading the books. By accepting I committed myself to a regime of getting home from *Newsnight* at half past midnight and then having to sit up until four in the morning, ploughing through the invention of zero, the latest contribution to our understanding of Potemkin, or how the eye works. While my store of general knowledge expanded, I could really have done with an expanded store of sleep. An additional problem became clear as time went by. A couple of years ago, an international survey disclosed that Britain published more books per head of population than any other nation on earth. There is really no excuse for this. As the *Start the Week* producers soon discovered, there are simply not enough generally interesting books published to merit discussing four of them to a mass audience each week. While some of the authors, like the palaeontologist Richard Fortey, were delightful, others turned out to be the most awful poseurs and should never have been taken seriously.

The beauty of radio is its simplicity. Television demands that you effectively tell the story twice, first to understand it, and secondly to find a way of illustrating it. Radio – a person with a microphone talking to a person with a listening device – is cleaner and quicker. The format on *Start the Week* was generally straightforward for the apprehensive author: you arrive at Broadcasting House with a publicity person from your publishing company at around 8.30 in the morning, feeling slightly resentful that you have been given all the other guests' books or lectures to read, and will be expected to divulge your unpaid homework on air. The two of you are shown into a drab room where there is a plate of biscuits under clingfilm, or if you're lucky, a soggy croissant or two. There is something claiming to be coffee in a Thermos flask. A couple of other contributors also eager to share their discoveries with the world look at you resentfully for perpetrating the book they have had to sit up reading at the producer's instruction. The producer explains the order in which things will be discussed: you hope you will be first, or at worst second, because you know that throughout the programme listeners are leaving the house, getting out of the car or fighting a losing battle with the noise of the washing machine. If you are scheduled to be contributing last, there is the additional danger that the previous interviews have been so riveting that your life's work will have to be compressed into two minutes – which includes the observations of the grumpy other contributors. A few minutes before nine the producer shepherds everyone to the studio, another very dull room, sometimes with what seem to be eggboxes stuck to the walls (something to do with sound quality) and probably smelling of last Friday's *Woman's Hour* cookery demonstration. A gaggle of people are visible beyond the soundproof glass that separates the studio from the control room. They seem to be very busy talking among themselves, possibly about you or your appearance. Then the red light comes on and the world can hear what you have to say.

Apart from the time when Henry Kissinger walked out of the studio after I had asked him whether he felt a fraud for accepting the Nobel Peace Prize (the event that Tom Lehrer said 'made political satire obsolete'), the programme generally continued a constant course for forty-five minutes. The occasion on which it was discovered that the Dalai Lama was to address a gathering of Buddhists in London was too good an opportunity to miss, though. Early one Monday morning we assembled on the fourth floor of a grim concrete conference-centre hotel in Wembley to meet the Living God. European flunkeys in hand-knitted jumpers and environmentally sound sandals worried that His Holiness might not be treated with sufficient deference. There was to be no eye contact, I was informed. I was to sit at a lower level than the great man. He would arrive two minutes before the interview started, and there was to be no irreverent chitchat. I was explaining that there certainly would be eye contact, and that we would have to sit at the same level, when the door opened and the fourteenth reincarnation of the Bodhisattva of Compassion walked in, shook hands and sat down. The prohibited chitchat was now inevitable. How did he enjoy travelling the world? He said he was a slightly nervous flyer. It was that sense of not being in control, wasn't it, I suggested. Yes, he replied. And what was that smell wafting in through the window? Sorry about that, I said, there's a burger van down below cooking bacon butties. They smell good, he said.

I was about to say, 'Hang on, you're Buddhist!' when the red light came on. We talked for the allotted forty-five minutes. I found him a man without malice or pretence, and with a slightly disconcerting frankness – especially when, at about 9.13 a.m., he held forth on the subject of masturbation. I liked him, and when he had left the room at the end of the interview I turned to the producer and said, 'What an amazing man!' She gesticulated in response. I turned around to discover the Dalai Lama's face peering around the edge of the door.

'I've forgotten my treasures,' he said.

'Oh no! What do they look like?' I asked.

'They're in a small cloth bag like this,' he said, gesturing to the maroon robe he was wearing.

'I expect it's under the table we were sitting at,' I suggested, and scrambled underneath to retrieve it. 'Here it is!'

'Thank you,' he said. 'Would you like one of my treasures?'

'I couldn't possibly,' I said, recalling the BBC's strict injunctions about corruption.

'Please.'

'I really don't think I could accept anything, Your Holiness.'

He reached into the bag, bringing out a clenched fist. 'Please,' he repeated, opening his hand. There was a toffee in his palm. I took it.

The experience was enough to convince me to spend another couple of years on *Start the Week*, but there were other opportunities too. For a few summers a group of us produced a topical television discussion show with a live national telephone vote called *You Decide*, a high-wire act which I was never really confident wouldn't fall off air. There were other offers to make radio documentaries and to chair discussions (much less interesting than participating in them as a combatant). National newspapers began to call asking my opinion on subjects like 'Is breakfast necessary?' or 'My worst mistakes with glue' – the ringaround and subsequent printing of comments from half-recognisable people being the laziest form of journalism; it got worse when mass emails removed the need even to lift the telephone. Each summer and Christmas there were requests from literary editors of national newspapers to recommend a few books worth reading. Appeals for support from charities came with great frequency. I soon discovered I was useless on committees, but three times I was invited to judge book awards, which seemed a bit of an impertinent thing to do, until I realised that if you're writing books for a general audience, it does no harm to have middlebrow people judging awards. I was flattered enough to accept some honorary degrees from universities, the main purpose of which seemed to be for them to get a photograph of a slightly familiar face wearing a silly hat and fancy dress in the newspapers, and to save some Vice Chancellor the chore of making a speech to new graduates – instead, those who are leaving must listen to someone who had to do virtually nothing to gain their degree

People accost you in the street or on the train. One or two colleagues have attempted to claim that as a result they cannot travel on the underground, and should therefore be allowed to claim for taxis. This is an absurd argument. If you put yourself into people's homes, they will recognise you. If you really don't want to talk to others, get another job, or at least carry a book or a newspaper with you. Being asked for a selfie is a bore, but it takes little time. And most people are immensely nice. I have met great numbers of human beings I should never otherwise have met simply through the false recognition that comes from appearing on television. A crowd of aggressive, drunk football fans isn't much fun, but the vast majority of individuals who have accosted me have been considerate, polite and friendly.

The time spent in Manchester for recordings of *University Challenge* provided the inspiration for my first television documentary series. The regional art galleries of Britain are seriously underappreciated, and almost every sizeable city has a collection. They are, predictably, dominated by nineteenth-century painting, since most were endowed by Victorian industrialists with a sense of civic pride. They are now sadly underfunded – the wonderful Walker Gallery in Liverpool seemed positively dingy last time I went, as if they couldn't even afford to replace the lightbulbs. But the treasures you can find there, or in galleries in Manchester, Leeds, Birmingham, Glasgow or Preston, are remarkable. The contents of these galleries are a treasure trove of unfashionable painting. Some of the art may be tripe, but cumulatively the collections provide a gloriously vibrant portrait of what Victorian Britain was like, for big canvases like William Powell Frith's *Derby Day* and *The Railway Station* or George Hicks's *The General Post Office, One Minute to Six* (i.e. in the last-minute rush before it closed) are crammed with stories. When you look closely at these pictures, or at moralising works like Ford Madox Brown's *Work* (there are versions in both Manchester and Birmingham), or Luke Fildes' *Applicants for Admission to a Casual Ward* (in Tate Britain), showing a line of homeless people in the snow outside a workhouse, to say nothing of the endless pictorial warnings about marital infidelity, you get an insight into nineteenth-century life as vivid as anything in Dickens or Hardy.

It was in Manchester City Art Gallery, moving between the soft pornography of well-breasted ladies of Greek mythology and Hubert von Herkomer's depiction of an unemployed labourer and his wife and children in *Hard Times*, that it occurred to me that these paintings would make a wonderful television series. Since Victorian art remains generally sneered at, it took some time before I was able to persuade the BBC that a series on the subject was a gamble worth taking. But it paid off – Jay Hunt, then rejoicing in the Orwellian title of Controller, BBC 1 (and later appointed to become Channel 4's Chief Creative Officer), took a risk, and found that there were millions of people who wanted to spend a Sunday evening seeing how their ancestors had lived. The two researchers and four directors assembled by Basil Comely, an old-school BBC eccentric saddled with the bizarre title of BBC Vision Studio Head for Arts, proved that you don't have to manufacture tat to acquire an audience. The modish term at the time for series with lots of beautiful scenery and sunshine was 'warm bath television'. Basil Comely said afterwards that *The Victorians* had really been 'a warm bath with edges', whatever that was, and suggested a series about the art of the British Empire. Mercifully, we were able to convert this into a series of films about the history of the Empire, with the promise that it would examine what ruling the world did to the British people. Jay Hunt was again keen to have the series, 'just as long as there aren't too many paintings, like that last one'. We promised that there wouldn't be. During the next year and a half there were trips to India, South Africa, the Middle East, Sudan, Kenya, Malawi, and then, in a dizzying single journey, Singapore, Hong Kong, Canada and Jamaica. It was wonderful.

Much of the success of the series was due to the fact that it was filled with blue skies and sunshine, and was broadcast in the dank days of British winter. No such considerations applied to the next series, a four-part history of the First World War. Broadcasting has a simple-minded weakness for anniversaries, and production companies are constantly deploying young researchers to discover the facts that will enable them to begin a pitch to a bored executive with words like, 'It is precisely two hundred years, three months and five days since …' The centenary of the outbreak of World War I in the summer of 1914 was a rather bigger deal, that calamity ultimately forcing mass enfranchisement, empowering women, fostering scepticism about government, enabling the state to meddle in almost every area of life – effectively creating modern Britain while triggering the collapse of the country's international power. I was keen to make a series about it. The BBC was contemplating all sorts of events to commemorate individual battles, notably the Somme, but had not commissioned a single documentary series which would explain what the war did to the country. They accepted the suggestion.

The locations were less glamorous this time – Preston, Poplar, Picardy, Ipswich, and a few soggy excursions to Flanders – but the story of how so many died for so little gain was sufficiently powerful that the sheer force of the narrative could grab and hold the viewers' attention. The style of all these documentaries was old-fashioned – man or woman stands in front of camera, telling a story, visiting locations, conducting the occasional interview and commenting on bits of archive film. One can understand the reluctance to abandon a format that works, but it is well past time that documentary producers invented a new idiom.

What few presenters of documentaries will admit is that the business of filming in this idiom is staggeringly dull. Spending weeks in each other's company, you make good friends with the cameramen and sound recordists with whom you work, but the truth is that the thrill of journalism is finding things out, thinking about them, and meeting people, while with documentaries, generally speaking the script has been written before you arrive anywhere. The presenter's job is, therefore, little more than an exercise in recitation and walking. I thought I had plumbed the depths of pointless walking when required to trudge for a mile through the desert along the railway track laid by Lord Kitchener as he advanced on Khartoum. But the other day, filming a documentary about van Gogh's time in Provence, I sank even lower, walking and listening for the sound of the cameraman's whistle – one blast to turn around and walk towards the camera, two blasts to swivel through another 180 degrees and continue in the original direction. I would have done well in a dog obedience competition. I realise that it is absurd to complain about the tiresomeness of such filming – the job is hardly like being down a mine – but the glamour is false, even if the spectacle and the companionship are not.

There is a story (almost certainly invented) about David Attenborough travelling with a cameraman for weeks into the depths of a jungle, climbing above the treeline and finally cresting the top of a hill to see a fabled, Shangri-La-like secret valley laid out before them.

'We may be the first Europeans ever to see this valley. How are we going to capture this magical moment?' he is supposed to have asked the cameraman.

'Well David,' the cameraman replied, 'the last time I was here, the presenter stood over there, and I put the tripod just here.' It is a venerable visual vernacular.

I wrote books to accompany all three documentary series, in the mistaken belief that the writing and the film-making would be complementary. Generally speaking, they're not: research for writing and research for television films are very different, and what makes an impression on the screen can look very thin on the page, while what seems astonishing in print is often untranslatable to the screen. Publishers like books linked to television series, because they view the exposure as a form of advertising. But I have yet to read a 'book of the series' which is worthwhile as a piece of writing. Better by far to treat the two things as separate projects.

My third book, *Friends in High Places*, an exploration of the British Establishment, had been published soon after I arrived at *Newsnight*. I followed that with books on a couple of questions that had been exercising me – what is it that makes people decide to become politicians, and why does Britain still have a monarchy? Producing books is a long, lonely slog, and there can be few authors who have not shared Dr Johnson's wonder at why a man would devour half a library merely to produce another book. There is really no adequate response, apart from saying that if you have an itch, it helps to scratch it.

When all else failed, I took myself off fishing. Reading back through my diaries I find page after page filled with accounts of days spent on the riverbank. My trout-fishing club demands that all members report at the end of the season how many fish they have caught, and whether any were of unusual size. This is by far the dullest way to assess a day on the river: only a fishmonger should care about the size or weight of a fish. The enchanting aspects are what you see around you, while stalking about on the banks.

A child doesn't think much about the world of work – it seems remote, dull and mechanical. But when I found myself having to earn a living I was able to look back at my grandfather's life, and it appeared to me that in many ways his work pattern was perfect: by that time in his life, he didn't do any. For the first several months of the year he was away four days out of every twelve, fishing for salmon on the river Eden in Cumberland. In spring and summer he played golf and fished for trout in the Yorkshire Dales more or less every week. When the autumn arrived he went out shooting pheasants, partridges and other game. He had earned it all, having started out as a travelling salesman on a motorbike and sidecar, building up a canning business and then retiring while he could still enjoy life. I have no idea how I'd have coped with his hard early years, and his interlude as a Salvation Army bandmaster was definitely not for me. But his last decades strike me as about as good as it gets. He had a study on the first floor of the family home in Yorkshire where he kept his guns and fishing tackle. It was small and dark and reeked of leather and gun-oil, still my favourite smell, for the promise of a day in the fresh air. The dim light from the lamp that stood on his desk shines across as I write this.

I have lost much taste for killing things (I plead guilty to once enjoying deer-stalking in the Scottish Highlands, which I thought the purest form of field sport, until I decided that since the fun was in getting close enough to watch the red deer, pulling the trigger was unnecessary). But I loved fishing from the very start, standing in short trousers and Wellingtons in the river in Wensleydale and usually not catching anything, while a few yards away my grandfather lured trout after trout to his fly. Occasionally he would hand me the rod to play the fish. There is nothing on earth that feels as energetic as a fish at the end of your line. It is struggling for its life, of course, and these days I put back into the water most of the salmon and trout I catch (which itself raises a complex set of ethical issues: why inflict the pain if not to provide food?). Nothing fascinates a child like the opportunity to see another creature close up, and sometimes I would sit on the riverbank and take the dead trout out of Grandpa's creel to examine their drying, dulling corpses and look into their unblinking eyes. It was like sneaking into an underworld. If I were only allowed to waste time in one way, I would choose to spend it trying to catch a trout on a dry fly.

Not long ago I went to a fishing tackle shop to buy a rod for a fourteen-year-old godson. 'Don't get him a very expensive one,' said the manager of the shop. 'But don't get him a very cheap one either. He'll probably give up fishing in a few years' time, because he'll be more interested in girls. But if you get him a decent enough rod, he'll be able to use it when he comes back to the sport later.' I realised at once that that was more or less what had happened to me: fishing is dull by comparison with chasing girls, but when you've grown up a bit, you realise that fishing doesn't break your heart. To the uninitiated it seems such a passive, pointless occupation – a stick and a string with a worm at one end and a fool at the other, to quote that old bombast Dr Johnson again. Everyone should give thanks that they do not have a sycophantic Scotsman writing down every damnfool thing they say.

'I could never do that. I just don't have the patience,' is the usual boneheaded response when I confess to enjoying fishing. The truth is that fly fishing requires no patience at all. It is essentially about trying to insert yourself into an environment where you don't belong, without being noticed. If you blunder about you won't catch anything – on a sunny day you will be able to see the trout darting off in all directions when they sense your footfall on the bank, their flicking tails a snub to your clumsiness. Be quiet. And then, when you're stalking a fish, things happen around you. A grass snake swims sinuously across the river. A water vole plops into a stream. Wagtails and oystercatchers dance at the water's edge. Swallows and martins swoop low over the water, snatching flies. A kingfisher flashes that spectacular iridescent blue above the river; it is gone in an instant. I was once standing in the bend of a river when an eel slithered over my foot. In Ireland, I sat for twenty minutes watching a big dog otter swim repeatedly up a sidestream, just to have the pleasure of drifting down the rapids on his back. To become absorbed in the natural world frees your mind: fish cannot survive in our element, and only imagination will allow us to live in theirs.

Dry fly fishing for trout is about observing a fish, working out what it is feeding on, and then presenting a confection of fur and feathers attached to a hook in such a way that the fish will mistake it for a fly hatching on the water. Salmon fishing, by contrast, is largely a matter of chance. As migratory fish, salmon hatch from eggs in fresh water, and migrate to the sea to feed. When they return to fresh water for the urgent business of laying or fertilising their eggs, they do not eat. In casting your 'fly' (actually it looks nothing like a fly) into the water you are hoping to provoke an aggressive reaction in which the salmon will seize your hook because it is irritated by something in what it deems to be its territory. It follows that unless your fly is somewhere in the vicinity of a salmon you are whistling in the wind. There are many easier ways to catch a fish, a net being just the most obvious; the difficulty is part of the point. Though I enjoy every occasion on which I go salmon fishing, I will happily admit that most of the day I am wasting my time. But that does not deter me. Either way, all the ingenuity of *Homo sapiens* is devoted to trying to deceive an organism with a brain smaller than the stones on a gravel beach. It's ridiculous. And I don't care.

In essence, it is a solitary occupation. But the best fishing days are those spent with friends, meeting for a picnic lunch on the riverbank, united in the awareness that we are doing something which defies rational explanation. And when salmon fishing you may spend much of the day in the company of someone you hardly know. Though the arrangement has distinctly Victorian or

Edwardian overtones, and therefore an image problem, being accompanied by a ghillie can significantly enhance the day. How often do we spend hours in the company of someone from an entirely different walk of life, united in a shared passion? His (or her – though they are a tiny minority, there are a few female ghillies) expertise can significantly alter the odds. Among salmon-fishing ghillies, the jobs are often handed down from father to son. Born bearded and swaddled in ancient tweed, they have red faces and hair sprouting from their ears like lichen on a stone wall. They live solely on white-bread meat-paste sandwiches and whisky. Oddly, when the midges are out they can smell quite fragrant, having discovered that reeking of Avon Skin-So-Soft is one of the better ways of deterring the little buggers, though nothing rivals utter indifference. Being a congenital optimist is one of the first requirements of the job. However empty the river is of salmon, they cannot say, 'You're wasting your time,' and they quickly realise that 'Ye'll nae catch a fash if yer flee's nae in the watter' is a long way short of a vote of confidence – as advice goes, it's not really up there with the Sermon on the Mount.

What you really want to know is the water temperature, the height of the river, whether it's rising or falling, and which side of a rock the fish tend to lie at this depth of water. (One of the reasons, incidentally, that the average woman makes a better salmon fisher than the average man is that they tend to listen to what the ghillie has to say, while men stride into the river to whack out the longest line they can fire off, regardless.) The ghillie will dispense advice on likely hot spots and effective flies. On big rivers, he will often row a boat as well. You will spend most of the day in his company, and it is generally a delight. They can perform minor surgery when you stick a hook in your hand, and are able to identify any bird by its call. On Orkney I heard the funniest story of my life, involving bagpipes and a septic tank. In Ireland, as we brewed tea on an island in the middle of a lough, the ghillie spun a fantastical story of poteen, a police raid and the annual shearing of a horse. I believed every word of it.

The first member of this tribe I ever met was 'Mr Thompson', with whom Grandpa fished in Cumberland. He had a flat cap the size of a bucket, glasses as thick as the bottom of a Victorian lemonade bottle, and wore an ankle-length black oilskin. There must have been days when he was out on the riverbank while the sun was shining, but I can only remember seeing him through a cloud of drizzle, as if he had a personal raincloud tethered a few feet above his head. Mr Thompson was too far my senior for there ever to be much conversation between us. But I have met many ghillies in the years since, and while, inevitably, most of the conversation has been about fishing, or what's wrong with the way I cast my line, we've covered everything from music to politics to horror movies.

Americans eschew the term 'ghillie', and prefer to talk of a 'fishing guide', thinking (rightly) that it sounds less feudal. I once fished with an American guide who arrived festooned with dangling bits of kit, in enormous waders, his face hidden behind polarised glasses, and netting hanging from his hat to keep off mosquitoes. Plastic tubes ran from the water container on his back to his mouth; this was a new stage of evolution, half man, half gadget. Though I have yet to meet his equivalent in Britain, the younger British ghillies are much more like friends and fellow enthusiasts than the caricature suggests. One of them explained the other day how the internet had transformed the loneliness of life in his remote corner of Scotland: he eventually had to stop switching on his computer for fear his internet dating partner would appear on Skype with no clothes on for the hundredth time.

Some of them dress like tramps, some like Edwardian gentlemen at York races, and some you just wonder why they're doing the job at all. I once rented a boat on a loch in the far north of Scotland, hoping to catch a few sea trout. The loch turned out to be about twelve square miles in surface area. Where to row the boat to? All I had was a sketch map, with helpful landmarks identified from which to triangulate the line the boat should drift. The landmarks were mainly identified with comments like 'stream', 'big tree' and 'stone wall'. Since the 'tree on skyline' had fallen down years earlier, and there were dozens of streams and walls, I arranged to hire a local boatman who knew the loch and the shoals beneath.

I realised something was not quite right when he arrived at the lochside dragging one leg behind him. A wiry man with a lived-in face, he stumbled into the boat and took the oars, while I pushed us off from the shore, for it turned out he had broken his leg. When I took a seat in the stern it became clear that he was in no shape to do much physical labour. 'Shall I row for a while?' I asked. 'Please,' he said.

I spent the rest of the day pulling the boat about the loch in aimless circles while he sat smoking cheap cigarettes and occasionally casting a line onto the water. £50 well spent.

'How'd you hurt your leg?' I asked him.

'Accident.'

'What happened?'

'It was in a bar,' he replied, in a tone indicating that more precise enquiry would be unwelcome.

'God, where's the nearest proper hospital?'

'Inverness.'

'But that's two hours away, on bad roads. It must have been hell.'

'Aye,' he said. 'They wouldnae let me smoke.'

10

Would You Answer the Question?

Here are some of the questions that get asked of people who work in television.

Do you still get nervous?

Television studios are essentially warehouses with a lot of wires running through them. Even when they have been decorated to look like a room in someone's house, they are nothing like such a thing: there is always at least one wall missing. Then there's the fact that there are so many other people on the set – on *University Challenge*, for example, there are half a dozen camera operators, a couple of sound people, lighting technicians, set designers, a floor manager and various producers and researchers, to say nothing of the eight contestants and two reserves, and a live audience (with marshals and a nurse in attendance in case anyone gets over-excited). Even news programme studios generally have a floor manager and a technician or two – though the bean-counters have tried their hardest to replace as many as possible of the human beings with robots. There are some television studios which try to appear as imposing as possible – light entertainment shows or election results programmes, for example – by giving a sense of enormous scale, and with lots of bright light. But the central illusion of the medium is of conversation – one person standing or sitting in his or her warehouse and the other sitting in their home.

Like some others, when I started broadcasting I was under the impression that I needed to shout, like a preacher at a revivalist meeting. This is a very foolish mistake to make, because however loudly you shout, you will not be heard by the viewer in Hull. The style has to be conversational, albeit a one-way conversation, and you must ignore the other people in the studio. Mostly, they will ignore you, anyway: the best way of telling whether a film or interview on *Newsnight* was any good was by seeing how many of the studio crew took a break from their screens or newspapers to pay attention to what was being broadcast.

Attempting to be intimate with the viewer is also easier said than done, because when we talk to fellow humans we tend to look into their eyes, to see whether or not they're registering any interest. But the television camera is unblinking and expressionless, and you have no idea what is happening in the room to which it is sending its image. Programme-makers fondly imagine that viewers are sitting rapt, on the edge of their seats. But they might equally well be having a family row, have fallen asleep, or have left the room altogether to make a cup of tea. Other things they might be up to do not bear contemplation, but they certainly wouldn't be at them if you really were in the room with them.

Then there is the environment in which you find yourself. Conversation tends to take place when we're seated. But in the last few years, news programmes have for some reason decided that presenters have more credibility if they are standing. Like other idiotic fashions, this will pass, and the men and women will be told to sit down again. But where is the chair to be placed, and what sort of chair should it be? Val Doonican liked a rocking chair, Dave Allen a stool, but most news people accommodate their bottoms on office furniture of some sort or other, and seated behind a desk, which is believed to add gravitas. For a few years Channel 4 broadcast a late-night discussion show, *After Dark*, on which the participants slumped in armchairs: the challenge was whether they would nod off before the viewers. Then there is the set. Along with many other news programmes, *Newsnight* had a taste for skylines (usually London's). We also had the night sky, world maps – sinusoidal, cylindrical, azimuthal – and for several years what appeared to be a giant orange toast rack. Coming across as having a conversation in these settings was something of a challenge, though they did impart a degree of authority to whatever form of words you had cobbled together beforehand (apart from the toast rack, that is).

The studio is ruled by red lights, which come on when the output is being transmitted or a camera is 'live'. It is, supposedly, the glowing light which induces the nerves. But anxiety is the product of anticipation, so the most nervous-making part of broadcasting – as of most activities – is the expectation. Sex therapists apparently call this 'performance anxiety'.* But as time goes by, you get used to the fact that when the red light is on anything you say may be shared with vast numbers of people, so studio twitchiness is reduced. If you felt no nerves at all, you probably wouldn't be much good at it: anxiety encourages you to make more of an effort. You probably wouldn't feel any nerves at all sitting safely in a heap in the middle of an ice rink, but if you want to move, you will have to live with the possibility that you may fall over.

---

* I learned the term from Tracey Cox, author of *Hot Sex*, *Superhotsex* and *Sextasy* and many other titles, who I used to bump into at the gym. We got to know each other when she asked my advice about her career. She had been offered a column in the late *News of the World*. 'Will it damage my credibility if I take it?' she asked. I thought not.

How do you decide who to interview?

The only honest answer to this question is that presenters don't get to decide who they interview. And nor should they. They're entitled to express a view about who is to appear, but in the end they should shut up and do as they're told. The contrast is with the American model, where the 'anchorman' really can have some pompous title like 'Editor in Chief'. It produces a Cyclopean breadth of vision. ITV shows – and many radio programmes, even on the BBC – are built around the front man or woman, but as we have seen, in television at least the BBC believes in producers rather than permatanned egomaniacs. It doesn't like anyone to forget it. For those whose faces appear on screen, and who are the ones who end up looking stupid, and possibly much worse than that, if things go wrong, the experience can be galling, but in the BBC producers' view of the world, if you're going to make a programme you need so many camera operators, so many lights, so many edit suites, such and such a sound system, and one or two presenters – they are just part of the equipment. Most of those documentaries claiming to have been 'written and presented by' an individual were actually written by the producer.

There are pleasurable exceptions to the rule of producer omniscience. Like the producer who rushed me into a *Newsnight* studio one afternoon to record a down-the-line interview with a prominent Minister in the post-invasion government of Iraq, who had driven himself to the studio we had booked in Qatar. When he was settled, I asked, 'Well, Minister, how much longer can this government of yours survive?'

A momentary look of bafflement crossed his face before he collected his wits and replied, 'Oh, it's my *brother* you want. He's the politician. I'm an engineer.' He added helpfully, 'I can tell you about the bridge I'm building.' Soon afterwards, the producer decided to give up television and become a barrister.

In general, the presenter should express enthusiasm for all projects, and when your producer says, 'You've got to interview Russell Brand tomorrow,' you should not reply – as I did on the first occasion this was mentioned – 'What on earth has he got to say that the world needs to hear?'

Mr Brand had just written *My Booky Wook*, which was on a subject he knew a lot about. It was about himself. My producer, Shaminder Nahal, and I were at the Labour Party conference in Manchester, and took the train to London to meet the great man – who, like many of the most eager apostles of revolutionary socialism, found it easier not to leave the Home Counties. At the appointed hour he arrived in the suite that had been booked at Claridge's, attended by a small claque of hangers-on, including his own make-up artist.* His book was about his ferocious desire to be famous. This ambition to be recognised, but not necessarily for any particular skill – as a great scientist, gymnast, philosopher or manufacturer, for example – is one of the most noticeable aspects of contemporary life.

Where, I asked, did he think the obsession had come from?

His reply – 'I suppose it's an idea that deeply permeates because it's omnipresent' – didn't take us very far. Things did not get much more precise after that.

The phenomenon of 'celebrity' would have been incomprehensible a generation ago, but it is a mark of our times. As I have suggested, it seems to me the obsession of a culture which has lost its religion. Brand himself was quick enough to point out (his mental nimbleness is his most striking characteristic) that the fact

---

* To be fair, the make-up artist made him look reasonably laid-back for someone so hyperactive, whereas I, with no such cosmetic assistance, appeared on the recording to have covered my face in Thousand Island dressing.

that the programme devoted fifteen minutes of its allotted span to our conversation meant that fifteen minutes was not given over to something more important. The interview was, however, undeniably popular, and there are few things a producer likes more than having lots of viewers.

In 2013 Russell Brand was invited to guest-edit the *New Statesman*, the left-wing weekly whose lurches from one funding and readership crisis to another over the past several decades have earned it the nickname 'the Staggers'. What its earnest Fabian Society founders, Sidney and Beatrice Webb, would have made of Brand's issue, devoted to 'Revolution', and for which he wrote a very long essay, is anyone's guess. Brand used his article to point out that young people are disenchanted with conventional politics – which is an observable fact, even if most mainstream politicians prefer not to observe it. He went on from this uncontroversial starting point to argue that they shouldn't waste their time voting. I was sent off to another luxury London hotel to sit at his feet.

Brand's idea struck me as just stupid. The political process has undoubtedly failed young people. Politicians endlessly bend the knee to the legions of old people, for two reasons. Firstly, there are more elderly voters than there are of their young counterparts. Secondly, politicians know that old people will actually make the effort to vote – it at least makes a change from the bingo, keep-fit classes and occasional outings to the seaside. The consequence of deferring to the elderly is that policies are increasingly skewed in their favour, with younger people having the misfortune of working and paying taxes to support them.* But young people's failure

---

* The suggestion is increasingly being made that the solution to the problem of young people's disengagement from politics is to lower the voting age to sixteen. But why stop at sixteen? The answer, surely, is not to expand the franchise, but to limit it, and to stop anyone over the age of, say, seventy-five from determining how taxes are spent unless they are still contributing to the public purse through direct taxation. We need to revise the cry of the American colonists: 'No representation without taxation.'

to vote does not mean that no one gets elected. It just makes the influence of those who *do* vote even greater – you cannot correct under-representation by under-representing yourself, as even Brand recognised when the next general election came around.

But the election was a long time in the future when we recorded the interview, and there is no doubt that Brand's comments hit a nerve in a way that interviews with dull old conventional politicians do not. At that time, about 600,000 people watched *Newsnight* each evening (down from well over a million a few years earlier – people had unfortunately discovered plenty of other things to do at 10.30, not the least of them being a need to go to sleep). But the Brand interview was watched nearly twelve million times, joining Miley Cyrus, talking animals and weather reporters falling over as one of the most-watched videos on YouTube. The total audience was, therefore, even bigger than the night the programme went on air straight after the notorious 1995 *Panorama* interview with the Princess of Wales, and Prince Charles's friend Nicholas Soames described her as in the 'advanced stages of paranoia'. However much I protested that my encounter with Russell Brand was just a bit of theatre, entertaining perhaps, but not signifying very much, back came the riposte, 'Look at how many people watched it.'

On the basis of a couple of meetings I decided that, for all his flakiness, Brand was a likeable chap, and his basic point, about the utter failure of mainstream politics to touch the lives of many people, rang true. His solutions might not have been profound. But his observations about the chasm between the political class and voters were heartfelt (and were later amply borne out by the results of the 2016 referendum on the European Union). A year or so after the interview, I thought it might be fun to make a film about the looming 2015 election campaign. My initial idea was a sort of road movie, driving around the country in an old ice-cream van, announcing our arrival at political rallies with the chimes of

'Greensleeves' and seeing what happened. I emailed Brand: did he fancy the idea?

'Fate has thrown us together,' he replied, adding, 'I can't believe either of us are actually considering this. It could be amazing.'

That was seven months before the vote. Needless to say, by the time the election campaign started (during which he changed his mind and told people they should vote after all), he had given up responding to my emails. There may have been something of the professional naughty boy about Russell Brand, but he was nice to his mother and had good manners, and he was definitely on to something about the extent of disillusion with the way politics works in Britain. Even if his solution was a bit silly.

Do you tell interviewees the questions in advance?

The answer to this is very simple. No. If you hand over a list of questions, and then merely recite them, you aren't listening to the answers. On the other hand, anyone who agrees to do an interview without checking what it's going to be about is a mug.

What's a silly question?

There really aren't any silly questions – they are either necessary or not. There were many times during Kenneth Clarke's time as Chancellor of the Exchequer when asking him about his passion for birdwatching would probably have produced a much more interesting interview than hearing the latest about fiscal policy. Of the several interviews I had with his successor Alistair Darling, I remember more about my conversation before one of them with his wife, in which we discussed marmalade-making and she passed on some tips for helping me to get mine to set properly. Having once been invited to join the same fishing party as George Osborne, I would have found discussing why fewer salmon seem to be returning to British rivers a great deal more interesting than hearing a lot of implausible claims about balancing the national books. But birdwatching, marmalade-making and fishing were not what we were required to discuss. Whatever the subject, it remains true that the best questions are the obvious ones. The more the questioner tries to show off their knowledge, the sillier they seem.

Do you know what you're talking about?

It is not necessary to be an expert – why bother interviewing someone if you already know it all? Brian Redhead, who presented the *Today* programme on Radio Four for many years, acquired the nickname 'Brian Bighead' because he appeared so omniscient.* It did nothing to endear him to his listeners. But there was a simple trick behind his knowledgeability. When his guest sat down, and before the interview began, he would ask, 'What's the really key issue here?' With the microphone safely off, the Chancellor of the Exchequer (or whoever) would then say, 'Well, it's complicated, but the real issue here is the Hicks-Marshall Laws of Derived Demand, but they're not talking about it down the Dog and Duck.' Redhead could then begin the interview by saying, 'Well, I suppose the real issue here is the Hicks-Marshall Laws. Why on earth aren't you coming clean about it?'

The presenter is there merely as the representative of the average, reasonably alert viewer or listener. You only need to know

---

* He also presented a radio programme called *A Word in Edgeways*, a broadcasting enterprise of such wonkiness that a friend who spent time there as a producer once received a report from the BBC Audience Research Department containing the warning that they were unsure whether they had discovered the listenership or a sampling error.

enough not to ask spectacularly stupid questions. That means working on the research, being able to use it, and then to forget it. Today it could be reform of the English school curriculum. Tomorrow it might be the state of the Dominican banana harvest.

Have you ever thought, 'This guy is going to hit me'?

I've never had this thought while talking to anyone in a television studio. But it has occasionally occurred to me during a barney in someone's office, after which the cameraman has muttered, 'I was sure he was going to punch you.' It hasn't happened yet. It may have helped that I met and interviewed plenty of guerrillas, terrorist leaders and death-squad commanders before spending much time with politicians, which tended to give a sense of proportion.

But both parties know that a television interview is a performance. To some extent, even a mass murderer will be on his best behaviour when he is aware that a camera is trained on him. This can be intensely frustrating for the interviewer, and as time went by I learned to match the content of an interview to its duration, the key thing being to get the killer question in early enough for there to be enough time for the interviewee to climb down from the ceiling by the end. If the concluding section was then straightforward or easy-going, sometimes they even forgot how testy things had been earlier. After the camera had stopped running, a question along the lines of 'Happy enough?' tended to calm things even more.

Once, when the Israeli army stood accused of a series of human rights outrages, we recorded an exceptionally crabby interchange with the government spokesman, at the end of which I thanked him for his time, saying it had been 'pretty robust'. 'It's just business,' he replied matter-of-factly. Conrad Black, the Canadian carpetbagger who became proprietor of the *Daily Telegraph* and was ennobled as Lord Black of Crossharbour before being convicted of fraud in the American courts, said he was rather proud of having survived his time in a US federal prison without losing his mind, and of being able to endure the sort of questions I was asking him without getting up and 'smashing your face in'. I rather wished he had done, as it would have made brilliant television. But he was only promoting a memoir. He signed my copy after our interview with the words 'For Jeremy Paxman, with thanks for a lively meeting and every good wish'. It was just business.

Did you plan to ask Michael Howard the same question again and again?

No. The background to the notorious interview is complicated. At the time (May 1997) Michael Howard was running for the leadership of the Conservative Party, which had just found itself dumped into opposition after eighteen years in government.

As Home Secretary in John Major's administration, Howard had invented a doctrine by which he could be held liable for policy questions, but anything to do with their implementation was 'operations', and the responsibility of the executives under him. Since the Home Office's responsibilities included everything from falling satellites to keeping lunatics out of the Queen's bedroom, on the face of it the distinction made a certain amount of sense, though it did raise obvious problems about accountability.

The Home Secretary was in charge of penal policy, and Howard was a politician who liked to boast that 'Prison works.' This flew in the face of all the evidence that nearly half of prisoners returned to crime when they had completed their sentences. But, as he pointed out, it was certainly true that while they were inside prison, offenders were not out burgling or beating people up. His claim only held water, though, if you could be sure that once they were in prison, offenders stayed there. When five IRA men and an armed robber escaped from the maximum security prison at Whitemoor in Cambridgeshire in 1994, the claim looked pretty threadbare, especially when it turned out that the lax security regime was partly the consequence of political decisions. Only weeks later, three Category A lifers escaped from Parkhurst prison on the Isle of Wight, using a home-made pass key, ladder and gun, making Howard's claim seem risible. The prison's governor was suspended within days, while Howard said that the breakout had nothing to do with policy. But then a retired general he had appointed to investigate what had gone wrong reported 'a chapter of errors at every level and a naïveté beyond belief'. Howard sacked the head of the prison service, Derek Lewis, who had been recruited to the post from business. Despite the fact that the inquiry had discovered ministerial meddling from top to bottom, Howard maintained that the buck stopped with Lewis. The Labour opposition mounted an attack on the Home Secretary's increasingly feeble excuses, but it was very ineptly managed, and Howard garnered enough support in the House of Commons to survive.

The scandal did nothing to dent his ambition, and in the wake of the Conservatives' 1997 election defeat he declared himself a candidate for the party leadership. But he had reckoned without Ann Widdecombe, the splendidly eccentric Conservative Member of Parliament for Maidstone – and future ballroom dancer and pantomime witch – who had been the Junior Minister responsible for prisons at the time he had fired Derek Lewis. She and Lewis had become friends, and now she delivered a scathing speech in which she accused Howard of 'semantic prestidigitation'. She wanted to know why he had not admitted that he had told Lewis to sack the Governor of Parkhurst. He was entitled to do so, she said, but as this was an 'operational' decision it would have destroyed his claim that he was only answerable for 'policy' issues.

When she also said that Howard had 'something of the night' about him, the story became irresistible, and we invited the former Home Secretary for an interview. That afternoon I called Derek Lewis, but he said he could tell me nothing, because he had signed the Official Secrets Act. I went to see Ann Widdecombe at the House of Commons, but she wasn't much more forthcoming, and was actually slightly worried that the 'something of the night' line sounded like the title of a pornographic novel.

During the live interview that night Michael Howard said first that he was 'entitled to be consulted' about the decision to remove the Governor of Parkhurst prison, but that he had not 'instructed' Derek Lewis to get rid of him. Lewis's version of events was that Howard had threatened to overrule him if he did not sack the Governor. Was Howard saying that Lewis had lied? Howard fell back on the 'I have given a full account of this …' defence, which explained nothing, and reiterated his version of events, repeatedly saying, 'I was entitled to be consulted.'

It was now that I asked, 'Did you threaten to overrule him?' for the first time. Howard did not answer the question, so I repeated it. I suddenly sensed that his evasions perhaps signified that I had stumbled upon the key issue. On the next iteration he began to answer not my question but another one which *he* had invented, about whether he had had *instructed* Lewis to dismiss the Governor. He found himself not guilty of that charge. But he had still not given a clear answer to my question about whether he had threatened to overrule Lewis if he did not get rid of the Parkhurst Governor, so I repeated it. Again and again. After twelve attempts, and with only two minutes of interview time remaining, I gave up, judging that it would by now be clear to anyone watching that Howard had ducked the question. As we were replaced by the next item and he got up to leave the studio, I asked him my usual 'Happy enough?' 'What do you think?' he spat out.

It had been an unusually tetchy encounter, but I was still astonished to wake up next morning and discover that the interview had become news. It did so mainly because the leadership of the opposition is a serious matter. But when the style of the interview itself, and my repetition of the same question a dozen times, later became a talking point, I was rather embarrassed – by comparison with penal policy and prison breakouts, interviews are, or ought to be, small beer. When asked about it afterwards, I would talk up other elements, such as the fact that Martin McGuinness, who was waiting in a studio in Derry to take part in the next item in the show, had got up and left the building, so suddenly there was more time, and I couldn't think of anything else to ask. It was true that the interview had been extended, but it is less easy to discern cause and effect. A few people have since suggested that the interview did politics a disservice, by 'treating the interviewee like a criminal'. I reject the claim: if as an interviewer you ask a question, it is your duty to get an answer.

The incident dashed Michael Howard's hopes of winning the party leadership in 1997. If only he had realised that he could have killed the thing stone dead had he said, 'It's some time ago now. I don't want to mislead you. I'll look at the papers and get back to you tomorrow.' That would have been an answer without being an answer.

Are the people who are interviewed different from the rest of us?

Tony Blair was once at a European Union summit in Holland at which all the heads of government had been invited to an evening reception. Like the other politicians, he worked the room with a grip-and-grin handshake introduction, at ease in his own importance. Thrusting his hand out to a rather older woman, he smiled, 'Hello, I'm Tony Blair.'

'And I'm Beatrix,' came the reply.

Before he could stop himself, Blair had asked the Queen of the Netherlands, 'And what do you do, Beatrix?'

Very few of the people I interview are troubled by self-doubt. But take away the trappings of office, the staff and outriders, the uniforms or guns, and they are little different from, and often less impressive than, the person who runs the local Scout group or works at the Citizens Advice Bureau. Quite apart from the capacity for blunders like that of Tony Blair, they may – like Gordon Brown or David Cameron – be visited by awful family tragedy, have embarrassing relatives, find that their bodies let them down or their children don't care for them. They're just human beings.

People who achieve eminence have often done things the rest of us have never done – made life-and-death decisions, earned millions, made astonishing discoveries, created wonderful art or gone into space. Some of them I found open, friendly and honest. Others were odious. The Palestinian commander who ordered a bombing which killed civilians was horrible. The Palestinian woman whose bomb exploded prematurely, driving shrapnel into her face, was tragic. But the greatest lessons I have learned from briefly rubbing shoulders with all manner of people are that different fields of life give licence to different ways of behaving, and human beings are just human beings. They were lucky, or they did unusual things because they grasped unusual opportunities. We're all just doing the best we can.

Who is the most impressive person you have interviewed?

That is impossible. Rummaging around in my memory would only guarantee that some people or occasions are overlooked. But assuming I could conduct a comprehensive audit, it would probably not be a politician, a business person, a trade unionist, or any other spokesman for a vested interest. The most striking individuals are those who do not prescribe, but attempt to understand. The big question is not whether or how, but why. Retaining a capacity for thoughtfulness is the key. That, and a sense of the absurd while others are taking you seriously.

Why didn't you stop him saying that?

Some surprisingly thoughtful people seem to believe that interviewees operate as ventriloquists' dummies. In 1998, after Tony Blair's Welsh Secretary Ron Davies had been involved in a 'moment of madness' on Clapham Common (he claimed he had met a Rastafarian, whose name he could not recall, and invited him to a dinner party at which he was mugged) we held a discussion about attitudes to homosexuality in public life. In the middle of the conversation the (gay) former Conservative MP Matthew Parris suddenly said he was certain there were at least two gay members of the Cabinet. I was caught flat-footed and wondered aloud, 'Two?'

'Well, Chris Smith is openly gay,' said Parris, 'and I think Peter Mandelson is certainly gay.'

At the time, though I knew Mandelson to be gay, he had not come out. I said, 'I think we will just move on from there. I'm not quite sure where he is on that.'

I was mortified. It was not that I wanted to collude in Mandelson's dissembling, but his sexual orientation was surely no one's business but his. That night I went home and wrote a note to stick through his letterbox the next morning. I said I was sorry that someone else had disclosed his sexuality, and that there had certainly been no plan for it to happen – I had had no idea what Matthew Parris would say.

As luck would have it, there was a reporter outside Mandelson's house when the taxi dropped me off there next morning. Seeing the letter, he exclaimed, 'Oh, I know what you're doing,' and within a couple of hours it was being reported that I had hand-delivered a note of 'apology' to a Cabinet Minister. The story had gone from a 'moment of madness' after dark on a public common, to speculation about how many members of Blair's Cabinet were gay, to whether the BBC was helping an unpopular Minister pull the wool over the public's eyes.

The storm blew over, of course, but not before Mandelson had sent a government driver to deliver his angry reply to my letter. He did not accept my version of events and the suggestion that there had been no plan to out him. The letter ended with the self-pitying words, 'I know how thoroughly *Newsnight* thinks about its output and interviews, and I know what licence it gives itself in traducing and demonising its pet hates. I have been one of these for too long.' Apart from the 'poor little me' tone, it was an unequivocal rejection of the idea that guests might say anything for themselves. It was a curious blind spot to have, considering that before becoming a politician Mandelson had been a television producer. I wrote back telling him to come off it. He was not mollified. But in live broadcasting you cannot predict what people will say. Which is one of the reasons for being careful to whom you give the freedom of the air.

How do you keep your own feelings out of it?

There is a long and not very glorious tradition of senior broadcasting executives claiming that their only concern is to ensure 'impartiality'. At its worst, this is one of the dullest ideas on the planet: for every point of view, some opposing position – however badly informed – has to be found. In a strict interpretation, every creationist would have to be matched against an evolutionary biologist, and they have much better things to do with their time. The idea is anyway defined very oddly – no mainstream broadcaster, for example, is impartial about racism. I share the anti-racist prejudice, but fascists have a case when they say that they are treated differently by the media from most other parties.

On the whole it is, I think, more practical to aim to be 'fair' than to expect to be 'impartial'. Political parties claim to be able to assess 'impartiality' by applying stopwatches to the amount of time given to each side of a particular argument. It makes for some very dry broadcasting. Even though 'fairness' is a matter of judgement, it is a better yardstick. Obviously, it can only be applied universally if everyone shares the same commitment and is willing to ask themselves, 'Am I being fair?' It ought to be possible. Once you remove personal feelings from broadcasting, you might as well have the job done by machines. For all the cold technology involved, it works only if there is some human transaction taking place between speaker and listener.

It would be simply dishonest for an interviewer not to acknowledge the extent to which they verbalise some of the assumptions of the society from which they come. Assuming the language difficulties could be sorted out, is there any reason why the whole of the European Union could not be served by a single newspaper? It would be dull as ditchwater, naturally, because things appear different, depending upon where they are seen from. That is the justification for the existence of hundreds of different newspapers in most countries, and it underpins the broadcasting authorities' commitment to diversity in television and radio. 'Fairness' is necessarily intuitive, but it makes for better interviews. In an interview one night with the hook-handed former nightclub bouncer and imam 'Abu Hamza', I found myself exclaiming, 'If you want to live in some fundamentalist state where they chop people's hands off and stone women to death, well then, why don't you go and do so?'

There *was* a notional question mark at the end of the sentence. But I knew it was a statement of opinion. No one ever rebuked me for it.

What are they really like?

This is as strange a question as 'What is a tree like?' A tree is a tree is a tree, whether it is an oak or a beech. Politicians are just human beings, like the rest of us. Some are entertaining, some are dull, some are clever, and some aren't. One of the silliest comments you ever hear is, 'They're all the same, aren't they?' No, they are not. They may all play a game that we recognise. But they do not all play it the same way. And some of them don't like the game very much, anyway. They often like to talk of their trade as 'public service', which puts the best possible gloss on what happens in Parliament or the council chamber. It is a noble generalisation, and some of them went into politics for high-minded reasons. Others are charlatans; and the reason still others went into politics is a mystery – they seem to have forgotten it themselves. On the whole, it is better that we settle what we disagree about by discussion rather than by fighting, and electing someone to Parliament is superior to trying to hire a mercenary or a prize-fighter. Those who are willing to do the job tend to be as variegated as the rest of us.

Do they all tell lies?

Not all of them, but the public image of politics suffers from the fact that its practitioners include people like Jeffrey Archer, a man prepared to sue for libel and then to lie in court (he would later go to prison for perjury and perverting the course of justice), and Jonathan Aitken, another Conservative who went to prison for the very same offences after a hubristic speech in which he talked about 'the simple sword of truth [wielded by him] and the trusty shield of British fair play'. Both men, and the half-dozen other parliamentarians who subsequently spent time at Her Majesty's pleasure for fiddling their expenses, had got into the habit of saying things and being taken seriously. All politics depends in the end on reducing things to simple, binary choices – do we do this, or do we do that? – which require you to assert that in an immensely complicated world there is only one possible answer to a problem. Certainty is a habit that is hard to break, and once you start to believe your own propaganda, you may easily come to believe you can walk on water.

Yet the outright liars remain a tiny minority. Much more common is a highly partial way of seeing the world, which is the consequence of the need to reduce everything to one perspective. The politician who says that 'Seventy per cent of cases are dealt with quickly and efficiently' is accurately citing the same statistics as the politician who says that 'A whole 30 per cent of cases are dealt with neither speedily or efficiently' – but the two are making contradictory points. And sometimes even the most important people can get the wrong end of the stick – as in all the ministerial warnings about the Millennium Bug and how planes would fall out of the sky and bank accounts void themselves as computers tried to cope with the arrival of the twenty-first century.

The Millennium Bug was at least worrying some computer scientists, but at other times politicians seem just to like making a noise. The Millennium Dome, Tony Blair's expensive vanity project in Greenwich to celebrate two thousand years of the Christian calendar, was justified by Peter Mandelson to the House of Commons as a place where citizens would be able to play a game called 'surfball', which, he said, was 'the twenty-first-century sport'. It has not been heard of since.

These are trivial examples, one based on a misapprehension, the other showing how front can see you through a great deal. There is no reason to believe that there is anything unusual about either of them.

What's with the make-up?

I've never worn make-up in civilian life. But the studio lights are bright, and the place can get very hot. Left to their own devices, most people's faces will assume a sickly pallor and then begin to glisten. When people perspire a lot, they can look decidedly shifty. In my own case – and that of many others – the visit to the make-up chair is pretty fleeting, though it does force three or four minutes of decompression upon you. Sometimes when sitting there you can learn things, although the Baroness who sat down, announced she was wearing no knickers and then gave me her hotel details was slightly more than expected. The students on *University Challenge* seem rather to enjoy the whole business – it proves they're really part of showbiz, I suppose. One who looked at the tub of brushes and creams and said to our make-up artist Jill Stansfield, 'Make me beautiful,' may take a different view.

'It's a brush, love, not a wand,' was the reply.

Can we believe what we read in the newspapers?

Sometimes. Outright lies are very uncommon in the news columns, although almost anyone who knows about a subject in any detail soon comes to accept that anything written in the press will be larded with inaccuracies, misunderstandings and false simplifications. The thing you immediately discover when people start to write about you in the papers is how much of what appears is just plain wrong. Even those of us who are utterly ignorant of how to write computer code, build a bridge, prune an apple tree or forecast the markets do generally know what we had for lunch, or which football team we support. We are, therefore, perfectly placed to know when something written about us is inaccurate. It happens all the time.

A veteran tabloid reporter once told me of the question he was asked when he returned to the newsroom having discovered that the story he had been sent to report on did not stand up.

'It's not true,' he told the gnarled news editor.

'Aye. But can you *write* it?' came the reply.

Most of the time the inaccuracies and misunderstandings are not intended, but are just the consequence of pressure or laziness – it never hurts to ask another question. For all the sneers of the broadsheet reporters, the tabloid papers often try harder. Though the headline may not be fully borne out by the story, there is generally the germ of a fact or two at the heart of things. It may be infuriating when the *Daily Mail* gets in touch to say they have it on 'impeccable authority' that you have done something or other (in consecutive months I had them asserting that I had secretly got married and then that I had 'definitely' split), but at least they are trying to check the story. Sometimes astonishing stories just fall into their laps. The *Daily Telegraph* once printed a paparazzo photograph of me on a bicycle turning right off The Mall. The sensational point was made by the caption: I was 'wearing a helmet and signalling clearly'. A reporter from the *Mail on Sunday* emailed my agent in 2011 urgently requesting a comment because 'We have some photographs of him inflating his bicycle tyres on Tuesday in London, and there's a couple of questions I wanted to ask.' I emailed back to say she'd better be careful Woodward and Bernstein didn't get a sniff of the 'Man Inflates Tyres' story.

Another time the same paper was in touch to say they had been told that I had had plastic surgery – though I doubtless need it, the tale was rubbish. A rule of thumb is that if something is in a gossip column and there are no direct quotes, it's probably tendentious or possibly made up. In its day, the diary column of the late *Independent on Sunday*, one of the most self-important broadsheets, was a particularly brazen offender.

The danger is that once something – true or false – gets into the newspaper cuttings it is likely to be repeated again and again. Someone once claimed on Wikipedia that I had been to school at Charterhouse in Surrey, an institution I have never set foot inside. It soon became part of my life story in numerous newspaper profiles. Broadcasters affect to maintain a superiority to newspapers, but are just as dependent upon the cuttings. The root of the problem is that there is far too much space to fill and far too few reporters. It is a great deal easier to recycle something or to make something up than it is to get out of the office and find something out.

Do you know all the answers on University Challenge?

Of course not. The English scientist Thomas Young is supposed to have been the last person who knew everything it was possible to know, and he died in 1829, which makes him too old even to be a quizmaster. The questions on *University Challenge* are the work of quite a large team, and are much easier to answer, or to seem to answer, at home than in a brightly-lit television studio. I have discovered that quite the best way to cope with a television quiz is to have the answers written on a card in front of you.

Incidentally, the questions are now not only much harder than they used to be, but get progressively harder the closer the contest gets to the final.

Why does everyone make such a fuss about television awards?

All television is showing off to some degree, and most people like to be acclaimed, especially by their colleagues. Some awards are genuine marks of appreciation by doctors, farmers, politics lecturers, or even travel agents. The BAFTA film awards are decided by members of a club who have been given the opportunity to watch the movies at home instead of undergoing the torture of seeing them on a big screen with a proper sound system and a room full of *hoi polloi*. Other awards are just given to people willing to turn up to collect them – I once accepted a Variety Club award simply because I was so surprised to have been offered it; I later discovered that had I not been willing to go to their event, they'd simply have given it to someone else. Still others are a way of making an organisation seem real: the Notty Ash Television Awards suggest that the Notty Ash Television Viewers' Association is to be taken seriously. And others are just rackets.

Every winter, producers are detached from doing something useful and set to assembling showreels for ambitious programmes and individuals. Quite apart from the waste of the producers' time, the broadcasters are also often charged money to submit their entries. Then there are tables to be sold for the dinner at which employees can watch the awards being presented – it is surprising how many allegedly 'edgy' individuals love to dress up like a waiter and get merry at someone else's expense. I often felt that if licence-fee payers were aware that money collected from them was used to enter competitions, instead of being spent on programmes, they would be pretty angry. But each time I suggested that the BBC should simply decline to play along with the Royal Television Society Awards, for example, I got the reply, 'But if we did that, then the RTS would collapse.' This was, apparently, self-evidently A Bad Thing.

Is there a difference between working for the BBC and ITV?

At the BBC I would never have worked on a programme that shared its production office with *The Jeremy Kyle Show*, as *University Challenge* does. While *University Challenge* producers beaver away on the relationship between Dadaism and Surrealism, their counterparts on other ITV entertainment programmes scour the land for people whose problems will provide work for the *Kyle* show, daytime-TV psychiatrists, or a broadcast small-claims court. 'Do you think there are too many physics questions in this show?' you hear a *University Challenge* producer worry, while on the next desk someone is earnestly asking on the phone, 'And how long have you found his toenails put you off sex?'

Underneath the raked audience seating of *University Challenge* is the little room where Jeremy Kyle takes his sobbing victims and promises them the eternal support of his staff if only they'll get back on the set and disclose more of their sad or sordid lives. One of my favourite idle fantasies is that the teams of students on *University Challenge* will somehow find their way into the *Kyle* studio, while the tattooed crack addicts attempting to prove by lie-detector test that they never slept with their grandmothers are fired questions about Petrarchan sonnets.

There was a period when the two shows shared a make-up room, and one day a young woman was being powdered alongside her father. 'I can't go on holiday because of him,' she said, stabbing a finger in his direction. 'He stopped me getting a passport.'

'That must be terrible. No foreign holidays?' asked Jill.

'It's worse than that,' said the young woman. 'I can't get any catalogues either.'

When the two programmes were recorded at the same time (in different studios), the beaming mothers and fathers of the over-bright young people would be marshalled alongside the *Kyle* mob, because there was only one metal detector – legend had it that a *Kyle* audience had once left the building with the entire contents of a room full of prizes for a game show that was to be filmed later in the week. The most astonishing thing about the heist was the fact that the items helped on their way included an entire set of garden furniture.

There are no prizes on *University Challenge*, which is part of its charm. Historically, the BBC always had a problem with prizes of much value anyway – a toaster or a bedside tea-maker was considered pretty well beyond the dreams of avarice – which is why the decision to broadcast a programme celebrating the dropping of balls in the National Lottery was such a watershed. A wagonload of monkeys could never write the works of Shakespeare, but they could certainly play the lottery, for it requires no skill whatsoever. When the BBC acquired the rights to broadcast the weekly draw it attempted to invest a game of chance with a fatuous dignity; but nevertheless, it marked the crossing of a Rubicon.

Independent television is not so encumbered, and is a business, which must satisfy its shareholders by producing programmes on which advertisers want to spend money. The BBC has no shareholders, and historically defined its mission in higher-minded terms than the mere attracting of an audience. One of the odd consequences of this was that very large numbers of people required by law to pay a tax to fund the BBC did not bother to watch what their money was spent on. In caricature, the BBC became a service watched by the respectable middle classes, while ITV, funded by advertising, was entertainment for the proles. Much of the distinction has vanished since the BBC determined to compete for viewers, and quite how muddy the water has become is shown by the fact that *University Challenge* is made by ITV for transmission on BBC 2, where it regularly achieves the highest ratings of the day, running against shows that ITV has lavished production resources upon. The fact that so many newspapers still begin to bay when the BBC lavishes money on shows which might just as easily have been funded by advertising demonstrates how much the old assumptions about the corporation serving some higher purpose are shared. For all the sound and fury, the papers help to keep the BBC honest.

Changed attitudes to broadcasting have blurred the distinction between the BBC and commercial television. Before I found a home on *Newsnight* I applied for jobs with Granada three times. Three times I was rejected.

The red rooftop sign 'GRANADA TV' still blazed across Manchester, but by the time I arrived at the slightly gimcrack 1950s building beneath to work on *University Challenge*, the company was already fading. It had once been considered the finest commercial broadcaster in the land, for its punchy current affairs show *World in Action*, superb dramas like *Prime Suspect* and *Brideshead Revisited*, its role as a patron of modern art, and its inner-city scholarship schemes. And it had done all of this while being, to its core, a north-western company, with a proud Mancunian soul. But changes to broadcasting regulations brought in by the Conservative government in the 1990s elevated business concerns above editorial regulation. And as in so many areas, when the Blair government arrived it just consolidated the changes, so programmes that made trouble for the powerful became progressively more morally and editorially neutered. One by one, obligations imposed on commercial broadcasters – to provide for children, to serve the arts, to deliver religious content – were removed or relaxed inside the corporate behemoth of ITV.

I arrived on *University Challenge* as the last vestiges of Granada's heritage were being extinguished under Gerry Robinson, its new boss, who was described in John Cleese's unpleasantly snobby words as an 'upstart caterer'. Oddly, the only food to be had inside the building appeared to be from vending machines, although later the company's dubious canteen reopened. Granada TV has now been swallowed inside the corporate behemoth of ITV.

But big cultural differences remain between the commercial sector and the BBC. As a performer, the first thing you notice is the very different attitudes toward 'talent'. At the BBC, the producer will always be on top. BBC Light Entertainment came to see the drawing power of personalities like Michael Parkinson, Terry Wogan or Chris Evans years ago, but news has never really shaken off its belief that what matters are the events being reported upon, not who is doing the reporting. I rather share the prejudice. On ITV, if the name of the performer is not in the title of the show, then it is 'The News' – pregnant pause – 'with Sylvia Nailvarnish.' The style is American. While the BBC has been growing out of its affection for anonymity for years, it has accepted recognisable newsreaders only grudgingly. There is still a feeling that the ideal Huw Edwards would be battery-powered.

As a consequence the BBC has, generally speaking, been hopeless at dealing with 'talent'. Occasionally senior executives are sent on courses to teach them 'talent management', and for a few months thereafter everyone who appears on screen gets a birthday card from their channel controller or whichever figure in the bureaucracy is their notional head of department. Sometimes the recipient has never met the sender. ITV manages these things much better, but I find it a hard issue to get exercised about – after all, if licence-fee payers want to send a birthday card to a favourite presenter, they're quite free to do so. Rather touchingly, some of them do just that.

Do you wear your own clothes on screen?

News presenters wear their own clothes, even though by the time of a late-evening transmission they may be pretty crumpled, or stained with lunch. Periodically, stories circulate about female newscasters getting dress allowances, although I imagine that such a gender-specific thing is no longer allowed.

University Challenge, being an ITV Entertainment show, comes from a different culture, and when I was first asked to work there I was sent off to be measured by a theatrical costumier in central London. He produced the two most uncomfortable suits I have ever tried to wear, and they were sent back. Now I just wear whatever is to hand in the ITV wardrobe store. Students turn up for recordings in their own clothes, and wear them on set unless they strobe on camera or bear obscene messages or commercial logos; then there is a rummage around in the costume department and some alternative is found which probably last had an outing on *Coronation Street* or on the shoulders of a fictional serial killer. The programme has a (small) budget to spend on presenters' jackets, shirts and ties, which come from the local shopping centre. Since my legs are hidden by the desk, I usually just change my top half between matches.

On news programmes, male presenters are expected to wear a subdued suit, on the theory that it is better that people pay attention to the content than spend their time wondering where on earth that awful jacket came from. News programmes and

University Challenge both have a thing about ties: in some ante-diluvian way they are thought to impart authority, even though they now tend otherwise to be confined to politicians, estate agents and car salesmen.

Are there some questions which never get asked? And others which shouldn't be asked?

The most important questions which never get asked are the questions it never occurs to anyone to ask. Since so many of those who report on politics share a large number of the assumptions on which the political class survives, entire swathes of life are simply excluded from discussion. It was this constituency for whom Russell Brand spoke. The simple questions – Who? Where? When? Why? How? – are the best.

'Is it true that you called Angela Merkel "an unfuckable lard-arse"?' is a question on the borders of tastefulness, even though Silvio Berlusconi, to whom I addressed it, gave no indication of considering it anything other than part of normal conversation. We were talking in June 2014 in the grounds of his lovely country house in the hills north of Milan: bizarrely, given his reputation, the place was once a convent. It was a beautiful Lombardy Sunday morning, but even so a great gaggle of hangers-on – courtiers, assistants, drivers – sat around in the shade: Berlusconi was not to be disturbed until midday. When he appeared, his face painted a strange shade of orange, his eyebrows stenciled dark and every follicle of his hair transplant shouting 'Look at me! This is not where I began life,' the courtiers all started to move, like the water in a harbour when the tide begins to flood. Berlusconi is a short, square man with the ingratiating smile of a restaurant *maître d'*, which doubtless served him well when he worked as a crooner on cruise ships. He is the sort of man who simply could not survive in public life in Britain – it would be like choosing Ken Dodd as Prime Minister.

In addition there was the inconvenience, by the time of our interview, that he was banned from holding public office because of convictions for fraud, to say nothing of accusations of underage sex with 'Ruby Rubacuori', a Moroccan belly-dancer who had joined him at 'bunga-bunga' parties. If Berlusconi was bothered by his reputation he gave no sign of it, and once the interview was finished he asked if I would like to see 'the bunga-bunga room'. Not surprisingly, I said yes. He then opened the door to a long dining room. It was not what I had been expecting. On the furthest wall hung a School of Leonardo portrait of a young woman. 'They tell me she is one month older than Ruby,' said Berlusconi with a rather unpleasant wink.

'Would you like to join me for lunch?' he then asked. Of course, I said. Perhaps the camera crew could join us? No, they could not – he insisted they ate in the kitchen. So I sat at a table in a former convent with a man with an orange face who had been charged with having sex with underage girls, eating fettuccine with a ragù sauce which had been prepared by his cook. He talked incessantly, mainly about how much the Italian people loved him – rather as they loved the Pope, he said. For pudding we were served his home-made ice cream, of which he was immensely proud, though I rather doubted that he had made it himself. When the door from the kitchen swung open I could see our cameraman and sound recordist surrounded by nubile young women doing the washing up. They seemed very content.

Is the BBC dominated by political correctness?

Yes. It is sometimes idiotic and sometimes frustrating. But on the whole what is derisively called political correctness is just a wish not to discriminate against people because of who they are, how they look or how they act. What's wrong with that?

Is the television industry a snakepit?

It is true that parts of it certainly have that reputation. At the time I was on *Panorama* the programme was especially poisonous, which I attributed to the particular mix of people who were there at the time – as one of the producers put it from deep within his built-up heels, 'It is not enough to succeed. Others must be seen to fail.' The programme is still pretty toxic, by all accounts. It comes, I think, from having several teams working on different stories at the same time. When one of them is chosen for broadcast, it means that others aren't.

And it's important to remember how compartmentalised the industry is – you could spend your career producing arts programmes and never meet the people who put sport on screen. But in the end, all of you are competing to arrest the eyeballs of the viewer. Just as it has had a good influence on the nation, the BBC has probably had a very benign influence on the industry, cultivating good practice, moderating rampant commercialism, limiting the clash of egos, and creating better working conditions than would be the case if everyone lived or died by their last production.

It's never been quite true that worry about the size of the audience always drives out good sense and judgement – the BBC invented *EastEnders* to give itself an audience platform in the schedules, yet it continues to televise the Promenade concerts every summer. But if no one is watching, there is really no point in going to the trouble of making programmes. The BBC stood for years against the idea that television was a mere 'industry'. Yet, however high-minded executives may claim to be, everyone cares about the overnight ratings. These demonstrate time and again that you don't need topless weather forecasters for commercial success: a channel of live sports events, talent shows and soap operas, interspersed with a bit of detective fiction, would have no trouble finding investors. The British have still not lost their taste for a bit of period murder and mayhem around the village green, or for endless reworkings of some bygone ideas about social class. Fill out the daytime schedules with cookery shows and property porn, and being a channel controller ought not to be very hard.

As an industry, television is also blessed by having its pick of creative young people. Because there is no shortage of supply, they tend to be treated worse than used to be the case, expected to work without pay in the early stages, and then to hop and hope from one short-term contract to another. Their problems tend to come just at the point when they enter the Bermuda Triangle of mortgage, children and anxiety about job prospects. Alasdair Milne, who rose to become Director General of the BBC and was then sacked for being intellectually arrogant and politically inconvenient, is supposed to have said that he thought he was too old to edit the *Tonight* programme when he turned thirty. The business remains a young person's game: if you haven't escaped the indignities of the daily graft by your early forties you will find yourself pitching ideas against people little more than half your age, blessed with more energy and unencumbered by your domestic distractions. Maybe that's where the reputation for unpleasantness begins.

But taking the industry as a whole, it seems to me to have no bigger a quotient of unpleasant people than most. In fact, because the majority of those involved are – or ought to be – thinking about serving the public good, it's probably better than many others. It's been a great place to spend a working life.

11

And?

I called a local taxi firm the other day, and couldn't help remarking to the woman who answered the phone (admittedly, it was a Monday morning) that she sounded rather dejected. I don't suppose it improved her day much to be told, but she answered, 'I am a bit. But it's a job.' I have been lucky enough to have had to think of earning a living in that way only rarely. I could usually convince myself that whatever I was doing, it was Important. It doubtless made me pompous at times. But constant observation of the human comedy tends to make you either laugh or cry, and I've had the good fortune to have laughed a lot. It is the relationships you form which make any job enjoyable, or even tolerable.

I have become a great deal less messianic about news than I was when I started in the business. Partly this is because genuine news – information about an event which causes you to gasp, or at the very least to say, 'Well, I never knew that!' – is very rare indeed. The British vote to leave the European Union, the subsequent chaotic battles to win the leadership of the two biggest British political parties, the shot in the arm the referendum result gave to those seeking to break up the United Kingdom, were genuine surprises. The 'I told you so' pieties it also gave rise to were not. But most of the time what is presented to us in the newspapers and on the news bulletins is hardly genuinely surprising.

There is something else, too, that is evident in the digests of important events which are presented at the end of every year by most news organisations. For every sudden death or terrorist outrage there are a dozen other, less sensational, events which are in fact at least as important in defining how we live now. We often don't register them, because they fit a general pattern. Some – politicians lecturing about 'family values' and then getting caught in a sex scandal – are simply part of the cavalcade of human folly. Others, like a clifftop lighthouse, briefly illuminate relatively constant aspects of our lives. One Prime Minister after another takes himself across the Atlantic to declare that Britain still has a Special Relationship with the United States, even though it clearly means less and less in Washington. For decades they took themselves, too, to European 'summit conferences' – an increasingly meaningless term, since there can be hardly a mountaintop in the world big enough to accommodate twenty-eight heads of government and their hangers-on. They were too high in the clouds to hear the rumblings of discomfort from the citizenry about the political elite's much-loved 'European Project'.

Each year also brings more graphs and tables to set off a further bout of hand-wringing about why other economies, notably in the east, are growing faster than that of Britain. Everyone swears faith in the National Health Service, but refuses to imagine ways of ensuring its survival. Moral panics come and go, about anti-social behaviour, drunkenness, drugs or child neglect: they all bring forth anxieties about whether the nation will ever recover a sense of purpose. British children are repeatedly found to know less than young people in some other countries. The British armed forces diminish in size while Foreign Secretaries posture as if nothing has happened – the country clings to its pretensions like Miss Havisham wandering around her decaying mansion in her wedding dress, decades after being jilted at the altar. The Church of England continues its amble into irrelevance, mumbling to itself about the ordination of women and what it should think about homosexuality.

Many of these developments are troubling, while others are positively beneficial. There is, however, a discernibly constant direction of travel. While many of its cultural, financial and educational institutions remain the best of their kind in the world, in terms of crude power Britain is a shadow of what it once was – even if the often not-very-impressive figures at the top try to pretend otherwise. Yet Britain remains an immensely civilised country, with deeply ingrained values – respect for the rule of law, 'I know my rights,' a sense of fair play, minding your own business, a commitment to democracy – which other nations, even in Western Europe, just don't get. The country has retained these values while travelling a long way in a short time. I have seen dozens of other countries, and there is nowhere I would rather live. A feeling that 'We're going to the dogs' is intrinsic to how we are.

There is a stock set of clichés which reporters tend to repeat when they reflect on their lives. Having 'a ringside seat' is one of them. And though I try to follow George Orwell's advice never to use a metaphor which you are used to seeing in print, I suppose I have had such a thing. I was in Belfast when the IRA declared its ceasefire, and in the Western Cape when Nelson Mandela walked out of prison. I watched black South Africans vote for the first time in history, travelled with migrants from Romania to Britain, was in Maastricht when the European Union was invented, and in Washington when Bill Clinton, George W. Bush and Barack Obama were elected President. I have met just about every significant British politician of the last quarter of a century, and sometimes our interviews made a few waves. I don't suppose I registered much with Henry Kissinger or Noam Chomsky, Christine Lagarde or the Dalai Lama, Daniel Barenboim, David Bowie or Maya

Angelou, but at least I got the chance to meet them all. I even once had to interview a chimpanzee that could count.

So what? The reporter's job is to watch, to pass on what he or she finds out, and to hold the powerful to account. But the limits of competence are strictly marked, and to attach particular importance to those who report the news is like being more interested in the handles on the coffin than in the life of the person inside. We could all do with remembering that making comments is easy, but making decisions is hard. There have always been grandees in the journalistic trade, spewing forth reams of self-important comment on the state of the world. The best of them have been at least raffish and entertaining. The most dreadful of those who fancied themselves 'opinion formers' have sought out the company of plutocrats and the esteem of the powerful. But journalism is in the end a life of spurious glamour. If you doubt this, just think for a moment what all those portentous political editors do when they are caged behind a crowd barrier in Downing Street and bursting to use the lavatory. One of the big changes that has occurred in the last forty years is that the rest of society has come to take so many journalists as seriously as they take themselves. A career in 'the media' is now seen as a respectable calling, and wanting to get ahead can be the enemy of decent journalism: a reporter should care about his story, not about whether or not it makes his bosses more likely to promote him. The best reporters and producers I have worked with have all been irreverent, humorous, down-to-earth and slightly fixated. The worst have been dullards or popinjays.

At the time I entered the business, journalism was regarded as a grubby trade. But the huge expansion of higher education and the accompanying growth of the professional class, the decline of many traditional occupations, the increase in the number of media outlets, the growth of leisure, the replacement of *doing* by *saying*, have led to a proliferation of courses teaching a media career as a 'profession'. Those who could not stomach the business itself can now carve out secure employment by teaching aspects of the trade to impressionable young people. It is high time someone initiated a prosecution for confidence trickery against the universities and colleges which purport to promise a career in the media when there are simply not enough jobs for the claim to be true. To echo Noël Coward's advice to Mrs Worthington about trying to get her daughter on the stage:

> The profession is overcrowded,
> The struggle's pretty tough,
> And admitting the fact she's burning to act,
> That isn't quite enough.

Finding things out is hard work, and can be pretty thankless; the plain fact is that there are too many people chasing too little genuine news. Too many bricks are being made with too little straw. There is something frustrating in the way the news machine operates. It is not just that the morning meetings to plan for the next edition or that evening's broadcast are dominated by what has been in that day's newspapers, and that so much of the 'prospects' or news diaries showing what is expected to happen has been vouchsafed by the PR offices of powerful organisations. It is also that specialist correspondents can too easily become the creatures of the people they report upon.

Then there is the language used by journalists – laden with jargon and cliché – which can deaden the very events it purports to describe. Every event is a 'crisis'; reporters do not inquire, they 'drill down'; travel disruption does not cause inconvenience, but 'misery'. A correspondent discussing the chances of a peace agreement in the Middle East once actually talked of 'the roadmap' being 'derailed before it was airborne'.

Nor is there much evidence that we have become broader-minded in the way we look at the world. The United States is over-covered. Much of Europe is under-reported. Africa is mainly bad news, the Middle East mainly menace. South America might as well not exist. Television thirsts for excitement, which is not the same as thirsting for understanding. Since technology now means that pictures sooner or later become available from the scene of most tragedies anywhere in the world, the viewing public is routinely assailed with images of suffering and distress about which they can do precisely nothing. Of course it is good that we feel a sense of kinship with those less fortunate than ourselves, but the reverse outcome is just as possible – a numbed indifference to the sight of yet more victims of events over which neither they nor we have any control. We pretend that all human life has the same value – the starving child in Sudan, the murdered child in Rotherham – but every news editor knows that it is the Yorkshire story they're talking about in the pub. Yet because technology has penetrated deeper in richer countries – as evidenced by the news's obsession with transatlantic weather porn – we are likely to be told in great detail about the latest high-school shooting in the United States long before we hear anything about the daily problems that beset teachers in classrooms at home or in Africa. Television remains an escapist medium even when it is most apparently rooted in reality.

What is to be done? Journalism is important: those who know nothing can have anything done to them. All our lives are affected by the laws passed in Parliament, which is one of the reasons we should all pay attention to politics. But perhaps the question we need to ask ourselves is how much we need to know of things about which we can do little or nothing – the Third World misery, the freakish weather in Alabama, most murder cases and other people's private lives. Less concern with impact might mean more depth. Take just one example: business and finance are covered appallingly on the electronic media, which tend to throw their hands in the air and tut when shysters get found out treating the economy as a game of chance, while failing to hold to account the immensely wealthy and powerful people who shape so much of our lives. The shysters get away with it because they *can* get away with it. Oh, we are told, but there is plenty of news – entire channels devoted to it. The problem is that the more there is of it, the less most of it seems to count.

At its most basic level news matters because disclosure is the enemy of tyranny and ignorance its ally. It cannot be repeated too often that a well-informed democracy is a healthier democracy. However much governments have freed commercial broadcasters from editorial obligations, information companies are not just another business: there is a special responsibility when you are shaping the minds of a nation. There is a deeper question, too. The proliferation of media channels means that anyone can say or hear more or less anything. The growing distrust of politicians is partly attributable to the fact that they can no longer claim any special grasp of information. Not all sources of information are created equal, and some of the wells have been laced with hallucinogenic drugs.

But most of the unpolluted wells were created in an age of fewer television and radio channels, long before the World Wide Web was invented – *Newsnight*, for example, was born in 1980. There is a particular challenge facing these shows: by the twenty-first century, people had a galaxy of alternative sources of information available to them. The audience appeared to be ageing, and attempts to appeal to a younger demographic group – with items on street fashion, or by making presenters dance or interview glove puppets – were frankly embarrassing. Was it time to invent something else? Certainly it was time to let someone else see what they could do with what was already there. I would have left *Newsnight* earlier had it not been for the fact that the programme was in such a terrible state.

* * *

In the autumn of 2011, Meirion Jones, a longstanding *Newsnight* producer, told me he was going to 'nail' Jimmy Savile. I was underwhelmed, for Savile had just been nailed into his coffin. But I had known Meirion for years as a dogged journalist with that obsessional, slightly nutty commitment that marks out all successful investigative reporters. Most of all, whenever there was some slick, highly paid corporate lawyer trying to get an inconvenient investigation canned, Meirion knew how far we could stick to our guns. He was brave and subversive, and if he said something was true I believed him. But Jimmy Savile, a shallow, loud-mouthed disc jockey? Really?

And what, I asked, was the point in trying to take down a man who had already been carried off? Meirion said that an aunt of his had run Duncroft, an approved school for teenage girls in Surrey, in the 1970s and eighties. While visiting her there he had seen Savile arrive in a gold-coloured Rolls-Royce convertible and take out some of the school-age girls. Meirion had guessed what he was up to, and, appalled by the eulogies which attended the death of the old fraud, persuaded Peter Rippon, the then *Newsnight* editor, to let him begin an investigation. In short order Meirion and his reporter, Liz McKean, tracked down a number of women Savile had sexually assaulted. But when he saw BBC news's uncritical coverage of Savile's ostentatious funeral in Leeds (golden coffin, mourners on the streets, obsequies led by the Roman Catholic Bishop of the city), he guessed – correctly – that his revelations about Savile's predatory paedophilia would create enormous problems for the BBC.

Even the mice in Broadcasting House were familiar with the stories about Savile's taste for teenage girls. The great question (which – too long afterwards – bothered the BBC enough for it to commission an outside investigation by a former High Court judge) is why no one had done anything about them. The answer, I think, is that Jimmy Savile was a small part of the hordes which invaded the stuffy old BBC when, in 1967, the corporation was instructed to provide a radio station for pop music. Throughout most of the sixties the BBC had remained wedded to cosy radio shows like *Workers' Playtime* and *Family Favourites*, and the men in tweed jackets and cardigans simply had no idea of how to manage a bunch of brash disc jockeys. Sex is intrinsic to teenage music, and the BBC was run by people who preferred pipes and sensible skirts.

On one of my first days in the BBC in the early seventies I walked past the murky studio where Alan 'Fluff' Freeman was broadcasting an afternoon show. There was underwear hanging from the mic stand. Even then, the rumours about Jimmy Savile's appetite for young flesh had been around for years, and I cannot have been unusual in preferring to file him in a box marked 'shallow, vulgar and distasteful', and to leave it at that. But now, thanks to Meirion's work, *Newsnight* had a piece in which, among other things, a former pupil at the approved school told of being obliged to service Savile in exchange for visits to the recording of pop shows at the BBC. She also talked of seeing the convicted paedophile Gary Glitter having sex with a teenage girl in Savile's dressing room. Yet the people who planned the BBC's Christmas schedules were envisaging a series of programmes portraying the man as a jolly (if inane) family entertainer. In the early stages of his investigation not even Meirion would have claimed that *Newsnight* was in a lather of excitement at his imminent revelations about an unsavoury disc jockey – and a dead one at that. But by now the team had unearthed numerous examples of Savile's abuse – they guessed the final total of victims, if it could ever be established, would come to over a hundred. They were especially angry that Savile appeared to have protected himself by cultivating friends in high places like Margaret Thatcher and Prince Charles. Any direct attempt to halt a highly embarrassing investigation was doomed to fail: our self-respect would demand that we ignore any request from elsewhere in the organisation to drop the story. But the BBC is full of clever, sophisticated people who could ensure that nothing so crude as a confrontation occurred.

At this point the editor Peter Rippon suddenly changed his tune. One week he was keen to run a piece on *Newsnight* about paedophilia. The next, he said the real issue was whether the Crown Prosecution Service had failed to prosecute Savile because he was too old. This was a story the team did not have, for the simple reason that it was not the story they were pursuing. Had someone leaned on him to squash the investigation? It is fair to say that Rippon, a stolid man whose previous career had been spent in radio, did not command the respect of the team. He never seemed to get to grips with the mechanics of the new medium, or to share our enthusiasm for a good scrap. I argued with him that we should broadcast the Savile piece as soon as possible, but each time I did so he replied, 'I can't do that' – which struck me as a strange choice of words. In the end an editor has to edit, and you can't go on indefinitely arguing the toss. I, Meirion, Liz and everyone else bit our tongues and accepted his judgement.

None of us was among the target audience for the Savile-related tat in the Christmas schedules, and the issue might have been forgotten, had it not been for the fact that many months later – a year after Savile's death – a documentary appeared on ITV exposing his paedophilia, some of which was said to have occurred on BBC premises. The film was very obviously based upon the *Newsnight* discoveries. The organisation now had two serious embarrassments. Firstly, there was the accusation that minors had been abused inside the BBC. Secondly, it became public that *Newsnight* had shelved its own investigation into the matter. With politicians calling for the BBC management to take action, two separate investigations were set up – one into the allegations themselves, and one into how the BBC's own inquiry had been suppressed.

The critical question, which was now part of the subject matter of yet another BBC journalistic investigation, this time by *Panorama*, was whether the decision to abandon the *Newsnight* inquiry had been taken because it would have compromised the BBC's plans to 'celebrate' Savile's life in various Christmas programmes. As if in a satirical novel, the key conversation about this was said to have taken place at a celebrity lunch. The new Director General, my friend George Entwistle, was called before the House of Commons Select Committee on Culture, Media and Sport, and prejudged the outcome of the second inquiry by declaring that the decision to can the *Newsnight* investigation had been 'a catastrophic mistake'. The editor of the programme was invited to 'step aside', whatever that meant. Soon afterwards, the BBC began using its press department to brief journalists against its own reporters, some of whom soon left the organisation in disgust.

The BBC – and *Newsnight* in particular – was therefore in a sensitive state when a man from an outfit called the Bureau for Investigative Journalism, based at City University in London, approached it with a story. Investigative journalism takes time and costs money – sometimes a great deal of money – because there is no guarantee where the research will lead you, nor how long it will take to complete: you might spend months on a story and never find the key fact or witness to nail the allegation definitively. The grand-sounding Bureau of Investigative Journalism had been set up in 2010, partly in recognition of the fact that reduced broadcasting budgets had made those sort of considerations more powerful than ever. The story it offered *Newsnight* was about how police had failed properly to investigate allegations of child abuse at a children's home in North Wales. In journalistic terms, the allegations were ancient, and they had already been exposed on a radio programme twelve years earlier. Angus Stickler, the BIJ reporter, contacted a man who said he had been abused at the home, and interviewed him about his experiences.

I was in Washington covering the re-election of Barack Obama, accompanied by one of the programme's two deputy editors, Liz Gibbons. Having been three thousand miles away when the previous night's edition, which included the BIJ story, was broadcast, I was at a bit of a loss when Ian Hislop, editor of *Private Eye*, called to say he had seen *Newsnight*, and warned me, 'I hope you've got more evidence than you put on air, because we once went to court with that witness, and when he got into the box, he completely changed his story.' The man had been judged by a government inquiry into the abuse allegations to be 'severely psychologically damaged' and an unreliable witness. I really had no idea what Ian was talking about, but found Liz in a room down the corridor of the improvised office we were using. When I told her of the call she looked alarmed. The first thing she said was, 'It's OK. We didn't name the perpetrator.'

'Whether you choose to name him or not is a matter of judgement,' I replied. 'But before you air the story you have to be certain you've got the right man.' She did not look as if she found this comment helpful.

In truth, she had been in an impossible position. The programme had had to rush the story onto the air because other outlets were openly saying that *Newsnight* had a story about the sexual abuse of children, which according to *Channel 4 News* involved 'a former senior Conservative official from the Thatcher era'. The show surely wouldn't squash a story of sex abuse *again*? Channel 4 had spoken to Lord McAlpine, who had been the Tory Party Treasurer at the time of the alleged abuse, and who was rumoured (wrongly) to have been identified from a photograph by one of the victims. Following the Savile fiasco, not to have broadcast the story would have looked like another example of self-censorship.

When gargantuan egos like the wife of the Speaker of House of Commons began throwing McAlpine's name around on Twitter, the formula that *Newsnight* had come up with, of not identifying the alleged perpetrator, was a dead letter. But – and this was the point at which the whole thing imploded, and one wondered why on earth no one had done it beforehand – when the victim was shown a photograph of Lord McAlpine, he said it was definitely not the man who had abused him. That Friday – a week after the fateful broadcast – Eddie Mair was guest-presenting the programme. The poor fellow, who is certainly one of the finest news broadcasters in Britain, and probably the best of all of them, was told to begin with an apology. He refused: he had had nothing to do with the affair. In the corporation's usual fashion, deputy heads rolled: and *Newsnight*'s deputy editor and the former deputy head of the News Division were removed from their posts (also in true BBC fashion, both were subsequently promoted). Nearly 1,300 licence-fee payers saw their annual contribution given to Lord McAlpine in damages, with plenty more money spent on lawyers.

'Is *Newsnight* toast?' Eddie had asked on air, voicing the question that was keeping most of the staff awake at night. He ended that evening's show with, '*Newsnight* will be back on Monday – probably.'

The BBC had been caught out by the utterly changed media environment, in which what was said *about* what was said on air could play a poisonous role. Soon, the organisation had begun yet another internal investigation. There was much talk of a lesson having been learned. By then, of course, it was far too late. The team on the original Savile investigation had quit, my friend George Entwistle – who would have made a rather good Director General – had lost his job, and the *Newsnight* editor had been sent to take on what the BBC described as 'a significant challenge', looking after the corporation's paperclip supply. In the way of these things, that Establishment pillar Lord Patten retained his job as BBC Chairman.

There was much fevered anxiety on the programme about rumours (spread by, among others, the BBC's own media correspondent) that *Newsnight* would be taken off the air. No show has – or deserves to have – an indefinite life, and doubtless sooner or later someone will dream up a programme which seems to suit the mood of the times better. But no one wants to be aboard a ship that's being scuttled. Though I had by now decided that it was time to move on, quitting at this point would have made me look like the proverbial rat. Instead, I went to see the acting Director General, Tim Davie, to see if I could plead for the programme's survival. He said that the rumours *Newsnight* was to be scuppered were untrue, but that the programme was to be placed under new management.

I decided I would stay until things got back on an even keel. I could not argue with the decision to install a new editorial team: the misjudgements about Jimmy Savile and the utter incompetence revealed by the later blackening of the name of an innocent man showed how desperate was the need for reform. In subsequent investigations Savile was revealed to have abused children and vulnerable adults at a range of institutions, of which the BBC was only one – the *Newsnight* journalists had been right. Probably the most depressing thing about the whole affair was its demonstration that the girl who had been assaulted by Savile had been right to guess that her allegations would have been ignored had she begged anyone to listen to her.

I was confirmed in my decision to move on when I was sent one day to interview the Chief Inspector of Schools, Sir Michael Wilshaw, a man I rather liked. I was sitting in his office before the interview teasing him about how old he was (he was then sixty-eight), and I asked the producer who had been sent with me how old *she* was. 'I'm twenty-seven,' she said. I realised that when I began at *Newsnight* she had probably been in nappies. It was definitely time to do something else.*

---

* My decision had nothing to do with the music played in one of the lifts of Broadcasting House, as was bizarrely alleged by the *Daily Telegraph*. (The music was awful, though.)

It might have been a sad moment, but I did not find it so, partly because I did not imagine that it would be the end of the road – had it not been for the Savile shambles, I would have left earlier. I recognised, too, that I owed the programme a lot. For a quarter of a century it paid me to have fun. I had worked with funny, interesting, irreverent people, and what we did required us to meet many of Britain's most influential individuals, and a healthy handful of the most powerful men and women of world politics. I am also neither vain nor naïve enough to believe that I would have been offered work on other outlets on television or radio without first having been seen on *Newsnight* – without it there would have been no *University Challenge*, for example, which I love. But we live in an ageing country, and there are too many older people hanging around, getting in the way and stopping others having a crack at things.

I have been lucky to have been given a special vantage point on important events, and to have met lots of people I should never otherwise have come across. Though it may not have felt like it at the time, I recognise that I had a privileged start in life. But I – and most of the other journalists I know – did not come to our jobs by inheritance or connections. If anyone asked what is the main lesson I have learned from my career in broadcasting, it is surely that you don't know what you can do until you try to do it. To be sure, I've been scared by one thing or another – war, loneliness, failure – but I have laughed a lot, and have enjoyed the company of lively minds. And, like many of my generation, I have hardly had to make any very big decisions. I've been fortunate to have worked in a prosperous country which needed graduates. Although it has been a slightly arm's-length relationship, most of my working life has been spent with the BBC, at a time when it had a pretty constantly growing income.

The BBC is now the biggest broadcast journalistic organisation in the world. There are many reasons for this pre-eminence, not the least of them being its insulation from market forces. In my childhood I encountered the BBC through valve radios warming up as households across the land prepared to sit down to Sunday lunch of roast beef and Yorkshire pudding, perhaps followed by suet pudding or treacle parkin. The BBC was the reassuring cooing of a nation which had emerged victorious from the Second World War, and thought it knew where it stood in the world.

The national picture since then may have been one of more or less constant relative decline (though life for most people has been increasingly comfortable). But for the BBC, the story has been one of almost constant growth in resources and influence. In the days of valve radios, no one could have imagined that the corporation would turn into the great behemoth it has since become: television was a luxury, and the internet had not been invented. Yet organisations have ancestral memories, and some of the cast of mind of the early days survives, especially in the BBC's apparent inability to admit that it has ever got anything wrong. Mistakes are inevitable anywhere, and the greater the diversity of output, the more likely it is that someone, somewhere will foul up. It is a fine and noble organisation, but it really could do with learning a little humility.

True, the BBC is too big, frequently badly managed, and often seems high-handed. But it cares about the state of the nation, it cares about truth, and it has nourished some astonishing creativity, from *Monty Python* to *Life on Earth*, and from *Top Gear* to innumerable classic series. Because of its unique funding system, everyone – rightly – feels entitled to comment on what it does, even if, like the creatures on *Animal Farm*, some citizens – a small number of listeners to Radio Four, for example – are more equal than others. It is the prisoner of its audiences, but it would be a very foolhardy government that tried to get rid of it. Like an instinct for justice, a taste for words and a resistance to pretentiousness, the BBC is one of the things that makes us who we are.

Its size is a good part of its problem: who'd be Director General when any plans you may be making for the next few decades can be overwhelmed in the furore over what some clown on BBC Radio Ramsbottom has said during an early-hours phone-in? It is too big and unwieldy. But tackling gigantism is an argument for evolutionary focus, not for putting it down.

Is the BBC institutionally biased? Yes, I think it is. But the bias is really just towards providing entertaining, thought-provoking content. Since this necessarily means challenging the status quo, the content can seem subversive. It does not mean that the organisation is 'left-wing', although – and I never asked – if I had to bet on how most of my colleagues voted, I would have guessed they were largely Labour or Liberal Democrat. But I don't know. And, frankly, we shouldn't care – journalists ought to leave their prejudices at the door. I always greeted Paul Mason, *Newsnight*'s economics editor, with a clenched fist and a cry of '*La lucha continua!*', but his political background as a Lancashire leftie seemed to me to give him a fresher perspective on economic affairs than the thoughts of some dreary cheerleader for red-blooded capitalism. He had been recruited to the programme from *Computer Weekly*, winning his place after what the then editor called 'the worst screen test I have ever seen' – but he had spotted a freshness behind the mumbling.

Having said that – and this is the opinion of a candid friend, for I admire the organisation's ambitions – the familiar protestations about 'balance' are fine only as far as they go. The BBC's coverage of the referendum on whether Britain should leave the European Union was doubtless well-intentioned, but it was not thoughtful: instead of exercising judgement, every time someone made a case on one side of the argument, the corporation preferred just to seek out someone to say the opposite, whether they knew what they were talking about or not. On a whole range of subjects, the BBC is not even-handed. It is not, for example, impartial on racism or gender prejudice, which is fine by me. By setting aside broadcast time for religious output it favours belief over atheism. It would be refreshing to hear some sceptical voices. But the question that anyone who wishes to abolish the BBC has to answer is 'Would the world be better off without it?' The answer is an unequivocal 'No.'

If that is the case, then the question to be settled is 'How do we pay for it?' Political interference in the content of programmes is one of the marks of despotism, so the BBC must retain its independence. It is highly unlikely that the potential advertising market is big enough to sustain several more television channels, and a dependence upon commercial funding would anyway just open the organisation up to a different sort of vulnerability. No one who has watched American public television, and sat through its constant tin-rattling and 'special offers' of *Downtown Abbey* tea towels, is likely to support that system as an alternative; and in any case the non-commercial sector in the USA still depends on tax funds from federal and state governments. The British system suffers from the fact that all politicians understand that any form of poll tax is hugely unpopular. But the BBC's tussles with government every few years over the licence fee imposed on anyone who chooses to watch or record television are a piffling matter compared with most alternatives. The privilege of an assured income allows the BBC to make programmes which might not be commercially viable. But, quite apart from penalising those who consume little or nothing of its output, it also distorts the market by punishing businesses – notably online – which must find a way of getting consumers to pay for the content they produce, when those customers can find out what they need to know from the BBC's 'free' content. Television is an intermediate technology, and the BBC is kept afloat by an intermediate funding mechanism: the licence fee belongs to the analogue world, and the distinction between computers and televisions is becoming obsolete.

Finally, everyone knows that the present system is unsustainable: no other electrical item in the home is similarly taxed. It cannot continue much longer, but it also cannot be beyond the wit of humankind to find a twenty-first-century replacement for a twentieth-century mechanism – scrambled signals which can only be decrypted on payment of a fee, perhaps.

The problem is that the BBC often proves to be its own worst enemy. The international services of the corporation are judged by the Foreign Office to be a hugely valuable form of 'soft power', and for decades were funded out of general taxation rather than by the licence fee. Yet since 2014 the BBC has paid for the international service out of the television licence fee levied on domestic consumers – an offer made by the BBC which must have made the Treasury think Christmas had come early. Similarly, the decision to give free TV licences to people over seventy-five was a political judgement made by a Labour government, and initially also funded out of taxation. When the BBC offered to meet the cost itself in 2015, it not only surrendered £650 million of income, it began to play politics. Why seventy-five rather than, say, sixty-five? Or even forty-five? Why do it at all? Each of these decisions was doubtless taken for what seemed like sensible reasons at the time. But each was a very big mistake.

The BBC is also caught in a bind. Despite the efforts of an array of stage bogeymen, it is a much-loved institution which has become part of the viscera of the state. That position imposes upon it duties which do not apply to commercial broadcasters. Yet its dominance of broadcast news obliges it to accept most of the imperatives of a helter-skelter trade, and compete to be the first and most authoritative voice telling people what has happened in the world. The two duties are bound to collide sometimes.

* * *

The first thing I did after getting off the treadmill was to devise a stage show to take to the Edinburgh Festival. 'Why?' was the question asked by all my friends. I had no satisfactory answer. Because it was there? Because my friend the comedy producer John Lloyd had enjoyed his own performances there so much? Mainly it was just because I was scared of doing it. The secret of successful television is to create a connection between the rooms in which the audience sit watching and the room in which the action of the show is taking place. 'What's going to happen next?' is the question you want the audience to be asking themselves, so they dare not take the risk of turning away. How much more difficult could a stage show be?

Very, it turned out. Live television is thrilling. But, on *Newsnight* at least, it has the great advantage that you cannot see the audience. The sight of even a few hundred eager faces staring at you, expecting to be entertained, is another proposition altogether. (Much the same applies to after-dinner speaking, with the additional disadvantage that when he or she gets to their feet the speaker is just about the only person in the room who is sober.) Eventually, with the help of Sarah Esdaile, a talented theatrical producer, we devised a format with the right combination of safety and unpredictability, in the form of a wheel with twenty-six categories marked on it, from 'Albania', by way of 'Impertinence', 'Spitting Image' and 'Y-Fronts', to 'Zeitgeist'. The idea was to spin the wheel and to have to talk on the subject on which it landed for a few minutes. With the addition of half a dozen wild-card categories, in which the choice of subject was left to the audience, it was quite sufficiently anxiety-inducing. I survived, and rather enjoyed it.

I briefly thought about doing something utterly different. Someone suggested a teaching post, but although I'm a Fellow of a couple of colleges, on the rare occasions on which I've been able to attend I've always felt something of an imposter by comparison with those who have devoted their lives to serious study. I was approached to see whether I fancied becoming head of a couple of Oxford colleges, but decided that the fact that I wasn't a committee man disqualified me, and the prospect of sitting through Governing Body debates about what type of biscuits should be provided with the coffee left me slightly cold. A contact in the Conservative Party tapped me up about running for Mayor of London when Boris Johnson stepped down. The plague of tourists at the time made my blood boil every time I went on the Tube, but I decided a bounty like the one they used to offer on squirrel tails wasn't a policy likely to turn out happily in the capital. The day after I had definitively said no, *The Times* printed a front-page photograph asking whether I was to be the Tories' nominee for the job. Just before the 2015 election I was asked if I'd like to try to become MP for Kensington. The idea initially attracted me as an opportunity to speak out about issues I believed in. But Parliament is not comprised of spiky independents (more's the pity), and one of the most dispiriting spectacles on the planet is listening to backbench MPs explaining why they're obeying the whips and supporting a policy they don't believe in. I decided that, too, wasn't for me.

Over the time since then there have been many other projects – documentaries, newspaper and magazine articles, and book projects. In May 2015 I was lucky enough to be invited to front Channel 4's election coverage. All the major broadcasters had entered into immensely tedious negotiations with the political parties about the terms on which their leaders would agree to share their ideas with the people who pay their salaries. A protocol was eventually agreed. It ran to over sixty topics, including the amount of time each politician was to be given to make his or her case, whether the moderator was allowed to interject or to ask supplementary questions, even the style of the set, and who was allowed to stand or sit. Each party would have an expensive lawyer or two sitting in the gallery to make sure nothing unexpected happened. The prospect was living death. Yet any serious broadcaster wants to play a part in a general election: it is one of the ways in which they justify their existence.

To avoid merely staging the same event in different places on different channels (which often happens), the broadcasters had agreed that they would submit different proposals. The poor old BBC, being the national broadcaster, knew that it would have to feature not just the parties from which a Prime Minister would be chosen and a government formed, but also the Welsh and Scottish Nationalists and UKIP. Though most of the interesting points in the BBC's broadcast were made by representatives of the small parties, you could not call the affair a prime ministerial debate. The Channel 4 pitch was very simple – we only wanted David Cameron and Ed Miliband, because they were the only leaders who might become the tenant of Downing Street. We got them, and furthermore we got them before any of the other 'debates'.

It was a joint project with Sky News, who fielded their star presenter, Kay Burley, to chair parts of the show in which the two men were to talk more or less directly to the studio audience. 'The election starts right here,' she declaimed, pointing her index finger to the floor, 'right now.' The pitch wasn't exactly subtle, but her bosses were quite clearly terrified of her – she had only to stamp her foot for them to tremble. Anyone who has anything do with the sort of event that allows voters to question politicians rapidly learns that the British public is, by and large, terribly nice and well-mannered. When they ask a politician a question and get a lot of meaningless verbiage in response, too many of them have a horrible habit of saying, 'Thank you very much.' (Though there has been more edge to the debates in recent years, as people have become progressively more cynical about politics and its practitioners, and producers more concerned about what things look like on screen.) Kay Burley tried to liven things up by asking David Cameron whether he'd ever eaten three Shredded Wheat.

The eighteen-minute interviews were my responsibility. The only way to get control, and to leave the thing looking simple and natural, is by hours of homework: you need to know how to deal with what will inevitably be a partial presentation of the facts. With three former colleagues, Rhodri Jones, Richard Danbury and Esme Wren, I kicked ideas about for a couple of days.

The Conservative leader, David Cameron, began badly, not knowing – and therefore potentially not seeming to care – about the extent of food banks feeding hungry people in Britain. The question was tough (how *can* a Prime Minister be expected to have at his fingertips the precise figures for everything from GDP growth to the number of cars on the road?), but in a medium of impressions, how you go about dealing with such a question is as important as the facts you deploy. A sensitive human being might begin by saying, 'I don't have the exact figures, but I fear the total has probably gone up, which distresses me. But when we've finished transforming our economy …' and then manoeuvred the discussion onto more comfortable ground. Ed Miliband, by contrast, knew that his main problem was whether, particularly by comparison with his former Foreign Secretary big brother David, he was up to the job. He had clearly been expecting the subject to come up, and when I raised it he replied with a rhetorical question – 'Am I tough enough?' – which he then answered with the words 'Hell yes.' I was astonished. It reeked of inauthenticity, which was why, unaware that the microphones were still live, I asked him after the interview was over whether he was all right.*

I did not know Ed Miliband especially well, although, apart from interviews, our paths had crossed on a couple of occasions. The previous year I had been swimming back to a deserted,

---

* It emerged after the election that the Labour Party had paid a firm of American public relations consultants £184,000 for advice about how Miliband should present himself in the debates. Such companies do not generally operate on a 'no win–no fee' basis.

scrubby beach while on holiday in Greece. There was something about the pale, spindly figure lying uncomfortably in the shade reading a book that seemed familiar. When I got out of the water it turned out that I had been right – Miliband was staying in a nearby villa. I don't imagine he was especially thrilled. When he was a mere member of the Shadow Cabinet I had taken him to lunch at a fish restaurant, recognising him as the sort of bookish, nerdy boy who gets picked last for playground football games and is then sent to stand in goal. I rather liked him, and for the first – and last – time in my life, I dispensed some political advice: it would be a big mistake for him to try to become leader too soon. The first opportunity he got, he ignored my suggestion and won the job. In 2015 he took the party down to defeat and – through the selection system created on his watch – handed on the Labour leadership to Jeremy Corbyn, who most of the party's MPs decided would take them down to another, even worse, wipeout. For while the choice of Corbyn may have addressed the question Russell Brand identified when he said that great numbers of young people failed to identify with mainstream politicians (most of Corbyn's career had been spent in opposition – either to the government or to his own party leadership), his leadership came at the price of the confidence of his parliamentary team. So within little more than a year both Cameron and Miliband, the two subjects of the extended interviews, were consigned to history.

At the election they fought in 2015 there had also been nine hours of live coverage on the night in question. For decades the BBC had engaged one of the Dimbleby family to anchor its programmes on election night. The incumbent from 1979 onwards was David Dimbleby: though one editor of the coverage after another asserted that 'this one' – the election of 1997, 2001, 2005 or 2010 – 'will definitely be his last', he generally managed to outsmart them, and in 2015, at the age of seventy-six, he was scheduled to present the election-night extravaganza once again – much to the fury of Huw Edwards, who thought he had been offered the job, and whose response to the news was unprintable. Though over the years I had repeatedly been told in so many words by senior figures in the BBC news empire that I would have Dimbleby's job at the next election, it never happened. I wasn't entirely sure I could play the role much better, and frankly Dimbleby anyway seemed to make a competent job of it. This meant that, had I stayed at the BBC, the 2015 election night would be spent in my usual little cage in a corner of Dimbleby's set, to which he would occasionally toss a bun in the form of a political figure to be interrogated. So I was receptive to Channel 4's invitation to anchor their many hours of live coverage: what was it like to live on your wits for that long, not knowing what was going to happen next, in the certain knowledge that all your blunders would be there for everyone to see?

It turned out that the first four hours – before any results were known – were to be devoted to comedy, preparation for which involved long hours locked in a room with a couple of writers and only the occasional Nando's chicken wing for comfort: the tyranny of the comic script which must not be deviated from turned out to be the polar opposite of think-on-your-feet current affairs. It turned out to be quite fun, if not quite what I had expected. The remaining five hours, from which I emerged blearily into the spring sunshine the following morning, had no script at all. It would have been good to have had the BBC's bottomless election-night pockets, but I decided that Dimbleby earned his money. It's exhilarating, but exhausting.

Before the referendum on EU membership the next summer, the BBC asked me to film a documentary explaining what had happened to British sovereignty inside the European Union. My conclusion that the EU was a wasteful institution, pursuing objectives often quite different from those of successive British governments, and worst of all with a gaping hole where there ought to have been some democratic control, was not, I thought, especially controversial. But it drew the response from Max Hastings, when I bumped into him a week or so after transmission, that 'It must have been worth half a million votes to the leave campaign!' He was blustering, but his reaction raised a troublesome issue. To what extent should a journalist temper his inquiries and conclusions to fit his personal views?

Like great numbers of British people, I had come to loathe the smug indifference of the European political elite to the Union's appalling lack of democratic accountability. The institution was both self-important and inept – a particularly deadly combination. But since virtually the whole of the British political Establishment was in favour of membership, I did not expect the nation to reject it: we are generally a cautious people. The exception to this rule is when we are roused. David Cameron chose to entrust the biggest foreign policy decision for generations to a popular referendum, while failing to recognise how roused public opinion had become. His misjudgement was at least the worst foreign policy mistake since Anthony Eden thought he could seize the Suez Canal by force in 1956, though you'd have to go back to Neville Chamberlain to find so serious a misreading of events. An Irish friend the other day suggested it was as big an error as Lord North's loss of the American colonies. I think he may have been joking. Not only are referendums quite alien to the British tradition of democracy, they are also abdications of leadership. And why did it happen? The short answer is that the fate of the country was entrusted to a referendum to avoid discomfort in the Conservative Party.

In the end I held my nose and voted to remain in the European Union, on the grounds that, for all its myriad faults, it was the only international organisation of its kind to which we belonged, that it is better to argue than to fight, and that in a world of big trading blocs it is better to belong than not. The leave campaign was run by journalists, and perhaps there was something in the accusation made by my friend, the journalist Henry Porter, that it is a bad idea to let our trade anywhere near executive decisions because we are innately oppositional. In making my documentary for the BBC, for example, to pretend that the faults did not exist would have been dim-witted and purblind. I had set out to investigate the issue of sovereignty, and honestly felt that there was no alternative conclusion to be reached than that membership of the EU had emasculated Britain's parliamentary sovereignty. No single programme can swing the result of a nationwide poll, especially when it runs counter to the general drift of coverage. But it did give me pause when the results came in.

On the eve of the referendum vote Channel 4 had invited me to chair a debate in an old bingo hall on the Commercial Road in the East End of London, with a bizarrely eclectic cast which included Delia Smith, Robert Winston and Peter Stringfellow, a couple of admirals, an angry Norfolk farmer and a curry-house proprietor who said he could only hire Poles to make his vindaloos. I defended the cast list beforehand, on the grounds that David Cameron had decided that membership of the Union was a matter for everyone, and not just for Parliament (greater love hath no man than that he sacrifice his country for his party), and that therefore the vote of any citizen is worth just as much of that of any politician.

The programme turned out to be a complete bunfight, more like *The Jeremy Kyle Show* than *Question Time*. The politicians of all parties and persuasions were quiet, even somnolent. But the audience just wanted to shout at one another. I concluded that many were simply angry at having to make up their minds, when they already paid a bunch of politicians to reduce a complex world to simple binary choices. Having gone through the pain of deciding what to think, they felt determined to get their money's worth. At one point Sandie Shaw, Britain's first winner of the Eurovision Song Contest, stood up in the audience to interrupt a discussion about collective security with a speech about music royalties. Selina Scott had apparently decided she wanted to leave the EU because farm animals were being transported in lorries. During the commercial breaks Will Self cupped his hands and shouted abuse at the panellists. Katie Price, who had been invited along as one of the undecideds, declared she was even more undecided than she'd been beforehand. Alastair Campbell, seated in the front row, drew my attention to a Tweet he'd received: 'Poor old Paxo. It's like watching a bear being made to dance.' I wasn't entirely sure he hadn't sent it himself.

The results of the referendum reversed over forty years of travel, although in truth the country had been growing less and less enthusiastic about attempts to build a European state for years. The tactics of the remain campaign had been dubbed 'Project Fear' by those fighting to persuade people that even the arm's-length relationship between Britain and the EU of 2016 was too much. The campaign for a remain vote was counterproductive: telling people that if the country left the European Union their pay, pensions and house values would fall, while their taxes would rise, came perilously close to threats, and voters do not like being threatened. Even President Obama was enlisted in the cause, to say that in negotiating a trade deal with the United States, a Britain outside the European Union would be at 'the back of the queue'. Whoever encouraged him to make this prognosis ought to have been fired, for the one thing British voters like less than being threatened is to be threatened by a foreigner.

But there was a deeper weakness in the campaign to sell the EU to a sceptical public – the argument was simply never properly made. It was left in that last debate, a mere nine hours before the polling booths opened, to the eighty-three-year-old actress Sheila Hancock to explain that she would be voting to continue living inside the Union for the sake of her grandchildren. Having grown up during the Blitz, she had come to hate the Germans. Now she just wanted peace. It was a passionate, artless argument. But no one had bothered to make it before.

In the end it was English and Welsh people furthest from the political elite who delivered the verdict – it had frequently been noted during the campaign that uncontrolled immigration from Eastern Europe was good for the middle classes, who could now examine quotes for building work from Polish plumbers, Lithuanian painters and Bulgarian electricians, as they sipped the coffee served to them by a young Spaniard. Membership was painful for the native plumbers, painters and electricians who saw their own incomes stagnate or fall. In the referendum they called the political class's bluff. Both Labour and Conservative governments had failed to control immigration (who now recalls David Cameron's 'no ifs, no buts' promises on the subject?), and in areas of failing schools, inadequate housing, high unemployment and poverty of expectation, the referendum gave people an opportunity to express their sense of betrayal. Voters in these disadvantaged communities were suffering the consequences of the combination of globalisation and austerity, and they took the opportunity to blame the only institution they were offered the chance to blame.* How long will it be before they realise they were deceived?

The peasants' revolt offended the metropolitan elite. But for those who bothered to look, the writing had been on the wall for years. Rather than political parties, people now belong instead to organisations which promote their interests – sports clubs, voluntary groups, the National Trust, birdwatching or line-dancing clubs. The politicians of Europe, from whatever country they come, seem to have more in common with each other than with the people they purport to represent. Giving the people the right to determine geopolitics, as if the referendum were a council

---

* That Scotland voted overwhelmingly to remain inside the EU probably testifies to the fact that it already had a devolved government which had come to power blaming everything on a culprit closer to home – in London.

survey on dog-fouling, was a very stupid thing to do. Cameron's speedy departure, pausing only to dish out 'honours' to cronies, seemed to show he had recognised his folly, if not that he cared very much.

There have been other professional pleasures. The *Financial Times* – in many fields a better calling card even that of the BBC – invited me to become a Contributing Editor, a Humpty Dumptyish title which allowed me to write features, opinion pieces and diaries. There was a documentary about van Gogh for the BBC, and a series about rivers for Channel 4. I hope this will go on for a while yet, though I recognise that I have now joined a club I never applied for.

It would be nice to be able to write that in the end, I came to understand our father. I certainly forgave him, but true understanding eluded me. Not long ago, visiting his ninety-two-year-old sister in Yorkshire a week before she died, I came across a photograph which must have been taken when Dad was trying to become a navy pilot. He is standing outside some drab pebble-dashed building, presumably at the training airfield in Luton, squinting into the sunlight. His dark hair is swept back from his forehead. He's wearing scuffed leather boots and an all-in-one flying suit, and in his left hand he's holding a leather flying helmet. It seems a picture full of promise.

He never achieved that ambition, nor others: never rose through the officer class, was merely a reasonably successful businessman brought low in the end, never achieved his ambition of sailing right round the world, never made a success of his marriage to our mother, never joined the county set. He never really fitted in, and remained a one-time clerk at the Midland Bank in Howden, Yorkshire. Later in life he would achieve a measure of success in Australia. But how cruel England had been to him once its hour of need had passed. For men of his generation, the Second World

War was such an intense experience that everything afterwards must have seemed pallid. What happened when your country didn't need you any more, and the dozy certainties of the old order began to reassert themselves? In the early seventies Dad joined a group of men and women setting off around the world on an old sailing barque – the sort of adventure others have during the youth which, because of the war, he had never been free to enjoy. He was back a year or so later, after the enterprise went bust (a writ was nailed to the mast in Singapore, and they sold the boat).

He was now in his fifties, and unable to find a job, when the phone rang one day. It was a man he had never met, calling from New Zealand. He introduced himself by saying he had been on Everest with Edmund Hillary and Tenzing Norgay, and now had a schooner which he planned to run as a training ship for teenagers. He needed someone with a Board of Trade licence to skipper it. Dad had such a thing, and left immediately for the other side of the world.

He never returned. The job lasted eighteen months, and then he fetched up in the Cook Islands in the South Pacific, running the local orange-juice factory. The sole perk of the job was a pair of company bicycle clips. After a couple of years there he moved to Queensland, where his early days were hard – he said later that he had lived in a working-men's hostel, and had spent his last Australian dollar on two tins of stew. But he picked himself up, got a job as business manager for a firm of accountants, and was given credit for saving the company.

During these years we usually only heard from him at Christmas, when an unseasonally sunny card would arrive with the words 'Love Dad' – one was never quite sure whether it was a statement or a command. After he had been away a dozen years, I went to Australia to seek him out, hired a car, found the house where he lived, and knocked on the door. An instantly recognisable figure emerged, wearing an orange sarong. After a fumbled mixture of handshake and embrace, his first words were, 'Come and look at the garden.' He was, of course, older and more careworn than I recalled, though as I discovered over the next few days, he was still playing the joshing Englishman among the Aussies. What an odd country we are, that there are roles an Englishman can play abroad that he may not play at home. I saw him once more, when I was sent on assignment to Australia. Then he moved to New Zealand, and no one gets sent on assignment there.

In these last chapters of his life my father had at last found a sort of peace. He had met a kindly New Zealand physiotherapist, and they moved to a little town in the North Island. She looked after him with a no-nonsense thoughtfulness, and one day he sent an email saying, 'Celia and I were married yesterday … We have enough toasters.' He died a couple of years later, in March 2010, at the age of eighty-seven, having announced his intention of synchronising his death with the exhaustion of his means. In this he was successful: when Celia came to England to scatter his ashes she brought our inheritance in cash – £140.22.

The American news anchorman Tom Brokaw once wrote a book about my parents' era which he called *The Greatest Generation*. My contemporaries and I – the post-war baby boomers – have been lucky to avoid being called the Worst Generation. The Greatest Generation grew up in the Depression, and fought through the most vicious conflict ever to take place on earth. My generation reaped the benefits of increasing prosperity, constantly improving medicine, breakneck technological advance and ever-extending personal freedom. Indulgence was offered to us on a plate. And what have we done with it? Not much – we hand on the world to our children and grandchildren in an appalling state. An impartial historical audit will not be kind to us. The generation that came of age in the sixties and seventies was the most privileged that has ever lived, and it continues to demand more than its share: at every election the politicians bend the knee to pensioners, sure in the knowledge that they're far more likely to vote than the young people whose futures governments are busy mortgaging. Where is Robespierre when he's needed?

It would do none of us any harm to appreciate how fortunate we have been. We have had to fight no wars, and have enjoyed freedom, peace and rising living standards. Apart from an unhappy few afflicted by the diminishing number of incurable diseases, our luck has been exceptional. My great-grandfather died in Bradford of TB at thirty-five, and his wife, a cleaner, two years later, also of tuberculosis and 'exhaustion'. We, by contrast, had the benefits of state-provided orange juice and cod liver oil, vaccination, tonsillectomy and antibiotics.

There comes a point when each of us has to ask, 'And what have you done with the chances you were given?' We each do what we can, and most of us have very modest talents. I have taken my own very modest talent quite a long way – I am interested in the world, and have done my best to satisfy that curiosity. I hope it has been a bit useful.

Illustrations

Unless otherwise stated, photographs are from the author's collection.

Journalist, conservationist and ambassador.
The sea, or a bit of river at least, is in our blood.
Father and sons about 1959.
Dad as would-be Magnificent Man, 1940.
Mother driving her ambulance in about 1945.
Training for a Boy Scout Cycling Proficiency badge on my new bike, 1961.
Doing my duty to God and the Queen, 1962.
Sunday lunch at the grandparents'.
My prep school was not overwhelmed with choice when picking its football team.
Gender and ethnic diversity in 1972 Cambridge.
Breakfast in an alpine refuge, 1978.
Knees That Tease in the High Pyrenees, 1975.
Though it seems improbable, this sort of haircut was once nearly fashionable.
Accommodating the BBC's pogonophobia. Sri Lanka, 1985.
In Iran with Simon Berthon, 1977.
Impersonating Detective Starsky. Nicaragua, early 1980s.

Interviewing an army officer in Norway, 1985.

Belfast, 1976. I think Gillian Chambers and I were making a programme about segregated education.

Beirut, 1976. I cannot explain the jacket.

El Salvador, 1982. Cameraman Alan 'Bulletproof' Stevens was less scared than I was.

Dinner to mark leaving *The Six O'Clock News*, 1986.

Breakfast Time, 1987, with Frank Bough and Sally Magnusson. (*BBC*)

Radio studio, 1989. (*Photo by In Pictures Ltd/Corbis via Getty Images*)

Newsnight, about 1994. (*BBC*)

Before the embrace of the tie, early 1980s.

Newsnight faces. (*BBC*)

How suits and ties grind you down, 2010. (*Photo by Jeff Overs/ BBC News and Current Affairs via Getty Images*)

1992 general election, with John Major. (*BBC*)

Michael Howard. (*Photo by Jeff Overs/BBC News and Current Affairs via Getty Images*)

2010 election, with Gordon Brown. (*BBC*)

2015 election, with David Cameron. (*Photo by Stefan Rousseau – WPA Pool/Getty Images*)

2005, with Tony Blair in 10 Downing Street. (*BBC*)

It is sometimes hard to convey the frenetic urgency of the news business. (*Photo by Jeff Overs/BBC*)

In the archives for *Who Do You Think You Are?*, 2006. (*Courtesy of Wall to Wall Media*)

Zambezi, 1989. I have no idea what this fish is.

Discussing world affairs. Chengdu, 2014.

Messing about in a boat, Glen Affric, 1993.

Deer-stalking in Glen Affric, 1995.

It is always a pleasure to hear from viewers.

2008. Reading a letter on a Kolkata commuter train.

2011. Waiting to be told to do some damn stupid thing by a director, Chennai (Madras).

2009. Being beaten at dominoes in Cairo.

2015. Outside the European Commission's lair. (*Courtesy of Brook Lapping Productions Limited*)

2011. Among the Ethiopian and Coptic churches defying Christian unity on the roof of the Holy Sepulchre, Jerusalem.

2010. A non-Test-match day at Sabina Park, Kingston, Jamaica.

2015. Admiring Rembrandt's *The Conspiracy of the Batavians*. (*Courtesy of Northern Town*)

2015. Interviewing the French provincial lawyer pretending to be Napoleon at the re-enactment of Waterloo. (*Photo by Giles Price*)

Cartoons: Geoff Thompson (p.22); Mike Williams (p.153); Kipper Williams (p.190); Nicholas Garland/*Spectator* (p.292); Peter Brookes (p.325)

Lyrics from 'Mrs Worthington' by Noël Coward, © NC Aventales AG, 1935, reproduced by permission of Alan Brodie Representation Ltd, www.alanbrodie.com.

Index